The Irish Mars

or,

A history of the war in Ireland for two years, from notes recorded by a fellow soldier

By Andreas Claudianus

Bilingual Facsimile Edition

Edited and translated by

Kjeld Hald Galster and Rasmus Wichmann

Legacy Books Press Classics

Published by Legacy Books Press
RPO Princess, Box 21031
445 Princess Street
Kingston, Ontario, K7L 5P5
Canada

www.legacybookspress.com

The scanning, uploading, and/or distribution of this book via the Internet or any other means without the permission of the publisher is illegal and punishable by law.

This edition first published in 2016 by Legacy Books Press
1

© 2016 Kjeld Hald Galster and Rasmus Wichmann, all rights reserved.

Originally published in Copenhagen by Ove Lynow, 1718. Facsimile pages reproduced with the permission of the Royal Library in Copenhagan.

Printed and bound in the United States of America and Great Britain.

This book is typeset in a Times New Roman 11- and 12-point font.

This copyright page joke has been translated from Latin.

Library and Archives Canada Cataloguing in Publication:

    The Irish Mars or, a history of the war in Ireland for two years, from notes recorded by a fellow soldier / by Andreas Claudianus ; edited and translated by Kjeld Hald Galster and Rasmus Wichmann. -- Bilingual facsimile edition.

Includes index.
Includes translation of Mavors Irlandicus, sive Historia de bello Hibernico
    biennium in Hibernia gesto, chartis consignata á Commilitone,
    originally published in 1718.
Text in English and Latin.
ISBN 978-1-927537-27-5 (paperback)

    1. Claudianus, Andreas, 1672-1720. 2. Ireland--History--War of 1689-1691--Personal narratives, Danish. 3. Ireland--History--War of 1689-1691--Sources. 4. Ireland--History--James II, 1685-1688--Sources. I. Galster, Kjeld Hald, 1952-, editor, translator II. Wichmann, Rasmus, 1985-, editor, translator III. Title: History of the war in Ireland for two years, from notes recorded by a fellow soldier.

DA945.I75 2016   941.506   C2015-905852-X

Table of Contents

Acknowledgements. ii

Preface. iii

Introduction. vi

The Irish Mars. 1
    Dedication. 5
    To the Sincere Reader. 17
    Claudianus' Account. 45
    A Humble Gift. 319

Epilogue. 324

Annex A – Order of Battle of Prince Frederick's Regiment
. . . . 328

Annex B – Glossary. 330
    Place Names. 330
    Titles and Military Ranks and Units, Military Weapons,
        Equipment & Tactical Expressions. 332

Index. 335

About the Translators. 338

Acknowledgements

This book – a commented translation of Andreas Claudianus' original narrative on the deployment to and war in Ireland 1689-91 of the Danish Prince Frederick's Regiment, published in Copenhagen in 1718 – would never have seen the light of day had it not been for Dr Harman Murtagh, President of the Irish Commission of Military History, who kindly encouraged me to endeavour making this important source accessible to the modern reader on the military events of this particular period.

I would also like to acknowledge the help and suggestions in the linguistic field provided by Professor Anna Chahoud, Head of the Department of Classics School of Histories and Humanities at Trinity College, Dublin.

Chief Consultant to the Royal Library in Copenhagen Søren Clausen has kindly facilitated permission to publish the original narrative written in Latin in parallel with the English text. For this I am truly grateful.

Last but not least many thanks are due to Dr Pádraig Lenihan, National University of Ireland, Galway, for help and encouragement throughout the work.

Kjeld Galster
Ormeslev 2015

Preface

Over the years many excellent books have been published on the War in Ireland from 1689-91: The War of Two Kings. Most have been based on source material such as the correspondence by commanders and diplomats, but very few have relied on eyewitness accounts by the soldiers who did the hard work on the ground, felt the adversity of weather, hunger and sickness, and took the brunt of the enemy's fire. However, such narratives do exist.

This book endeavours to convey in a way comprehensible to the modern reader the observations and messages that appear in the 'post-action report' written down in Latin by the Danish soldier, Andreas Claudianus. A Danish infantryman, he joined the expeditionary force raised by the Danish King Christian V in 1689 in support of the new British rulers, King William III and Queen Mary II, who – in the wake of the 'Glorious Revolution' of 1688 – had ascended the English and Scottish thrones. Claudianus remained with the Danish contingent throughout the War in Ireland and for most of the subsequent campaigns in Flanders. After he returned home in 1696 he matriculated as a student of divinity – a study he was never to finish. Although he intended to write a comprehensive history of Ireland, time and resources did not suffice, and eventually his endeavours resulted merely in this history of the War of Two Kings as seen through the eyes of a common soldier serving with the colours of Prince Frederick's Regiment in the Danish expeditionary force.

As a private soldier, Claudianus was not privy to strategic

deliberations or operational and tactical decisions made by the national or allied high commands. His work is based on his own observations and information volunteered by his fellow soldiers and others, as well as on encyclopaedic works on Irish history and geography which he seems to have consulted during the years of writing. It is unlikely that he would have had command of the English language, but, probably, and apart from Latin, he understood French and German.

During the years of writing, Claudianus not only studied theology, but he also worked as a teacher in a primary school in the village Stenstrup on the island of Funen. He finished his work in 1717, only three years before his death, and it is likely, as he had undoubtedly hoped for many more years of intellectual productivity, that he wished some kind of patronage. It is in this light that we must see his elaborate dedication of the Mavors Irlandicus to the Dano-Norwegian King Frederick IV, who was – at the time of publication – the country's absolute ruler, generalissimo and the patron par excellence of art and literature.

The book you are now holding in your hands is not an exact word-by-word-translation of the original text. Claudianus is not too consistent as to sequence, here and there one finds elaborations which would have made more sense had they been made earlier, many names seem to confuse the Danish contingent's establishment with those of other units (though some may belong to volunteers, i.e. young noblemen wishing to distinguish themselves with a view to someday obtaining a commission, or unknown NCOs and soldiers who have been given acting rank as officers due to casualties and lack of reinforcements from home), and quite a few names are given in a Latinised version which gives little clue as to the Danish, English, French or German names from which they have been derived. Thus, conveying this account to the modern reader has required a choice between serving the dedicated linguist and grammarian sticking rigorously to words, grammar and punctuation as the author chose them; or making the alterations necessary to today's military historians and others reading for the sake of historical comprehension. Being ourselves historians, we have chosen the latter option, which, we believe, will best serve the majority of readers. However, this does not imply that this translation will be useless to the Latinist. Page by page the translation is an accurate representation of the content of the original, and the Latin page has been placed precisely vis-à-vis its English opposite. We have moved paragraphs around where these seemed placed in an illogical sequence, but generally only within the scope of the same page.

The dedication is obviously intended to attract government attention and royal favour and it is for this purpose that it is phrased in a somewhat intricate – not to say sycophant – style, setting it apart from the actual historical narrative of the work. Keeping this in mind we have, nonetheless, endeavoured to translate it into a simpler, modern English, conveying the meaning rather than following the original's breathtaking and elaborate verbosity. That consideration goes for Claudianus' introduction "To the Sincere Reader," too.

Like the dedication and the introduction, we believe that the actual historical and geographical descriptions of Ireland, as well as the diary-like presentation of events on the battlefields, in camps and in winter quarters, must be translated to convey matter rather than style. Therefore, the main part of Claudianus' work – which includes the military historical narrative – is phrased in a way likely, we hope, to give a meaningful impression to today's readers of what actually happened. Military terminology – in particular in the fields of organisation and weapons technology – has therefore been adapted to modern English military parlance. Titles, organisational units, tactics and outdated weaponry will be explained in the introduction and in footnotes throughout the text, and for the sake of clarity a select glossary has been attached as well (Annex B).

Throughout the text Claudianus mentions a number of castles and minor fortifications by name. Most of these edifices were destroyed during fighting or have disappeared due to inadequate maintenance over the years. For this translation it has been assumed that most of the names of these strongholds were those of the owners.

Kjeld Galster & Rasmus Wichmann
Ormeslev and Copenhagen, May 2015

Introduction

Andreas Claudianus' eye witness account of the Williamite coalition's war in Ireland 1689-91 is one of the very few narratives on that war written by common soldiers. Claudianus entitled his work *Mavors Irlandicus, sive Historia de bello Hibernico biennium in Hibernia gesto, chartis consignata á Commilitone* [*The Irish Mars, or a History of the War in Ireland for Two Years, from Notes Recorded by a Fellow Soldier*], and it is presently to be found in *Det Kongelige Bibliotek* [The Royal Library] in Copenhagen, where it is now digitally available for any keen historian or linguist to download. The two Irish historians Danaher and Simms have not included Claudianus' narrative in their otherwise impressive and very useful translation of the Danish sources. However, in their introduction they have mentioned this work and described Claudianus as a pastor and army chaplain with Prince Frederick's Regiment. This portrayal, however, cannot be corroborated by any Danish biographical or bibliographical account.

According to a contemporary diarist, Jacob Thomassøn Bircherod, and to the author of the *Forfatterlexicon omfattende Danmark, Norge og Island indtil 1814, bind II* [*Danish, Norwegian and Icelandic Authors until 1814, vol. II*], H. Ehrencron-Müller,

Introduction

Andreas Claudianus was born in 1672 in Trondhjem,[1] Norway, the youngest of four brothers. When, in 1689, he joined the Danish contingent bound for Ireland as a *Martis Comes* [private soldier] in Prince Frederick's Regiment, he was a young man of seventeen. His elder brother Frederick was serving as an army chaplain with the very same regiment, but neither of the two was a commissioned officer. Claudianus died as a poor school teacher in Stenstrup on the island of Funen, Denmark, in 1720.[2]

Although in the overall strategic and operational sphere Claudianus' work is opaque, his description of the campaigns in Ireland is a rich source of information on the daily life within the contingent and on the impressions made by actual combat and by the Irish environment as well as on the social life in Prince Frederick's Regiment, where he served.[3]

Claudianus' book focuses on the Danish troop contribution to the war waged by Great Britain in Ireland 1689-91 with the general aim of frustrating the French King Louis XIV's quest for dominance in Europe, and with the specific goal of keeping the ousted King James II Stuart from resuming the throne of Ireland and indeed those of England and Scotland. The Peace Treaty of Westphalia, which had been signed in 1648, had ended the Thirty Years War and established a code of conduct for sovereign European countries and their rulers, laying down norms for civilised interaction among states, including regulations on the conduct of armed conflict. Post-Thirty-Years-War warfare was in many respects civilised and not particularly bloody. Manœuvres and sieges were key features, opposing armies were comparatively small compared with those of the Napoleonic and later eras, and fighting normally took place only in the summer season when

---

[1] Trondheim in today's Norwegian spelling.

[2] *Jacob Thomassøn Bircherods Optegnelser* [Diaries], Rigsarkivet (RA) [Danish National Archives], Gl. Kgl. Saml. 3018 b, 4to.

[3] H. Ehrencron-Müller, *Forfatterlexicon omfattende Danmark, Norge og Island indtil 1814, bind II* [Danish, Norwegian and Icelandic Authors until 1814, vol II], (Copenhagen: H.Aschehoug & Co, 1925).

fodder for the huge number of cavalry and dragoon horses as well as draught animals was to be found in the fields. However, although the art of war was mostly practised in a comparatively decent manner, this did in no way mean that atrocities did not occur.

In the period of interest when reading this book, Louis XIV of France possessed a power base large enough to dictate and enforce his will throughout most of the continent – and, consequently, he believed he had a right to do so. Since his accession to the throne of France in 1643, his main concern had been territorial aggrandisement, persecution of the French Protestants – the Huguenots – and creation of dynastic ties with likeminded Catholic monarchs. His initial successes were spectacular and his prowesses caused pervasive admiration and envy amongst many a fellow monarch.

King Christian V of Denmark was no exception and he could easily see himself in a similar position. Having taken over from his father, Frederick III, who died in 1670, he was merely the second absolute monarch on the Danish throne. From the outset he adopted an activist and aggressive foreign policy. He wanted to dominate what he saw as his own backyard in northern Germany, and he wished to re-establish Danish rule in the provinces east of the Sound recently lost to Sweden. To a certain extent he was militarily successful, but great power interests stood in the way, preventing Denmark from cashing in on the Dano-Swedish Scanian War of 1675-79, which Denmark had fought successfully – at least as far as operations at sea and on the battlefields were concerned. For this enterprise his forces had been equipped with the state-of-the-art weapons technology of the age, and in the years subsequent to the peace of 1679 they were much larger – and a lot more expensive – than what was required for the protection of the kingdom's borders and waters.

However, King Christian V of Denmark had been sorely disappointed by France, which had failed to support him when, at the end of the Scanian War, the chance had arisen to regain the lost provinces east of the Sound. Thus, like other princes and individual Europeans Christian found reasons for turning away from his alliance with an obviously egotistical France.

Introduction ix

For many reasons the newly proclaimed British King William III and Queen Mary II needed coalition partners in order to combat the ousted King James, who was a de facto proxy of King Louis.

Christian V of Denmark seized this opportunity and initiated negotiations to hire out a large portion of his military – ca. one fifth of its total strength of 34,000 – to William and Mary. Should any such agreement materialise, this would give his officers combat experience, keeping the military instrument sharp until the day might come when he would need it himself to fall upon Sweden, and save his treasury the burden of paying the troops, as this obligation would fall on Britain.

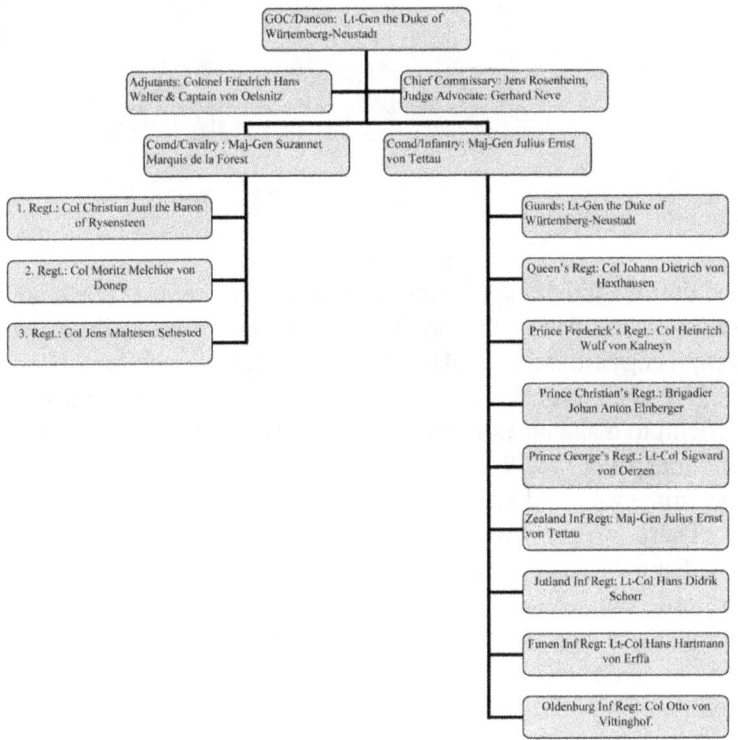

There were, thus, shared interests afoot, and negotiations facilitating an agreement were conducted in Copenhagen in the summer of 1689 between representatives of the two monarchies.

Introduction

These talks led to an agreement on the dispatch of a Danish Contingent of 6,000 infantry and 1,000 cavalry to England or Scotland before the end of that year.

The part of the Danish Contingent's organisation, within which Claudianus fought, was Prince Frederick's Regiment; one out of nine Danish infantry and three Danish cavalry units (see page ix).

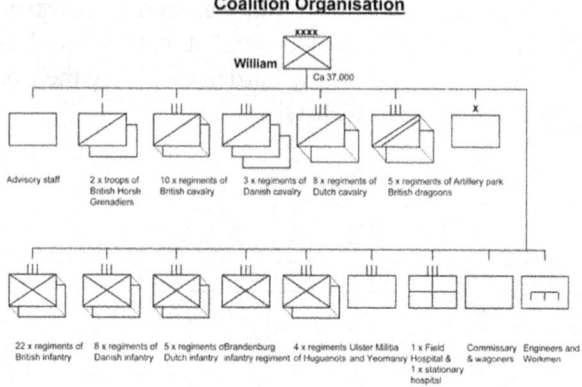

The entire Danish expeditionary force of ca. 7,000 officers and men was included in the British-led coalition-of-the-willing also comprising British, Dutch, Brandenburg and Huguenot formations; ca. 37,000 all told. While a lack of available information makes it difficult to make up a diagram showing the Jacobite army exactly the same way as the Williamite coalition, the illustration opposite goes some way to doing so.

There were some peculiarities setting these military establishments apart from what is general practice today. In the era concerned, it was customary for a general officer also to hold nominal command of one of this army's regiments. This secured him an extra income, but in reality he rarely served as the 'commanding officer' of the regiment, which normally consisted of only one battalion, albeit a large one compared with today's organisation. The tasks of the commanding officer of a regiment/battalion with a general officer in nominal charge were normally carried out by a lieutenant-colonel. Similarly as far as the other commanding officers were concerned, the CO – in the case

Introduction xi

of Prince Frederick's Regiment: Colonel Heinrich Wulf von Kalneyn – would have nominal command of A Company but leave the practical leadership to a major or a captain-lieutenant. For a detailed order-of-battle of Prince Frederick's Regiment, see Annex A.

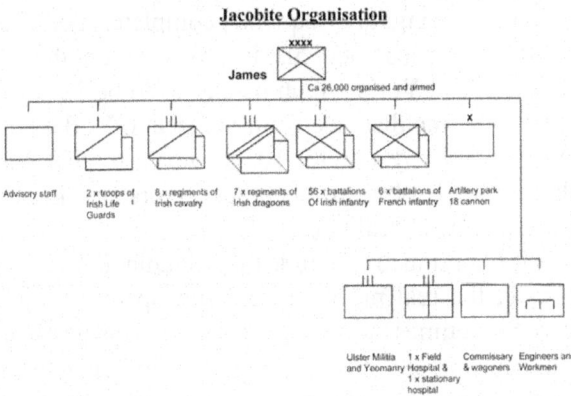

The armies at that time were generally composed of only three arms, viz. infantry, cavalry and artillery, though with auxiliary elements of engineers, wagoners, administrative personnel, hospitals, baggage train and a considerable tail of 'camp followers' such as women folk, children, sutlers, bakers, etc.

While infantry was in the process of rearming with modern flintlock firearms and bayonets, the time-honoured pike as an anti-cavalry implement was still seen, in particular amongst the Irish. While the cavalry was armed with swords and pistols, dragoons, who mostly fought dismounted, were issued with carbines. The artillery was subdivided into field artillery consisting of 3, 4 and 6 pounder guns, and siege artillery with mortars, howitzers and heavier guns such as 12, 18 or 24 pounders.

At the time of the events dealt with in Claudianus' narrative, the Gregorian calendar had already been adopted by nearly all western continental countries, but not by Britain. Claudianus sticks to the Julian calendar, the system which is commonly known as the 'Old Style' or merely 'OS'.

Claudianus must have had access to some kind of maps or

atlases, but his topographical information is flawed, nonetheless. Distances, in particular, are given in a manner which is not conducive to the reader's understanding of the movements of the troops. Claudianus uses the Roman measures of stadium [furlong] and passus [pace]. A furlong is one-eighth of a mile, equivalent to 220 yards, 660 feet, or 201 metres. A Roman pace is 1.5 metre. His measurements in furlongs are frequently completely detached from reality (such as for instance his information on the distance between Skipsea and York, which he claims to be 32 furlongs or 6.4 km). In reality, the distance from Skipsea to York is closer to 60 km. This is wrong by a factor 10. However in other places his miscalculations are off by various other factors and, in a few, the distances are relatively realistic.

While it is tempting to conclude that Claudianus simply had no sense of scale, the real problem lies with opaque geographical descriptions. Sometimes the points of departure and destination are towns, but occasionally the locations given are geographical features or townlands. The latter proceeding makes sense considering contemporary mapping conventions – but unfortunately Claudianus does not always discern between them. For example, the 56 furlongs from Clitheroe to Blackburn make no sense, unless he has meant the old Blackburnshire as a whole. Finally, it is not always obvious if the troops simply marched so and so many furlongs in a certain direction or if they actually arrived there. In yet other instances they are passing through an area covering a certain number of furlongs in the process. Moreover, Claudianus does not always provide information on the starting point. So, while Claudianus' measurements are not given at random, he has left his readers at a loss as to their precise meanings. Thus, though we have chosen to leave Claudianus' distances as he gave them, we recommend readers not to take them at face value.

To facilitate scholarly use of the original Latin text, the Royal Library (*Det Kongelige Bibliotek*) in Copenhagen, Denmark has kindly permitted us to copy their digitised version of Claudianus' work in its entirety. This version may also be found by using the library's on-line catalogue 'REX', which is available at the website http://www.kb.dk/da/index.html.

Introduction

Claudianus' Latin has some peculiarities, for which some explanation might be useful. His use of diacritical marks should be understood as follows: Unlike in French, the *accent grave* is not used for phonetic reasons, but in order to mark assimilation in prepositions (à = ab..., è = ex...), adverbs (adeò, verò m.fl.) and conjunctions. The *accent circonflexe*, however, serves the phonetic purpose of telling us that the vowel should be pronounced long. At the bottom of each page one sees one or two syllables of the first word on the following page. This was standard of many languages at the time – remaining so in Denmark until the last half of the 19th Century – and, as illiteracy was then pervasive, it might have been intended for easing the reading process when read aloud.

MAVORS IRLANDI-CUS,

Sive

Historia de bello Hibernico biennium in Hibernia gesto, chartis consignata à Commilitone

A. C.

HAFNIÆ,
Characteribus OVIDII LYNNOW
Anno 1718.

The Irish Mars

or,

A History of the War in Ireland for Two Years,
from Notes Recorded by a Fellow Soldier

Elegans hoc veterani Regiæ hujus Universitatis Hafniensis Civis & SS. Theologiæ Studiosi Præstantissimi ANDREÆ CLAUDIANI scriptum, cujus titulus est Mavors Irlandicus, sive Historia de bello Hibernico biennium in Hibernia gesto, tam bene, fide, accuratè & nitidè est compositum, ut tam ipsa Historia belli exinde scitè innotescat, qvàm qvantam etiam operam, fidelitatem, dexteritatem & virtutem in conspicuam ac perpetuam rerum gestarum memoriam Danicæ copiæ, qvæ a beato gloriosissimæ memoriæ Daniæ, Norvegiæ, reliqvorumqve Ducatuum, Provinciarumqᶻ, qvæ ad Danicum imperium pertinent, Monarcha Augustissimo & Serenissimo CHRISTIANO QVINTO in Britannici Imperii subsidium missæ erant, præstiterint. Qvocirca hoc scriptum publicum prelum meretur, & author gratiosissimam in tantorum discriminum præmium exopto promotionem. Hafniæ d. 5 Febr. Anno 1718.

Johannes Bircherod
Jani fil.
Facultatis Philosophicæ in Reg.
Universitate Hafniensi p. t.
Decanus.

This elegant work by a veteran member of this, the Royal University of Copenhagen, and a most excellent student of Sacred Theology, Andreas Claudianus, the title of which is *Mavors Irlandicus*, or History of the IrishWar fought for two years in Ireland, has been composed so well, faithfully, carefully, and clear, that the very history of the war is made just as much known, as how much the Danish troops surpass in their effort, fidelity, readiness, and virtue, in the present as in the lasting memory of their deeds. They were sent as auxiliaries for the British Empire by the blessed Monarch of Denmark, Norway, and the rest of duchies and provinces, which belong to the Danish rule, the Most August and Serene Christian V, of the most glorious memory. Therefore this work deserves the public press, and I wish the author the greatest promotion in recompense for such high risks.

Johannes Bircherod Jensen
Acting Dean of the Faculty of Philosophy
at the Royal University of Copenhagen
Copenhagen February 5th in the year 1718.

AUGUSTISSIMO MONARCHÆ FRIDERICO QVARTO,
REGI DANIÆ ET NOR-VEGIÆ &c.

Serenissimo Regi ac Domino meo clementissimo!

Inter alias, AUGUSTISSIME PATRIÆ PATER, divinæ providentiæ indagines, vix qvicqvam rerum à sanctiori populo gestarum commemoratione jucundius, nullumqve homini præsertim in Reipublicæ administratione occupato studium esse utilius agnosco, qvàm qvod historiis discendis evolvendisq; impenditur; nemo enim fit prudens & ad res benè gerendas in Reipublicæ administratione aptus, nisi face histo-

Dedication

To the noblest Monarch
Frederick
The Fourth
King of Denmark and Norway etc.

My honourable and merciful King and Lord,
Recognising our Heavenly Father's guidance of human destiny, Sir, you will hardly find anything more pleasant than the recollection of the deeds performed by your blessed people, and no passion more helpful to a man tasked first and foremost with the conduct of state affairs than learning and reading history.

DEDICATIO.

hiftoriarum prævia ex aliorum damnis & miris in orbe revolutionibus cautior evaferit, namq; fic ex alieni periculi lectione fanioris trutina mentis ea ponderantibus accedit lux, animos fuô fic illuftrans fplendore, ut ab exitiofis infcitiæ tenebris pedem eripiant. Sanè fi fcire aliqvis defideret temporum viciffitudines & varietates mutationesq; rerum in Republica geftarum, confilia & acta Regum, Principum, aliorumq; virorum illuftrium, tum in Imperiis, tum in Ecclefia, Regni unius alteriusq; ruinam & interitum, initia bellorum eorumq; res geftas & exitus, oborientes in animis invidos rebellantium motus, qvietis & tranqvilitatis publicæ confervationem & ufum rectum; fi qvis & explorare cupiat, qvàm inconftantes ac flexibiles hominum fint voluntates, qvantùm fimultatum, infidiarum vanitatumq; in ingenio mundi delitefcat, hæc omnia Hiftoriæ qvafi vivis & immortalibus exemplis demonftrant. Qvem in finem ego nec volo nec poffum filentiô hanc meam ut oculati teftis ex vera rei
appre-

Dedication

For history is the torch which leads us along the safe path, avoiding the pitfalls that others have fallen into. This torch helps the clever statesman to steer a flawless course where others err. Because he who has a grasp of the dangers at hand and those who know how to evaluate perilous events on the scale of a trained intellect are fortunate enough to have the intuition and the mental capacity to stay aloof from fateful decisions taken on the basis of ignorance.

Obviously, he who wishes to understand the change of times can do no better than to delve into history. Such scholarly activity may open the view to the important developments in the state, councils and actions by kings, princes and other enlightened men, be they in temporal or spiritual office. It will reveal causes of the ruin and destruction of kingdoms, the breakout of wars, the fighting and the end state. It might demonstrate political ambitions with those responsible for decisions on either war or peace and the way war is being instrumentalised. Moreover, close scrutiny of historical facts may disclose the inconstant and wavering aspirations of decision-makers, disagreements, political manœuvres and deceit.

DEDICATIO.

apprehensione consignatam Hibernicæ expeditionis narrationem prætermittere, qvin potiùs omnia qvæ, dum Martis comes essem atq; ejusdem sortis æmulus cum Regiis copiis, in Britanniam, Hiberniam, Belgiam transportatis, mihi & auditu & oculis & tantùm ipso rerum usu sunt comperta, ea aliis qvoqve tradam, ut ab oblivione & interitu vindicentur; etenim haud me fugit, præclara qvædam Reipublicæ hujus lumina magnô ejusdem non ab Anglis tantum, sed & Danis obtinendæ narrationis desideriô ardere; huic debitus ardori amor & obseqvium post diuturnam cessationem tandem me impulit operi manum admovere, & hoc qvantulumcunq; sit rerum in bello Hibernico gestarum, meisq; ipsius oculis usurpatarum compendium, eâ, qvâ jam est adornatum facie, chartis consignare, & publicæ luci expositum ad pedes Serenissimæ Regiæ Majestatis Vestræ unà mecum provolvere; Serum & præposterum fortasse diceres, Rex Augustissime, fœtum posthumum! Sed con-

A 3   ceden-

Dedication

Being an eye-witness to the Irish expedition, I see it as my duty to convey my experiences of the war. Thus, I have written down the following narration in faithful accordance with my own and others' recollections of events. Rather than leaving all this knowledge to oblivion and obliteration I shall deliver testimony to others so that it may be saved with them. For all the experience has been registered by my own ears and eyes, as well as by my engagement in the events mentioned during my time as a private soldier, when I bore my part of the hazards facing Your Majesty's troops transferred to Britain and Ireland and eventually to Belgium.

I am not ignorant of the fact that certain high-ranking men of this state are also eager to preserve the tale of this particular war, not only covering the deeds by the English, but those of the Danes, too.

After long suspension, my enthusiasm and obedience to the task did eventually urge me to continue the work. Thus, I sat down, resuming writing this humble narrative of the actions in the Irish war, which I had witnessed with my own eyes. I have endeavoured to do so in the form by which it now appears, to place it together with myself at Your Noble Majesty's disposal, in order to subsequently make it available to a wider audience.

You may find this a tardy and no longer relevant product, Sir, a fruit of yesteryear. However, I believe that this ought

DEDICATIO

cedendum hoc putavi partim injuriis temporum paupertatisq; ftudiorumqve inter pulveres fcholafticos denuo abfolvendorum, partim acerbæ lædentis fortunæ invidiæ, qvæ fummas ad infelicitatis incitas miferrimé me redactum retinuit, partim deniqve pœdagogicis per tria luftra functionibus, qvibus diftrictus diftentusq; né in ordinem qvidem redigere potui, qvæ tumultuarié congeffi, & inter ftrepitus militares, tumultus bellicos, & itinerum faftidia, qvotidianis pabulationum famulitiiq; periculis ac moleftiis obnoxius obfervata notavi: Statutum qvidem habui apud animum meum ac deliberatum, totius Hiberniæ Regionum, urbium, locorum, fituationum fluminumqve ordines ac defcriptiones tanqvam vivis coloribus ad Lectoris applaufum adornare, fed abfterruit me ab onere Ætnâ graviore res angufta domi, & nervi rerum defectus agendarum edendarumq;; Animum ergo revocavi ad ea, qvæ in tam turbulento rerum bellicarum ftatu per continuas occupationes,

itine-

Dedication

to be excused, partly because of difficult times and privation, and partly because of studies amidst scholarly dust that needed to be concluded. Moreover, a bitter fate striking me to the ground held me up, most regrettably bringing me to the end of my tether. Finally, my teaching obligations during three terms have occupied my time to the extent that I could not bring any system in what I have collected in those tumultuous days.

My original intent was – based on the observations I made during the years of martial clamour, the commotion of war, the nausea from the voyage and the daily dangers and troubles – also to describe the conditions and characteristics of provinces, cities, places, sites and streams of the Irish kingdom in vivid colours so to speak for the benefit of the reader, but tense conditions at home and a lack of means persuaded me not to take on such a task more taxing than climbing Mount Etna. Thus, to the best of my efforts I rallied my wits to the affairs that I had already made notes on. These covered the chaotic conditions of military activities throughout continuous employment, the marches, the din of

DEDICATIO.

itinera, armorum strepitus, classica, obsidia aliasq; obviarum imagines rerum in stativis & hybernis, qvoad fieri potuit, annotaveram; vix enim ac ne vix qvidem commisi, ut notatu dignum aliqvid praeterlaberetur, qvod non verborum compendio in locum sibi satis congruum insereretur.' Ut ergo unum alterumve splendoris Augusti Nominis Tui radiolum clementissime patiaris, tenuem atqve exilem hunc laborem illustrare, illumq; Serenissimo vultu adspicere, Te, Augustissime Monarcha, devotissime supplex oro, clementissimo fretus ipsa intra viscera ingenerato Vestrae Majestati affectu & propensitate erga meritos & miseros omnesq; pauperes fortunae immitioris ictibus & malevolorum hominum plagis injuriisq; expositos, eandem Gratiae magnitudinem mihi submisissime imploranti non defuturam. Qvod superest nocte atqve interdiu Deum Regem Coeli & Terrae ardentissimis suspiriis ac votis imploro, ut Reg: Maj: Vestram omni felicitate, in-

A 4   colu-

battle, the battle cries, the sieges and various impressions received in camps and in winter quarters. For all this I have found places to write down. I believe that I have hardly, if at all, let anything important go unmentioned – merely because of lack of adequate space – though where needed I have scribbled down in abridged form.

Therefore, Sir, please let this unassuming piece of work add whatever possible to the grandeur of your fame and your noble name. Moreover, Sir, it is my sincere hope that you in turn will look approvingly on this. I humbly and devotedly beseech you from my heart to show mercy and kindness towards those deserving, those suffering and all those impoverished by misfortune and subject to injuries and wrong-doings. And I beg most humbly that I, too, may not be excluded from similar greatness of favour.

Finally, both night and day I pray to our Heavenly Father that He shall crown and reward Your Majesty with every kind

DEDICATIO.

columitate, triumpho, pace, brabeô coronet remuneretq;, ut sub altissimi clypeo Numinis, & sub Vestræ Majestatis regimine & celebratissimo pietatis Zelo ad nominis divini gloriam Ecclesia Christi extremos usq; ad Indos nova indies incrementa capiat, & Regna Provinciæqve Vestræ Majest: semper vigeant atq; omni pace beatitateq; floreant: Qvod ità oro, ut majori studiô magisq; ex ardentiori suspiriô & intimis cordis penetralibus orare nunqvàm possim.

Ser; Reg; Majest: Vestræ

Dabam Steenstrop   humillimus Subditus & devo-
d. 29 Junii 1717.   tissimus Servus

                     ANDREAS CLAUDIANUS,
                      S:S: Theol: Studiosus.

Dedication

of happiness, soundness, triumph and peace now and hereafter. And I pray that – shielded by His will and Your Majesty's leadership and piety – the word of the Church of Christ may be spread daily all the way to far India, and that your reigns and provinces may for ever thrive and flourish in complete peace and joy. This I pray sincerely and with great zeal from a burning desire and from the bottom of my heart.

Your Majesty the King's Servant
  Your most humble and devoted servant

  Andreas Claudianus,
   S:S Theol: Studiosus.

Ad Lectorem Candidum.

Illustria inter Romanæ Eloqventiæ Parentis Ciceronis monumenta, qvorum non solùm propter dignitatem styli ad sublimitatem surgentis, verùm etiam ob sententiarum gravitatem magna Eruditum Orbem subit admiratio, emicat gravissimum hoc ejus Elogium: CEDANT ARMA TOGÆ, animadvertit qvippe Prudentiæ ille Ocellus, nihil in vita singulare aut egregium præstare posse viros excellentes & graves ad gubernacula Reipublicæ accessuros, nisi animos doctrinâ excoluerint, neq; æqvô animô ferre magnam posse contentionem, nisi Doctorum præceptis atq; literis non leviter tincti inde ab adolescentia usq; essent, sed penitùs imbuti; Verùm enimverò mirandam esse illorum puto imprudentiam (dicerem impudentiam) qvi artium cognitionem humaniorum respuentes, alia, qvæ vel corpori vel fortunæ

A 5

To the Sincere Reader

"Let arms yield to the toga"* is among the principal proverbs coined by Cicero, the father of Roman eloquence. His works inspires admiration throughout the erudite humanity, not only because of the dignified style, which is indeed magnificent, but also because of the significance of his maxims.

It is obvious† that at the helm of the state even excellent and dignified men can accomplish little in this life, which is singular or distinguished, unless they develop their minds by learning. Moreover, in controversy they cannot prevail in equanimity unless since childhood they have not only been influenced by the doctrines of teachers and studies, but immersed wholly in scholarship.

I am acutely aware that ignorance and impertinence are pervasive with those who despise human scholarship while

---

* The phrase has later been exploited by the Swiss war theoretician Antoine Henri Baron de Jomini in his *Précis de l'art de la guerre* (*The Art of War*), where he claims that you should not *séparer la toge de l'épée* (separate the toga from the rapier), or separate politics and war.

† The precise translation would be; "Obviously the Little Eye of Prudence observed..." With this Claudianus may refer to Cicero's dictum that "Rashness attends youth, as prudence does old age."

Ad Lectorem

tunæ debentur, multis huic gradibus anteferant, qvippè qvod ad Magistratum aut administrationem Reipublicæ nihil emolumenti, multò minùs existimationis ab illa redundare credant tristes illi & bruti Divinarum rerum Censores. At si, rejectîs opinionum involucrîs & tegumentîs, qvæ illi rei ipsius veritati obtendere solent, comitem eruditionis Honestatem, Jucunditatem & Utilitatem rectâ rationis trutinâ ponderare velimus, multa profectò ipsis ejus in visceribus & ad vitam rectè instituendam, & ad arcana naturæ perscrutanda, & ad politias sapienter gubernandas apprimè necessaria latere deprehendemus; Nam si Honesti nos movet ratio? qvid studiis literarum honestius? qvæ nos non modò à feris & rationis expertibus animantibus, sed ab incultis etiam & (si dicere liceat) obbrutescentibus hominibus egregium qvantum secernunt, ut nihil dicam de gravioribus antiqvorum censuris Philosophorum, qvi aliàs inter hominem & pecudem nullum esse discrimen statuerunt. Qvid iis honestius? qvæ nos ad

preferring doings, which depend either on the body or on chance. I am certain that the verdict of the prominent, firm and fair judges of things Divine will be that such activities produce neither advantage nor honour for the civic offices or for the administration of the state.

Laying aside the opinions of ignorant people who tend to conceal the truth of the matter, we want to weigh on the scales of the intellect respectability, which is the companion of learning, enjoyment and efficacy. We must realise that precisely respectability is a prerequisite for a decent life, for investigating the secrets of nature, and for the wise government of society.

Choosing respectability as our source of inspiration we shall see that nothing is more respectable than attention to learning. Not only does this set us apart from savage animals and matters without intellectual challenges, but also from uncivilised and brutish people. Neither can these say anything about the important thoughts of the ancient philosophers, nor do they see any dividing line between men and cattle.

Now, what can be more respectable than studies? They lead us on to the path of reflection on God, to a notion of the

Candidum.

ad ipfius Dei contemplationem, cœleftium rerum cognitionem & verarum perducunt virtutum amplexum, fine qvibus haud fecùs ac porcus qvidam de grege Epicuri nulli rei homo magis, qvàm ventri atq; abdomini addictus terrenis inhæret, & æternis neglectis perituris mundi falebris inhiat: At fi Delectationem qværamus? fic ea in re literarum cum Honeftate conjuncta eft, ut nefciam profectò, utrum plus honeftatis in ftudiis, an jucunditatis inveniamus: delectant enim in omni ætate atq; fortuna non fine maxima omnium admiratione, adeò ut mihi perfvaferim nullam potiorem & fvaviorem unqvàm fuiffe in Orbe voluptatem, qvàm in caftris Mufarum militare, & indefeffum cum eisdem habere commercium. Qvòd fi fortè (ut fubindè fieri folet) plus ea, qvæ Utilia fint, qvàm qvæ vel honefta vel jucunda fpectemus; qvid ad Utilitatem literis & eruditione præftantius? nè dicam plus neceffarium, fine qvibus neq; virtus neqve Philofophia nobis cognita, neq; divinarum neq; humanarum fcientia manifefta,

next world, and a fond embrace of true virtue. For without virtue man is like a pig in the herd of Epicurus,* favouring greed and materialism. He clings to temporal matters, sticks to the perishable, and is indifferent to the thereafter.

However, can we call ourselves respectable if we seek enjoyment through our learning? Yes, for joy is as connected with learning as is respectability. In every age and under any circumstance learning has brought delight and admiration. I am convinced that no enjoyment in the world has ever been stronger and more pleasant than that of serving the Muses, and to maintain an indissoluble bond with them.

However, even if we rank usefulness higher than both respectability and delight, we shall find that learning and erudition still remain of central importance. Without erudition we can understand neither virtue nor philosophy. We cannot obtain a clear perception of either divine or human matters.

---

* Greek philosopher, 341-270 BC. Father of the school of philosophy called Epicureanism, a philosophy recommending a happy, affluent and tranquil life.

Ad Lectorem

festa, sine qvibus nec Senatoris in curia gravitas, neq; Magistratûs in Republica authoritas, neqve Imperatoris in castris prudentia', neq; Oratoris in cathedra eruditio inclarescet. Rationibus ego adductus neq; frivolis neq; ineptis, liberalium cognitionem artium maximi pendo: qvia earum studia profunt hominibus non solùm ad delectationem, verùm etiam ad utilitatem in facultate dicendi, nam si qvi in pace & florente ac beata Republica militiæ navant operam, plus Arte, qvàm Marte, & exercitatione qvàm viribus sæpenumero proficiunt. Qvid juvat, armis indutis hostibus obsistere, nisi & opportunè sciant circumire, in cornua discurrere, pugnam mutare, ut vir viro, armis arma, dolus dolo, virtus virtuti opposita conferantur & sic ad exercitationes accedat usus, ut officium qvisq; suum strenuè faciat; Et qvis non exponendis rationibus inductus crediderit, non necessarium esse studium Eloqventiæ illis, qvi vel ad præcipua Regum & Principum munera & consilia, vel ad sacra rostra sunt adhibendi, & in augusta
audi-

And without such insight no senator will stand out in the council, no magistrate can wield authority in the state, no commander can exercise his military genius, nor can a professor excel in his chair.

Being guided by neither hollow nor futile considerations, I most of all appreciate the acquisition of knowledge of the liberal arts.* The study of these does indeed benefit human beings not only by their pleasantries, but also by their usefulness with regard to the ability of speaking. It is obvious that those responsible for the defence of a peaceful and prosperous Republic oftentimes achieve more by art than by war and by contemplation rather than by strength. Although, at the call to arms we will fiercely oppose the enemy, this will be to no avail unless we discern also how and when to envelop him, turn his flanks and manage the battle so that man faces man, weapon confront weapon, deception deceives the opponent's trickery, courage is shown in face of the enemy's courage, and that every soldier master his trade so that everyone can perform his rôle efficiently and promptly. Not even those, who were not themselves trained in scholarly fields, would doubt that the study of eloquence is necessary for men who either hold distinguished office or sit in the councils of kings and leaders or in the sacred chairs, and those

---

* The "liberal arts" (Latin: *artes liberales*) are those subjects or skills that in classical antiquity were considered essential for a free person to take an active part in civic life. Grammar, rhetoric, and logic were the core liberal arts. During medieval times, these three subjects were called the *Trivium* and were amended to include arithmetic, geometry, music, and astronomy called the *Quadrivium*. Together the *Trivium* and *Quadrivium* constituted the seven liberal arts of the medieval university curriculum.

Candidum.

auditoria panegyri orationem sunt habituri, publicô dicendi officiô funguntur. Diversa Magistratuum est ratio, qvi opus habent duobus, νῷ κυβερνῶντι καὶ λόγῳ ἐγκελευσμένῳ, mente gubernatrice in se ipsis, & oratione jubente ac mandante aliis, qvid sit faciendum, qvid omittendum; deinde Magistratus tractant populum admodùm insolentem, contumacem, refractarium, in omnibus non morigerum, necessitas igitur omninò flagitat antiqvitatis veterumqve disciplinas Scriptôrum, similemq; eorum in dicendo facultatem ad flectendos auditorum animos, ad conciliandas ac devinciendas hominum voluntates, & captandam omnium, si fieri poterit, gratiam ac favorem, ad multa fingenda atq; conformanda verbis & oratione. Hujus rei non immemor præstantissimus olim Philosophorum Coryphæus Aristoteles, cui tanta fuit dicendi copia, ut illum Parens Eloqventiæ Tullius, aureum manans Eloqventiæ flumen appellare haud dubitaverit; Id secum reputans Togatorum Doctissimus Idem, qvi ex limpidissimo
velut

giving speeches to the esteemed audiences, and those who speak in public.

The decision-maker will generally have two needs:* a mind devising adequate schemes, and persuasiveness telling others what to do and what to avoid. Such a leader may rule even the most conceited, obstinate and stubborn people who are unwilling to comply. Thus, necessarily leadership requires mastery of the disciplines of the writers of antiquity as well as their ability to speak well enough to bend the minds of the listeners, to win over and fetter men's preferences and, if possible, to captivate everyone's attention.

The leader Aristotle, whose rhetoric was so sophisticated that Cicero – himself the most outstanding of philosophers and eloquence personified – labelled him 'the fair torrent of expressiveness.' Cicero, the learned Roman, whose own language was as clear as spring water, thereby acknowledged

---

* Claudianus writes this in Greek.

Ad Lectorem

velut fonte suam hauserat facundiam, Eloqventiæ Studiosum apud sese in maximo futurum honore publicé fatetur; id etiam considerârunt omnes, qvos non sine communi omnium laude decoravit administratio Reipublicæ Literariæ, dum Philosophiam & Eloqventiam habere commune qvoddam vinculum, & qvasi cognatione qvâdam inter se contineri putârunt: At si qvis existimet sine studiorum adminiculo felicem posse acqviri Eloqventiam, & sibi & aliis insidiatur, nil agens, nisi ut omnibus persvadeat, meliorem aliundè qvàm ex literis crescere facultatem dicendi, qvæ tamen infelici teste Experientiâ arescat, almâ nisi doctrinâ alatur, sed & omnis in studiis labor nihil est aliud, teste Tulliô, qvàm cœca qvædam & muta scientia, nisi accedat ratio qvædam confirmatioq; ornatè dicendi. Progrediatur jam nostra consideratio ad majorem utilitatem ex literis capiendam; Authoritate enim earum commoti, nihil hâc in vita antiqvius hâc virtute rerum omnium Dominâ ducimus.

that those devoted to acquiring the art of eloquence were the most likely to win public esteem.

Within the so-called Republic of Letters,* too, the thought was prevalent that philosophy and eloquence constituted a common bond amongst members of this society, which was held together by a certain affinity through common scholarly references and ways of expression.

However, no one should make himself believe that successful eloquence can be acquired without study and that it lies waiting for him and others to take for free. In my experience won by bountiful teaching, doing nothing but trying to convince the world that oratorical talent materialises out of the blue and not from dry learning, is a vain ambition. Cicero is my witness that the toil of study is nothing more than unconditional acceptance of old maxims unless reason and improvement is added.

This may encourage us to go on considering the greater advantages to be derived from learning. For when first its

---

* *Res Publica Literaria*: A belief common amongst academia prior to and during the Enlightenment that their occupation with learning and erudition constituted them as a cross-national 'republic' exempted from national rules and regulations governing the lives of ordinary citizens.

Candidum.

mus. Ipsa omnium dignitates hominum omnesq; felicitatis gradus superat; Ipsa sola regno bene gerendo sufficit, vitia verò non nisi ad perdendum sunt idonea: Hæc duo sunt, qvæ hominem ad amplissimum dignitatis gradum atq; Majestatis fastigium evehere solent, virtus nimirùm & honestarum disciplina artium, nam ut aspectus ab aëre circumfuso accipit lumen, sic animus à disciplinis liberalibus novô qvasi splendore ornatur, qvibus in perseqvendis omnes corporis cruciatus & omnia mortis pericula parvi sunt ducenda. Videmus etiam consignata literis modestissima sapientissimorum hominum præcepta, qvibus & hâc & omni aliâ qvâcunq; hominum actione, qvicqvid aut agendum sit, aut omittendum instrui possimus. Videmus exempla, qvæ qvotqvot viros illustres, totidem illustrium monumenta meditationum nobis commendant, idqve non aliâ de causa, nisi ut tanqvàm expressas non solùm ad intuendum imagines, verùm etiam ad imitandum eorum virtutes

clout is realised, we shall see that no virtue in this life is more crucial. Erudition transcends the merits of us all and is the true source of pleasure. Although faults are inevitable, wisdom is what is required for a reign to be conducted well. There are two preconditions for a man to reach the highest degree of merit and the summit of magnificence: virtue, certainly, and discipline in the study of the liberal arts.

Just as our vision is clear on a bright and cloudless day, the intellect derives from the liberal disciplines a sort of new brilliance through which all earthly anguish and all the worries about the life hereafter assume reduced importance. The literature, which has been written by the wisest of men, offer fair instruction in what ought to be done and what should be left aside.

Similarly, we emulate examples set by eminent men and admire testimonies of their illustrious deliberations. We do this for the simple reason that we create imagery and write commemorative literature not only for admiration, but because we wish to copy the virtues of our forbears in order

Ad Lectorem

tes literis proditas ita nobis proponamus, ut sedulâ earundem pensitatione ad fervidam studiorum æmulationem animos ac mentem confirmemus. Deniqve literæ nostros fingunt formantqve mores ad vitam recte instituendam, & utilia ad Rempublicam capessendam consilia suppeditant, ut non minorem Togatis Reipublicæ Præfectis in civitate gerenda utilitatem afferat artium humaniorum cognitio, qvàm armorum exercitatio Ducibus militiæ Martisq; æmulis in bello gerendo: Eqvidem nihil foris prodesse arma puto, nisi gens Togata & viri prudentes domi suis ea regant consiliis, &, né qvid detrimenti Respublica patiatur, provide caveant. Interim utrobiq; palma virtuti & laurea lingvæ confertur, dispari verò sorte, in civitate modestia, in castris constantia, ibi enim toga, hic arma, ibi Feriæ, hic Furiæ, ibi lingva, hic plus etiam valent manus; ibi severitate cohibentur cives immorigeri, consilioq; & rationibus obstinati ad peccandum, hic salvîs Ducis auspi-

to strengthen our spirits and minds. Thus, learning shapes and forms our way of life in order for us to establish a decent existence and provides guidance in handling the business of the state. In this way the scholarly occupation with humanities is as useful to our state administration as it was to the prefects of Rome, and as important as is weapons training to the military commanders.

Honestly, I believe that military might is worthless unless it is governed by a wise political élite in councils at home. Their foresight should be the guarantor that the state suffers no harm. Anyway, while the palm of victory is bestowed upon the military commander the laurel adorns the political leader. However, while the political leadership must demonstrate humility, the army should be known for its steadiness. While the government is mostly made up of civilians the army is manned by military professionals. The society enjoys celebrations, the army is characterised by its fighting power; the political leadership functions through arguments, the army by wielding its strength. In society wayward citizens are held in check by laws and sanctions. With the colours the enemy is conquered by the correct and timely decisions by the commander's 'military genius.'*

---

* This is an expression coined by the Prussian war theorist Carl von Clausewitz in his magnum opus *On War*, published posthumously in 1831. Obviously this phrasing was not used by Claudianus publishing in 1718, but was found fitting by this translator. It means that the commander must possess a certain informed intuition based on his erudition, military training and sound judgment, but it does not imply that he is of necessity a 'genius' in the more common sense of that word.

Candidum.

auspiciis & non Arte minùs qvàm Marte ferocissimi hostes superantur: Sed qvoniam artium & literarum studia omni encomiô & prædicatione digna esse censeo, qværet forte non nemo, an vir magnus sine doctrina & studio Eloqventiæ nullus unqvàm vir magnus & præclarus extiterit? siqvidem domi for sq; multos & vidimus & audivimus fortes & prudentes viros & Reipublicæ regendæ sine studiis literarum aptos fuisse & salutares, Doctissimos autem noxios & damnosos. Homerus prudentissimos Ulyssem & Nestorem, atq; omnibus in rebus sapientissimos fingit, dum multorum ille hominum & urbes & mores vidit, prudentiam illam assecutus est, hic trium seculorum spatiô, plurima tum videndo, tum audiendo atqve etiam gerendo rerum maximum omnium usum adeptus, ac sapientissimus & eloqventissimus existimatus est. At difficile erit de omnibus unum & idem affirmare, Hoc tamen certô certius esse non dubitabo asserere, multos scilicet præstantes viros

B   ros

It is my opinion that interests in and learning of the liberal arts are commendable. Thus, some might inquire if there has ever been a great and intelligent man without any kind of education.

There have, nonetheless, been men of little education, both at home and abroad, who have turned out to be successful and compassionate statesmen. On the other hand, there have been many, though very learned, who caused havoc and mischief.

The ancient Greek author Homer described Ulysses and Nestor as two wise and insightful characters. Through his far-reaching journey Ulysses experienced both cities and customs of many people, thus developing forethought. Nestor, who had a reputation for insight as well as eloquence, acquired a practical understanding of all of the greatest events which had happened during three generations by experience and listening as well as by participation.

Although Homer's descriptions of the two is difficult to prove, I do not doubt that it is likely that many outstanding

Ad Lectorem.

ros ex ignorantiæ umbra atq; tenebris in lucem scientiæ ac virtutis protractos ex multarum rerum usu atq; experientiâ Duce sine doctrina, sine longo & laborioso Literarum studio ad administrandam Rempublicam, variaq; negotia pace belloq; tractanda, rem bene scienterq; gessisse; multos qvoqve, qvi salem sapientiæ primoribus tantùm labiis præguftârunt, mox in arcem sapientiæ se penetrâsse persvasi, & rebus saltem ad votum fluentibus prudentiæ famam aucupati, facta rerum revolutione sub onere corruerunt, nec sibi nec aliis frugi, saltem frugiperdæ. Illud etiam adjungo tantam multis ingeneratam esse vim naturæ, ut ad virtutem atq; laudem conseqvendam plus sæpiùs valeat ingenium sine doctrina, qvam doctrina sine sale, sine sapore judicii, id eft, invitâ, ut ajunt, Minervâ, & reluctante ingeniô & naturâ. Ad hæc autem accedit id qvod constantissimè affirmare ausim, omnibus absolutum numeris dari sapientiæ ac virtutis donum, cum ad naturam eximi-
am

men, who have grown up in the darkness of ignorance, have advanced towards the light of science and high merit. By experience from personal participation in many events, though without long and laborious studies, many such men have become successful statesmen, conducted negotiations both in peace and war, and governed well and skilfully.

Others though, who had paid only scant attention to learning, but believing themselves to be the epitome of wisdom, did well as long as things went according to plan. However, remiss in the field of forethought they faltered under the burden of command as soon as the situation changed and took the wrong decisions detrimental to themselves and to others.

Moreover, I want to suggest that learning with no skill is of little value compared with a natural disposition for the task at hand. Operating under adverse conditions, the man of a natural disposition and power of resistance will prevail. Furthermore, I should like to declare that the gifts of high merit and acumen are given unconditionally to those who combine in themselves reason with exceptional and noble

Candidum.

am atqve illuſtrem acceſſerit ratio & doctrina conjuncta cum Spiritus Sancti ſigillô; Ipſe enim ſolus in debilitate noſtra potens eſt; ſumit enim impetus qvosdam à natura virtus, qvæ ſtudioſis alitur obſervationibus, creſcit exemplis, Literis & doctrinis roboratur, conſummatur peritiâ, ingeniô exercetur, & à Spiritu Dei obſignatur; Hâc ratione Literariæ noſtræ juventutis verſatur ac circumvolvitur fortuna, qvippe ſi à primo ſtatim ætatis exordio in delectationes leviſſimas ineptiasq;, aut in ſummam prolabitur ignaviam, ſumpta jam prætexta & virili togâ eidem inhærere luto, eademqve frui levitate & ignaviâ unicè dat operam, ſi verò benignis naruræ dotibus ornata, felicitatem ingenii & judicii ſui, ad tractanda optimarum rerum ſanctiorum ſtudia applicuerit, & magnitudinem animo inſitam neutiqvam ſocordiâ ſinit torpeſcere, indies magis magisq; magna & magnoperè expetenda concipit, concepta conatur, conatusqve ſimul perficit, ut gradatim ad perfectæ

B 2   eru-

nature and learning blessed by the Holy Spirit – our trusty support in times of need.

Merit stemming from nature may be nourished by keen study, good examples and perusal of adequate literature. It is consolidated through practical experience, kept going by natural ability and impressed by the God's spirit.

It stands to reason that our youth's fortune is fickle. Obviously, if at an early age the young ones take to the easiest of pleasures or to great laziness, when they grow up they will reject great pain and hard labour and enjoy superficiality and inactivity.

However, if blessed with nature's favour our youth may combine the happiness of natural ability and own good judgment to accomplish studies of important matters. If they do not allow the greatness of their minds to be obscured by dullness, they may achieve great things. Day by day they might undertake new tasks and, while trying, realise that this endeavour lifts them further and further to the summit of accomplished erudition and of scholarship.

Ad Lectorem

eruditionis scientiarumq; culmina aqvilinis, qvod ajunt, pennis evehatur. Sed pluribus rem declarare supersedeo: Veterum exempla producere possem, qvi nunqvam eo usq; sapientiæ ac eruditionis, universam terram ut illustrarent, pervenissent, nisi peragratis fere mundi partibus incredibilem omnium sibi rerum experientiam comparâssent: qvod nunqvam fecissent, nisi hæc studia humanitatis magnum ad colendam virtutem regendamq; Rempublicam afferre emolumentum intellexissent. Qvis igitur mortalium est tam nullius ingenii aut rationis? qvis est tam aversus à vero? hospes in rebus anteactis, & cœcus in agendis, ut ex hoc non animadvertat, cum ad gubernacula Reipublicæ accesserint imperiti, maxima Reipublicæ fore naufragia: Testantur enim Historicorum cætera gravissimorum monumenta, qvæ fidem merentur apud omnes indubitatam, & non minus sacris qvàm profanis exemplis evincunt, summa Orbis Imperia & inclytas Respublicas

But I shall not dwell on what is evident: I might have given examples of people who, having been to almost any part of the world, had attained insight and sophistication enough to explain the dealings of nations; men who had gathered extensive experience on a wide variety of matters. They would never have advanced that far if they had not grasped that high merit and good governance benefits from cultivating the interests of humanity. Would anyone be oblivious to this? Who would not recognise this simple truth? A stranger to taking decisions on an informed basis, one who is blind to what is obviously necessary, or one who is inexperienced may not hesitate to take a seat in government. But disasters will occur; history, which should be trusted, abounds with examples. Examples from the spiritual as well as the temporal worlds show that the world order and many great nations have been shaken because of the leaders' ignorance and negligence.

Candidum.

cas ob infcitiam & temeritatem Præfectorum ità effe labefactas, ut nec vola nec veftigium Reipublicæ ullum appareat, nec fpes emergendi tandem aliqvando ulla fit relicta. In gubernatione navium reqviritur peritus gubernator, navem enim regere rei ignarus nauticæ pertimefcit, ad liberorum informationem eruditus & prudens debet adhiberi pædagogus; nec periculofa minus eft minusve difficilis Reipublicæ adminiftratio, qvæ felicius nunqvam geri poteft, potuit aut poterit, pvam per homines omni doctrinâ, prudentiâ, & longô rerum ufu præftantes. Eft, ut fcapham fcapham, & fcyphum fcyphum dicam, doctrina, veræ laudis fundamentum, juventutis alimentum, fenectutis oblectamentum, fecundarum rerum ornamentum, adverfarum perfugium ac folatium, Virtutis, Prudentiæ, actuumq; magiftra & moderatrix, fons veræ felicitatis, magnum utilitatis incrementum, egregiumq; virtutis præfidium, Qvæ cum ita fint, cumqve artes humaniores

B 3   adeo

To the Sincere Reader

For that reason risks to the Republic of Letters have emerged with dire prospects for the future.

Like steering a ship requires a trained captain, an educated and far-sighted teacher should be employed for teaching of children. Governing a state is no less complicated. It should be conducted by individuals of extensive knowledge, discretion and experience with state affairs.

Learning – the sustenance of our youth, the delight of old age – forms the basis for handling dangers, for virtue, for care and for actions. It is the precondition for sensible development. Since this is so, and since scholarship is necessary for man to improve, it is our obligation to make sure that our abilities and qualities of the mind are given a fertile ground to mature.

Ad Lectorem Candidum.

adeò hominibus fint neceffariæ, feqvitur inde nexu prorfus indiffolubili has divinorum opes ingeniorum, & hæc animi indolisq; ad optima erectæ bona, hasq; mentis folidas & immobiles divitias hominum præftantiffimis & qvibus è meliore luto finxit præcordia Titan, ita omni laude, prædicatione, literis monumentisq; commendari debere, ut majori ftudiô magisq; ex animo nihil poffit ab æqvioribus rerum Cenforibus commendari.

Impe-

Thus, the riches of the intellect characterise the most excellent of men. Fair judges of these matters will rule that such men, who have been blessed with a fine soul, who possess great zeal and a great spirit, are destined for renown and praise in writing and by monuments.

Impetrârunt ab Augustissimo Daniæ Norvegiæq; REGE CHRISTIANO Vto Angli auxilia, periclitante ad extremum usq; naufragium Religione, Salute, Libertate & Lege Patriæ in propria jam jam viscera sæviturae; Mittitur ergo alacriter et omni abjecta cunctatione agmen septem millium, selectâ eqvitum peditumqve constans manu, sub ductu imperioq; illustrissimi Ducis Ferdinandi Wilhelmi de Wyrtenberg in subsidium Auspicatissimo & Potentissimo Magnæ Britanniæ Regi Guilielmo hujus nominis Tertio, adversus exulem dejectumq; Regem Jacobum Stuart Secundum, initiô itineris factô mense Septembri, Anni æræ Christianæ MDCLXXXIX, per Selandiam, Fioniam & Jutiam, tandem qvatuordecim decursu dierum ad urbem

Claudianus' Account

The English asked for military assistance from the noble King Christian the Fifth of Denmark and Norway. They saw their Protestant faith, their welfare, liberty, and the laws of the country menaced by looming dissolution, which seemed to be afoot in its very centre at that very time.[*] Thus, willingly and without unnecessary delay, a troop contingent of seven thousand men was dispatched. It was a select corps[†] consisting of horse and foot under the command of the illustrious captain-general, Ferdinand Wilhelm Duke of Württemberg-Neustadt. The task was to deploy in support of the propitious and potent William the Third, King of Great Britain, fighting against the overthrown and exiled King James the Second Stuart.[‡]

The journey began in the month of September in the year 1689 during King Christian's Reign. The troops proceeded through Zealand, Funen and Jutland, until eventually, after a

---

[*] On 12 July 1689, he King William III empowered Sir Robert Molesworth, his envoy to Copenhagen, to negotiate the details of Danish military assistance with the Danish government.

[†] In Denmark the national contingent joining William III's 'coalition-of-the-willing' is mostly designated the 'Danish Auxiliary Corps'. That is true for the primary material found in the State Archives as well as for most literature. However, although a lieutenant-general commanded this 7,000-strong entity, it was not a corps in the modern sense of this word.

[‡] Although James was James II in England he was James VII in Scotland.

❋ 2 ❋

Ripas perventum eft; indeqve longius tria milliaria apud pagum Hierpftadienfem in finibus Slesvigæ & Jutiæ haud procul à mari disfitum ftativa habuit. Spatio qvatuor hebdomadum ibi fub tentoriis hibernavimus, priusqvàm omnia, qvæ ad navigationem reqvirebantur, parata effent ac inftructa, namq; claffem ad littora Liftrenfia fluctuantem confcendere militibus admodùm fuit difficile, qvippe qvi non nifi per qvotidianum maris receffum fcaphas, qvibus ad naves vehi oportebat, petere poterant. Horrendum vifu audituqve fuit, miferrimos omnium agricolas, qvibus ea tempeftate fæviori edicto ad fuos reverti lares interdictum erat, vitam degiffe adeò calamitofam, ut partim deficiente ipfis victu, eqvis pabulo, qvòd bruma jam maxime fæviret, nivesqve terram obruerent, fame geluqve exanimarentur; partim impedimenta plauftris impofita ad claffem vecturi, dum in plauftris exonerandis retardarentur, à præ rapido æftuantis maris acceffu cum
cur-

course of fourteen days, they arrived in the city of Ribe. From there they went on more than 3000 paces, to their assembly area in the village Hjerpsted near the border between Schleswig and Jutland and not very far from the North Sea.

Under wintery weather conditions we camped in tents there for four days, until all which was required for the voyage had been prepared and provided for. It was quite difficult for the soldiers to embark, since the transport fleet was moving to and fro off the coast at Lister Dyb. Moreover, because of the daily ebb and flow the men were hampered in making for the barges, which were necessary for transfer to the ships.

It was also terrible to see and hear the peasants, who were in a pitiful state. By a strict decree they had been driven out from their homes and forbidden to return throughout that season. They were leading an unlucky life due to lack of victuals for themselves and fodder for their animals, since winter was already raging and snow covered the earth. Many died of starvation and as a result of the frost. Moreover, in their efforts to carry the troops' baggage to the waiting vessels and while they were hampered in unloading their wagons, quite a few were swept away by sudden rises of the foaming

❖ 3 ❖

curribus & eqvis abforpti mifere perirent. Tertiô deinde Nonas Novembris nos reliqvi edictô Generali ad pagum Höier dimidiô milliari ab Hierpftadienfi diftantem, ut naves confcenderemus, proficifci jubebamur. Pridie Nonas nos cum aliqvot centuriis ex legione Principis Friderici navem Falconem album dictam confcendimus; Ipfis autem Nonis ob adfportationem commeatuum abundatiorem ad anchoras naves omnes fteterunt. Octavô Idûs manè folventes non longiùs unô milliari in altum progreffi anchoras jecimus, qvòd omnia fimul è portu egredi cum maris refluxu neqvirent navigia, impingentibus aliis, aliis ad exeundum fignô datô in procinctu non ftantibus. Sub lucis verò ortum feqventis, fignô iterum datô paffis plenisqve velis & ventô Subfolanô ftridente pleraqve in altum vehuntur, tum circa vefperam inhorrefcens mare paulatim levari, deinde acrius vento concitatum cœcos ac nigros fluctus Alpium inftar, horribili cum fonitu ma-

B 5   gnis-

sea, perishing together with their carts and horses.

Then on the 3rd of November – on the decision taken by the general presently in command – in order to embark, we were ordered to move to the hamlet of Højer, which lay 500 paces from Hjerpsted.* On the 4th we embarked the ship White Falcon together with other companies of Prince Frederick's Regiment. Then, on the 5th, all the ships remained anchored waiting for more abundant supplies to be taken on board. On the 6th of November, having set sails in the morning, we progressed but one nautical mile into the open sea. Not all the ships could exit the harbour at the same level of the tide, but while some lay rubbing their gunwales against one another other, and some still were not equipped for battle, sign was given to exit the harbour.†

At sunrise the following morning, with the easterly wind blowing, the departure was signalled, and with all sails set the fleet pulled out to sea. Then, around midnight, the rough sea began to smoothen little by little, though it was stirred up again by an even fiercer wind rising, setting in motion large, black waves with a horrible sound and a loud whistling.

---

* For the Danish Auxiliary Corps as a whole embarkation was begun on 14 October (see e.g. Gerhard Brammer, *Livgarden 1658–1908* (Kjøbenhavn: Trydes Forlag, 1908) p. 112).

† The Danish task force was hardly in the open sea before the pilots managed to ground the flagship *Christian IV* and two minor vessels.

4

gnisq; stridoribus ciere atq; provolvere cœpit. Nocte intempestâ triplici impetu oculum navis nostræ perfregit procella, adeò ut omnes fluctibus superfusis supremam horam adesse rati, divinâ tamen ope, licèt aliqvot diebus sævissimè perduraret tempestas, ab ulteriori malo simus liberati, qvamobrem & nautæ omnium sinus velorum, excepto uno minori in summo mali fastigio, nempe thoraciô, planè demissos contraxêre. Sæviente hacce tempestate, naves adeò disjectæ sunt ac distractæ ab invicem, ut ad oras Norvegicas aliæ, aliæ Edenburgum Scotiæ, qvædam Novum Castellum Angliæ appellerent; nos verò cum reliqva classe Ducem Würtenbergicum secuti iter porrò pergentes, qvintô Idus sub lucis ortu promontorium Flamburgi in conspectum duximus. Octavum jam milliare à Novo Castello Classis distabat, cum vel ob incuriam vel imperitiam Gubernatorum navis prætoriæ Christiani Qvarti nomine celebratæ, à recto, qvi Edenburgum ex instituto

That night, a forceful blast of wind completely crushed the hawsehole part of our vessel so that, with the overflowing waves, everybody imagined that their final hour was near. However, with God's help, even though the rough weather lasted for several days, thanks to the sailors who managed to reef the sails, we were saved from further mischief. While this wild weather was raging our flotilla was scattered and many ships went astray, one after another. Thus, some of our vessels reached the coast of Norway, others Edinburgh in Scotland, which the English call New Castle (sic).[*] However, following the Duke of Württemberg we proceeded onwards with the remaining ships, and on the morning of the 9th we caught sight of Flamborough Head. The fleet was now eight thousand paces away from New Castle[†] when, either because of the captain's inexperience or his inattention to the navigation of the vessel, the flagship bearing the illustrious name of *Christian IV* turned away from the right course. Originally, it was bound for Edinburgh, but, throughout

---

[*] Possibly Claudianus has misunderstood what he has been told about Edinburgh. There is a Newcastleton in Scotland, but this is situated inland. The distance alone between the landing site of the main force at Flamborough Head and Edinburgh indicate that the vicinity of Newcastle-upon Tyne more likely is where the stray ships anchored.

[†] Although the distance does not fit with the map, this time Claudianus possibly means Newcastle-upon Tyne.

❋ 5 ❋

tuto tendere debebat, curfu adeò effet deflexum, ut retroacturi ad stationem optatam navigia, per aliqvot dies & noctes fruftrà renitentibus ventis obluctaremur, qvippe iterùm atq; iterùm ad promontorium Flamburgi recurrimus; hinc mutatô propofitô portum Hulli ad jaciendas anchoras tertiô Idus Novembris intrare decrevimus. Poft Occafum verò Solis, Lunæ beneficio lucentis per amnem Humbrum provectos obvia Liburna Anglicana explofione tormentorum, ut ipforum ufus ferebat, falutavit, cui refponfum fignô Danicô dedimus; Hinc illuftriffimus agminis Præfectus Dux de Würtenberg duos veloces, alterum Londinum ad imperata afferenda, alterum Edenburgum ad inqvirendos, fi qvi ex noftratibus eò delati effent, ablegavit: nam ut anteà diximus claffe fic difperfa navibusq; a fluctibus & vento huc illuc actîs, aliæ Norvegicis, aliæ Scoticis appulfæ littoribus; prætereaq; duæ naves à piratis Gallicis interceptæ erant atqve direptæ. *Jam* decimô tertiô Calendarum

several days and nights it struggled with adverse winds while trying to return to our pre-planned route. However, more than once it ran into the roads of the promontory of Flamborough Head.* From that position it was decided to heave to at the Port of Hull and to cast our anchors there, which then happened on the 11th of November.†

But after sunset, on our way in and illuminated by the moonlight, an English vessel emerging from the River Humber greeted us by a gun salute, as is the custom, which we reciprocated by a Danish Salute.‡ The captain-general of our troop contingent, the eminent commander Württemberg, sent off two fast ships – one to London carrying our credentials to King William, the other to Edinburgh in order to investigate into the fate of the stray ships. As already intimated, the fleet had been sorely scattered and ships had been driven by waves and wind soon here soon there. It was realised later that while some had gone to Norway, others had reached the coast of Scotland, and two ships had been intercepted and looted by French privateers.

---

* On 9 November, partly due to the storm and partly to faulty navigation, more than half of the fleet reached Flamborough Head on the east cost of Yorkshire.

† Over the next few days the Danish expeditionary force trickled ashore, as 61 ships landed between Bridlington and Grimsby – a beachhead stretched across more than 40 km.

‡ Danish Salute [*Dansk Løsen*] was a gun salute consisting of the discharge three – or more rarely nine or twenty-seven – guns.

6

rum Decembris, anchorîs solutîs obliqvô ad urbem Hullum contendimus cursu, instructi scilicet mandatô Ducis ac Præfecti nostri. Vesperâ autem ejus diei impingentes in arenam pedem laxavimus, usq; qvò sex orgyarum fundum prehenderemus, sicq; illâ nocte navem in anchoris tenuimus, & cum diluculo, vela dantes, densa licet involuti nebulâ, urbi appropinqvamus feré ad unius milliaris distantiam. Postero die urbem intravimus, ubi singulis sua assignabantur hospitia; biduum hac in urbe datum curandis longô maris itinere defessis corporibus, & mox indè Hullo relictâ CCXL stadia Eboracum usqve triduano itinere agmen processit; hinc elapsis qvatuordecim diebus qvædam legiones in circumjacentes vicos sunt distributæ. Johannes Henricus de Calnein tribunus legionis Sereniffimi Principis Frideriei cum cohorte sua in pago Shipdonia hibernavit aliqvo temporis intervallo, cœteræ autem legionis ejusdem cohortes in pagis vicinis. Qvarto
Idus

As on the 19th of November our place of anchorage had been approved, our general and commander-in-chief obviously ordered that we rally to the city Hull.* In the evening of that day, our ship ran aground, though we had understood that we had 36 feet of water under the keel. We could now stretch our legs while, overnight, the ship lay at anchor. In the morning, we set sails again – and though we were surrounded by dense clouds – we were as close to the city as about a mile. On the following day we entered the city where everyone was then billeted. Two days of rest were granted to the bodies worn down by the long voyage, and soon our troops were able to proceed 240 furlongs towards York; three days of travel when first the city of Hull had been left behind.

After a fortnight, the Danish regiments were allocated quarters in the surrounding villages. While Colonel Johann Heinrich Wulf Kalneyn, the commanding officer of Prince Frederick's Regiment, went into winter quarters with his company in the Skipsea area, other companies of his regiment stayed in the neighbouring villages.†

---

* The landing might be considered successful, but the place of disembarkation was hardly in accordance with the terms agreed. Thus, to avoid any misunderstanding or bad feeling among coalition partners Württemberg dispatched Captain Suzannet of the Royal Life Guards as a liaison officer to Hampton Court, where King William III presently resided, to seek his approval of the new and improvised selection of staging area. On 19 November royal approbation was obtained.

† Andreas Claudianus, who moved with Prince Frederick's Regiment commanded by Colonel Heinrich Wulf Kalneyn, relates that the regiment left Skipsea on 9 February and marched via Otley, Skipton, Clitheroe, Preston, Ormskirk and Liverpool to Hoylake, where they arrived on 11 March 1690. Being the colonel of his regiment, Kalneyn was also the officer commanding A Company.

7

Idus Februarii, Anno MDCXC relictis hibernaculîs é Shipdonia XXXII ſtadia ad urbem Eboracum remenſa eſt legio Calneni; Poſtero die adjunctîs cæteris copiîs Calatum LXIV ſtadia pervenit; tertiâ luce XCVI ſtadia Otlegam greſſu tendit. Seqventi die ad reqviem militibus datâ, mox Skiptoniam LXXX ſtadia, altero die LVI ſtadia ad Gisburnam venientes, poſtridié qvieverunt. Decimo autem tertio Calendarum Martii XL ſtadia Clithoroam, qvartoq; LVI ſtadia Blaeburnam, ſed qvinto LXIV ſtadia Preſtoniam usq; proceſſerunt; hic vires corporum longo itinerum labore attritas tres feré hebdomadas recreabant milites; intereà à milite qvodam è cohortibus Calneni cædes in nobilem Anglum perpetrabatur, ilibus mucrone perfoſſis defunctum. Pridié Nonas Martii relictâ Preſtoniâ XCVI ſtadia ad Ormskirch, indeq; oriente luce amplius LXIV ſtadia Liſerpalum in comitatu Lancaſtrenſi profecti ſunt, custodibus autem impedimentorum ſub veſperam flumen Mer-

On the 10 February 1690, as soon as we had left our winter quarters behind, Colonel Kalneyn's regiment moved out of Skipsea, marching 32 furlongs to the city of York.* The day after, our regiment arrived in Appleby having marched 64 furlongs. There we joined the other Danish troops, and as soon as the sun rose the following morning we covered the third leg of the route, and 96 furlongs onwards we reached Otley. The subsequent day the soldiers were allowed to recuperate after the march. A few days later and after another 80 furlongs we reached Skipton, and after one more day we marched 56 furlongs to Gisburn. Then a day was spent resting. On 15 February we advanced to Clitheroe, on the 16th a further 56 furlongs to Blackburn, but then on the 17th we covered as much as 64 furlongs, which brought us all the way to Preston. Here officers and men were allowed three days to regain their bodily strength, having been worn down by many days of travelling.

At this point in time, a soldier of Kalneyn's regiment murdered an English nobleman – who had his groin pierced by the point of the soldier's sword.

On 6 March, as we had left Preston we continued 96 furlongs to the town of Ormskirk and onwards the next morning. When the sky was lit by the rising sun, we proceeded 64 furlongs further to the city of Liverpool in the county of Lancaster. However, while the troops remained in the city for a few days, the same evening the baggage train guards crossed the River Mersey.

---

* 6.4 km. In reality, the distance from Skipsea-York is closer to 60 km.

※ 8 ※

Merſeum tranſeuntibus paucis diebus agmen in urbe permanſit. Qvarto Idus ejusdem menſis tempore matutino extra muros urbis pœnas patratæ cædis dedit miles Nobilis prædicti interfector, cujus abſciſſo capite truncus humo mandatus eſt, mox flumine trajecto XLVII ſtadia ad portum Highlaci agmen proceſſit; aderat ibidem claſſis, qvâ milites in Hiberniam transportarentur; militibus igitur navibus impoſitis, manè refluus invehi cœpit oceanus exæſtuans, arenasqve ſiccas inundare; ergo levatis anchoris ac ventô Libonoto favente, curſum caurum verſus flectentes ad Winderii fluvii oſtia unius modò diei noctisqve itinere penetrârunt. Ipſis Idibus Martii in arenam Withuſiæ pari intervallo à Carrigfergo & Belfaſto diſtantis expoſiti milites ad deſtituta diſcedunt hybernacula; Legio Calneni primò XXXII ſtadia Carrigſergum, qvam urbem Angli ante adventum Danorum occupatam præſidio tenebant. Inde poſt biduanam reqviem XLVIII ſtadia Learnum

On the morning of 12 March 1690, the soldier who had committed the abovementioned murder of the nobleman was executed outside the city walls. By means of decapitation he paid the price for perpetrating the crime, and his body was buried on the spot.

As soon as the river Mersey had been crossed, the army advanced about 48 furlongs to the harbour at Hoylake.* There the transport fleet lay moored ready to transfer the troops, the horses, and their equipment to Ireland. As in the morning the water began to surge while foaming up and overflowing the dry sand, the soldiers had already been safely embarked.

Thus, with anchors aweigh the fleet set sails for Ireland. There was a favourable south-south-westerly wind blowing and, taking a northerly course towards Belfast, they reached the Bay of Carrickfergus in just one day and night's voyage. On the very same day, 15 March, the soldiers disembarked on the beach at Whiteabbey in order to move into winter quarters, Whiteabbey being approximately as far from Carrickfergus as the latter is from Belfast. Colonel Kalneyn's regiment marched a distance of 32 furlongs reaching Carrickfergus first. This is a town that the English had occupied and held prior to the arrival of the Danes. Then after two days rest there, the Danish troops headed for Larne, a

---

* Apparently, there had been plenty of time for the Danes to move, as the Williamite war machine and the political decision-makers were far from ready. The budget for the enterprise had yet to be approved by Parliament and the British troops necessary for reinforcing those already in Ireland had to be selected – some of them even recruited afresh. On 3 March, however, the Duke of Schomberg, the English commander in Ireland, requested that the king 'despatched some Danish infantry as soon as possible.'

❊ 9 ❊

num petiit, ubi alii in urbe, in vicis proximis alii hofpitio funt excepti. Sed qvoniam hafce in regiones venimus, operæ pretium effe duxi, priusqvàm initium faciam de egregiis ac memorabilibus Anglorum rebus in Hibernia geftis, hâc uti occafione ad cœtera illuftranda, modò eadem qvafi lineâ fitum & imaginem Hiberniæ depingam, & ingenia naturamq; incolarum, qvibuscum nobis priùs bellum, deinde concordia fuit, attingam, non enim fufficit unum aut alterum membrum inepti adinftar pictoris delineare, nifi omnes corporis partes nativis adumbrem coloribus, id qvod ut pauciffimis abfolvam. Accipe, Hiberniam unam effe ex infulis Britannicis, Regionem Occidentalem, ultimam & extremam Infulam Magnæ Britanniæ, qvæ Oceano undiqvaqve alluitur, à Septentrione Islandiam è longinqvo refpicit, & interjacentem Oceanum Deucaledonium habet; ab Occidente Occidentalem Oceanum amplexatur; à Meridie Hifpaniam fpectat, & fimul O-
ceano

distance of about 40 furlongs, where some found accommodation in the town, others in the neighbouring villages.

Before I commence my narrative of the illustrious and unforgettable actions of the English during the war in Ireland, I believe it sensible to use this occasion to illustrate the conditions on the ground, i.e. to describe the setting and the scenery that we faced in Ireland. I shall do this in a kind of sketch and touch upon the attitudes and nature of the Irish with whom, first, a war was fought but, later, reconciliation was reached. Just like a painter, who cannot acquiesce with painting only one part of his model, I shall have to create a comprehensive portrait showing all the parts of the environment in an appropriate manner and with the true colours.

Let us start noticing that Ireland is but one island amongst the British Isles. It is the western-most region, the last and remotest island of Great Britain, which is completely surrounded by the Ocean. To the North, Ireland is neighbouring Iceland, though at considerable distance, the western part of the Scottish Ocean lying in between. To the West is the Western Sea; to the far South it faces Spain, though at the same time it is cut off from the continent, but to

10

ceano Vergivio cæditur, ab Oriente autem Britanniam respicit mari Hibernico a se disjunctam; Longitudine à Septentrione in Meridiem trecenta milliaria Anglicana occupat, latitudo verò ab Ortu in Occasum centum viginti milliarium æstimatur. Dividitur Regnum hodiè in qvatuor Regiones, Ultoniam, Lageniam, Momoniam, Connaciam, alii addunt qvintam Mediam in Insulæ medio sitam, tandemq; Regioni Lageniæ adjunctam. Multiplex & varia est natura hujus Regionis, nulla nix gelu aut rigore constricta obruit terram, cœlum verò mite clemens ac serenum est, qvod asperitatem frigoris prohibet; Verno igitur tempori similis est hyems, pari ferè salubritate pratorumqve fertilitate fœcunda; Terra omnium ad usum vitæ humanæ necessariarum rerum fertilissima, agrorum cultu, urbium vicorumqve multitudine ac nitore amœna, magnâ ovium pecorumq; vi abundans, fluviis, lacubus & stagnis freqventer rigua, variis ditissima commerciis,

the East across the Irish Sea one beholds mainland Britain. While from north to south the Irish Kingdom measures 300 English miles, from east to west it is estimated to cover 120 English miles across.

These days, the island is divided into four regions: Ulster, Leinster, Munster and Connacht, although some count the county of Meath as a fifth region. This county is situated in the middle of the island and is actually part of the province of Leinster.

The climate of the island is diverse and varying; snow rarely covers the earth, which is hardly ever bound by frost or cold. No, the sky excludes the harshest of cold; it is mild, temperate and tranquil. Mostly, the winter is felt like spring-time, with nearly the same healthiness and abundantly fertile meadows. The earth is extremely productive, providing everything necessary for humans. Ireland abounds with farming fields plentiful with beasts and cattle, and presents a multitude of lively cities and villages wealthy in a variety of commerce. There are numerous rivers, lakes, and ponds,

11

ciis, arborum dives ad ædium navigiorumqve ſtructuram aptiſſimarum, frugum valde ferax & pabuli fertilis, omni fere ferarum genere maxime freqvens, ſerpentum adeo expers, ut eos nec generet nec alat terra, neq; aliunde advectos patiatur, ſed extingvat; adeo ut nihil agris uberius, nihil ſolo benignius, nihil mari & fluviis ſit hoſpitabilius, qvorum nobiliſſimi ſunt fluvii, Boanda, Brigus, Neorus, Svirius, Dabrona, Liffius, Sauranus, Ravius, & maximus omnium Senus, continetqve præterea multos ignobiles amnes, qvibus Regio non dividitur; Fluviorum alii in Occidentale, alii in Vergivium, alii in Deucaledoneum ſeu Hyperboreum, alii in Hibernicum mare decidunt. Hic promontoria Boreum, Venicnium, Robogdium, qvæ ad Septentrionem ſpectant; Notium qvod ad Occidentem, Hieron vel Sacrum promontorium qvod ad Meridiem, Iſamnium qvod Orientem verſus vergit. Hic inclytiſſimi lacus Argita, Auſoba, Logia, Neaghus & ſpatioſiſſimus Ernus. Non

C   omit-

riches of trees suitable for making beams for houses and vessels. Ireland is a highly productive society and it is fertile as to fodder for the livestock. Almost every kind of wild animal can be observed in the field, although snakes are not found, not bred or nurtured, and if someone should inadvertently bring a snake to this island it will be instantly killed.

Nothing is more bountiful than the Irish fields, nothing more fertile than the soil, nothing more welcoming than the sea and the rivers, of which the most prominent are: Lagan Water, rivers Boyne, Barrow, Suir, Avonmore, Liffey, Suck, Roughty, and Shannon, the greatest of them all. Moreover, there are many less known rivers, by which the island is not divided. Some rivers flow out in the West, others in the Scottish Sea, others still in the Irish Ocean.

The headlands of the island are Malin Head, Horn Head,* and Fair Head that look to the North; Mizen Head facing the West, Greenore Point or Carnsore Point, which faces towards the South, Ifamnium, which lies opposite the East. The most prominent lakes are Lough Foil, Lough Corrib, Lough Neagh and the spacious lake system of the river Erne.

---

* At Claudianus' time, this was in all probability still known as Rams Head.

✤ 12 ✤

omittendum videtur, qvòd hìc veteres Topographi & rerum geſtarum Scriptores de lacu Erno & monte Kevineo referunt. Ernus lacus triginta millia paſſuum in longitudinem & qvindecim millia in latitudinem vaſtô per regionem Ultoniam tractu diffuſus, piſcibus & & inſulis refertus, ab utroq; latere perpetuis montium jugis aſperis & præruptis clauditur, montes verò ſunt arboribus contecti. Ravius fluvius inde per Ultoniam & Connaciam currit, terrasqve ſcindens in mare ſe evolvit. Meminit Giraldus Cambrenſis de lacu Erno, qvòd olim fons fuerit & ſcaturigo, ſed ob incolarum veneream cum beſtiis nefandam conſvetudinem, Deô irato in tantam aqvarum diluviem erupiſſe, ut totum illum tractum unà cum incolis Noachicâ qvaſi qvâdam inundatione ſubmerſerit. Mons Kevineus ex habitatione & Oratorio Sancti Kevini, qvem ibi habitâſſe fama vulgaverat, clarus eſt, locus omni turba vacuus, horrida in eremo à Glandologia viginti qvatuor

The information of the old authors, who wrote on the topography and the history of Lough Erne and Mount Kevin, should be related too.* Lough Erne is thirty thousand paces in length and fifteen thousand across; it follows a rather diffuse course through the region of Ulster and it abounds with fish and islands. It is closed in at all sides by unbroken ranges of tree-covered mountains. The river Roughty flows through Ulster and Connacht, rolling itself into the sea while dividing the landscape. The 12th century clergyman and historian *Giraldus Cambrensis*† conveyed the tale that once Lough Erne had been a bubbling spring, but because of the local inhabitants' revolting affection for the wild animals, an angry god had set on a great flood, that submerged that whole river bed together with the locals as in the tale of Noah's Ark.‡ Mount Kevin – once the lodging and chapel of Saint Kevin – is a stunning place, free of any commotion, lying isolated in the waste about twenty-four furlongs from Glendalough.

---

* Here Claudianus describes a peak in the Wicklow Mountains, which today is called Lugduff. He may or may not have designated it as he has because of the cave called Kevin's Bed.

† *Giraldus Cambrensis* is a personal name given for the 12th century cleric/historian Gerallt Cymro (better translated as Gerald of Wales).

‡ It is surprising that Claudianus, at the time of writing a student of divinity, is not aware that, in the case of Noah, one pair of each species of all the living creatures were actually preserved from the flood.

✹ 13 ✹

tuor stadia dissitus, à natura velut opere atq; industria præceps aspectuq; tristissimus, ab uno latere sexaginta cubitorum spatium æqvat summa montis altitudo, radicibus ejus lacus subnascitur profundus, præaltis asperisq; ripis, ab altero latere in triginta cubitorum altitudinem eminet, unô perangusto aditu relicto, qvi in acutum exsurgit cacumen, & qvasi per scalas crescit gradatim, per qvas ab infima radice in sublime ascenditur fastigium. In medio verticis parva est planities, partim herbis viridata, partim arboribus opacis consita, dorsum montis lacui imminens fontem dulcissimis aqvis è scatebris jugi exilientem præbet; Specus etiam conspicitur, qvem ex industria manuumq; arte & nexu sibi ipse Kevinus contexit. Jam ad urbes: pluribus sparsis tuguriis qvàm urbibus freqvens est regio; urbes ad mare Roboretum, Carrigfergus, Dunkeranum, Drogheda, Watterfordia, Jagolia, Corcagia, Kinsalia, Limmericum, Gallovadia, & ipsa caput urbium Du-

C 2   bli-

Its nature is not appealing to either work or industry, it has a gloomy appearance, and from one side the highest point of the mountain equals the space of 60 ells.* There is a deep lake at its foot, with high and very sharp banks. From the other side the height seems to be about 30 ells. Right behind there is a narrow passage which turns into a path leading all the way up to a sharp peak. The path takes the shape of stairs which, little by little, ascend the slope from the lowest foot to the highest summit. There is a small turf at the top, which is partly covered with grass, partly with shady trees. The mountain top, hanging over the lake, has a spring with the sweetest water, springing from the mountain.

Saint Kevin's cave is still to be seen. He had constructed it for himself; it is said, by his own industry and his trust in God.

Let us now take a look at the cities. Across the country, lots of villages and towns lie scattered. The cities that lie facing the sea are Derry, Carrickfergus, Dunkerrin, Drogheda, Waterford, Yougal, Cork, Kinsale, Limerick, Galway and Dublin itself, the capital of all of these cities.

---

* 1 ell being 1.14 m, i.e. less than 70 meters, which does not seem a very impressive mountain, but again Claudianus is not very precise with measurements.

❊ 14 ❊

blinium, aliæ. De Hibernia & ejus colonia prima memorat Walfinghamus: Hibernia, inqvit, poft Britanniam omnium Infularum eft optima, qvæ qvamvis Britanniæ divitiis cedat, latitudine, falubritate, ferenitate præftat, qvæ ficut verfus Aqvilonem brevior eft, ità verfus Meridiem trans illius fines protenditur. Hæc autem propriè patria Scotorum eft; nam ficut legitur, Ægyptiis in mari rubro fubmerfis, illi qvi fuperfuerunt, expulerunt à fe qvendam Nobilem Sciticum (nomine Sruthum pronepotem Gatheli, ut exiftimat Petrus Walshius) qvi degebat apud eos,

Concerning Ireland and the first plantations, Walsingham[*] recollects that, after Britain, Ireland is the greatest of all islands. Although its riches are second to those of Britain, it surpasses it in autonomy, happiness and tranquillity. While the land is narrow in the North, it widens to the South. But first of all it is the homeland of the Scots; for one may read that when the Egyptians had been waterlogged in the Red Sea, those who survived expelled a certain nobleman Sciticus who lived among them, (with the name Sruthum, the great-grandson of Gathelus, as Peter Walsh relates), so that he

---

[*] Sir Francis Walsingham (c. 1532-90) was principal secretary to Queen Elizabeth I of England from 20 December 1573 until his death and is popularly remembered as her spymaster.

❋ 15 ❋

os, ne dominium super eos invaderet, expulsus ille cum familia pervenit ad Hispaniam, & progenies ipsius familiæ suæ multiplicata est nimis. Inde venerunt Hiberniam post annos mille duobus additis, à transitu filiorum Israël per mare rubrum & de Hibernia pars eorum egressa, tertiam in Britannia Brittonibus & Pictis gentem addiderunt; pars eorum qvæ remansit in Hibernia, Hiberni vocabantur, & adhuc eadem utuntur lingvâ. Hæc ille.
Gens regionis incola, maximé qvæ nemora, sylvas, paludes & montes inhabitat, olim inconditis erat moribus effe-

C 3 ra-

should not be allowed to rule over them. When ousted, he fled with his family to Spain, and their brood reproduced greatly. Two thousand years after the crossing of the Red Sea into Israel, they went to Ireland. While, in their turn, some of them left Ireland for Britain and added a third clan to the Britons and Picts; those who remained in Ireland are called Hiberni, and they still use the same language.

So much for Walsingham. The clan remaining in Ireland, who mostly took to living in the groves, forests, marshes and mountains, were once savage and of anarchic habits and

16

ra, animo sæva, vultu ferox, furore barbaros omnes superans; namq; fuerunt homines, qvos infamiæ libidinisq; suæ neq; pudebat neq; tædebat, utpote in effrænatam libidinem & inhonestas voluptates, atq; adeò ad omne nefas maximé pronos, qvibus nulla in voluptatibus unqvam fuit satietas, latrocinii potiùs qvàm bonarum artium studiosis, nullius legibus aut imperio obnoxiis, itaqve immani hâc barbarie sævientes in armis semper errârunt, eò qvòd, qvantum qvidem conjicio, melioris morum & virtutum culturæ essent ignari, hisce flagitiis deditos per multa secula Hibernos fœdera humani diviniqve juris violantes tandem Henricus Secundus Rex Angliæ ad obseqvium armis subegit, Qvibus de barbaris Bernardus Clarevallensis Abbas in vita Malachiæ sic loqvitur: Sicut piscis in mari non sapit salem, ità Malachias inter barbaros, inter qvos Archi-Episco-

minds, they were hot-tempered and they fiercely opposed every outsider. They were men, who were indifferent to infamy and yearning, their craving and dishonesty knew no bounds, and they gave themselves to every kind of wrongdoing. There was no limit to their hankering, and they were prone to piracy rather than enjoyment of arts complying with no one's laws or command. By this hideous barbarism they stuck together and therefore, as to my understanding, they remained ignorant of culture and virtue, dedicated as they were merely to perpetuating their shameful way of living.

Eventually, the army of Henry the Second, the King of the British, managed to subjugate into compliance those who violated the accords of mankind and divine law. In his *Life of Malachy*,* Saint Bernard of Clairvaux† stated: "Like the fish in the sea does not taste the salt, Malachy, while living among

---

* Saint Malachy (1094-1148) was a 12th century Archbishop of Armagh, Ireland. He became known for "the Prophecy of the Popes" published 1595, which is generally believed to be a forgery.

† Saint Bernard of Clairvaux, a contemporary biographer of Malachy who recorded the saint's alleged miracles, makes no mention of the prophecies, nor are they mentioned in any record prior to their 1595 publication.

❀ 17 ❀

piscopus Ecclesiam rexit, nullam barbariem traxit. Hæc ille. Sed ut asperitas ferri usu & attritu tollitur, sic genuina feritas eorum postea deferbuit, desenuitq; pristina illa barbaries; Hiberni enim nostræ ætatis sunt durum atq; velox hominum genus, natura ferox, bello promptum, jugi ac laborum patiens, sunt homines omni deliciarum genere instructissimi, ut qvi solo amœno & feraci, venatione tamen magis qvàm terrarum cultu, ad implenda naturæ desideria invitantur; satietatem inter epulandum ludis & tripudiis interpolant. Vetus ille mos Ethnicorum deplorandi mortuos hodiernô etiam die apud illos observatur, cadavera enim demortuorum honestè priùs involuta, non communi modò omnium mortalium matri reddunt, verùm etiam ad loca sepulturæ adeunt sæpissimè, vultus in terram incurvantes, manusqve barbarô ululatu planctuqve vexantes, funera & obitum amicorum aut conjugum

foreigners where the archbishops rule the church, he did not feel estranged. There is no more to say about him."

But like a sword, which is blunted by wear and tear, their innate wildness subsided and the old savagery vanished.

The Irish of our time are tough and industrious, they are fiery by nature and prepared for war. They endure burdens and toil, but they know how to please. Their country is delightful and fruitful, but they enjoy the nature more by hunting and shooting rather than by cultivating the land.

They love festivities indulging in games and dance. At funerals they pay their respect to their dead friends and consorts. Even today, those indigenous to Ireland observe the old tradition of honouring the dead by first respectfully enveloping the corpses and then committing them to the ground. Frequently, they convene at the burial sites where, bending down their faces and shaking their hands, they beat their chests under barbaric howling.

18

gum mactant; sic miserabili hoc spectaculô & gestibus externis internam cordis devotionem & ardorem doloremq; animi satis plus æqvô exprimunt, à more Africanorum, ex qvibus originem duxêre, haud multum abludentes. Qvi nobilitate aut opibus excellunt, modestô sunt habitu, erectâ indole & præstanti formâ, formamq; virtus honestat, vestibus non ad ostentationem luxus aut opulentiæ, sed ad usum qvàm pompam pertinentioribus utuntur, & hæc vestium vilitas fœminarum virorumq; nemini est dedecori. Victu parco & frugali victitant simplicissimè; cibus enim illis adversus famem non libidini nec luxuriæ est, neq; alia gulæ ad perniciem irritamenta qværunt. De colonia prima, de antiqvitate hujus Regionis, de implacabilibus odiis & simultatibus istius gentis, qvibus ad stragem alius alium persecutus est furiosè, de variis cruentis præliis inter sese commissis silentiô præterire satius puto, qvàm magnam rerum congeriem, qvam vasta
hist̆o-

Thus, they display their heartfelt devotion and passion and the pain of their bereavement. Obviously, this depressing spectacle and these superficial gestures seem exaggerated and not at all unlike the habits of their African ancestors.

The Irish are neither particularly noble nor rich people and they have a modest disposition. While by nature they are proud and resourceful, virtue adorns their lives. They use their best clothes not for public displays of luxury or wealth, but for the everyday toil, and this stinginess of clothes shames neither women nor men.

They subsist on a limited but carefully selected diet; for famine has afflicted this people more than once. Therefore, eating is neither for pleasure nor extravagance, and hence the Irish are careful not to let gastronomy become ruinous.

The merciless hostility and rivalries among the Irish of ancient times, and the bloody battles of numerous civil wars caused widespread devastation as well as early plantations,* of which you may find volumes of historic evidence. I believe, we should pass by in silence, rather than abbreviate.

---

* Plantations in 16th and 17th century Ireland were the confiscation of land by the English crown and the colonisation of this land with settlers from England and the Scottish Lowlands. The lands were then granted by Crown authority to the colonists ("planters"). This process began during the reign of Henry VIII and continued under Mary I and Elizabeth I. It was accelerated under James I, Charles I and Oliver Cromwell.

※ 19 ※

historicorum volumina evolvendo reperies, in compendium redigere; Ad ordinem igitur rerum, à qvibus me cotemplatio imaginis Hiberniæ averterat, ut redeam; Victor primus totius Hiberniæ fuit Jacobus Secundus, ab arce Regia Londini deturbatus atq; expulsus, qvi ubi intellexit, qvòd regnum aut relinqvendum esset aliis, aut armis redimendum, Galliam adiit, indeq; copiis aliqvot Gallicis instructus Hiberniam adortus est, ubi ex magno incolarum concursu, qvi ex suis passim pagis urbibusqve ad eum sicuti in sentinam confluxerunt, ad delenda Anglorum præsidia non solùm prædatoriam sibi turbam, sed eqvitum etiam peditumq; manum sat numerosam sed obscuram & rudem coëgit; mirum dictu qvantô in arma fervore traherentur, adeò ut ejus auspicium qvocunq; terrarum eos abducere vellet, seqvi se paratos, & ad ultimum vitæ pro ultione magis ejecti Regis, qvàm pro Penatibus invictâ dimicaturos esse fide pollicerentur. In-

C 5 genti

Let us rather turn to the events which have not, so far, been covered. James the Second* was the first conqueror of all of Ireland.† Having been dethroned‡ and driven out of London, he fled to France. Subsequently, and reinforced by French troops, he landed in Ireland with the purpose of re-conquering the island. A great many Irish gathered from their districts and cities, just like water flooding the country. They were a marauding crowd, who wished to destroy English property and defences. A plentiful horde of horsemen and foot-soldiers joined them, although these were unskilled as well as badly turned-out.**

I wonder how they had accumulated so much fury that they took up arms and were prepared to follow King James to wherever on the earth's surface he might lead them. They proved themselves ready to fight to the bitter end, though probably more because of loyalty to their ousted king than to defend their homes.

---

* The Stuart King James II of England was actually James VII of Scotland.

† Here Claudianus is inaccurate. The lordship of the English kings date further back. The Parliament of Ireland conferred the crown of Ireland upon King Henry VIII of England during the English Reformation. The monarchs of England held the crowns of England and Ireland in a personal union. The Union of the Crowns in 1603 saw the accession of James VI, King of Scots, to the thrones of England and Ireland. The personal union consisted thereafter of the three realms of Scotland, England and Ireland.

‡ By the 'Glorious Revolution' of 1688.

** Claudianus is possibly referring to the 'rapparees.'

20

genti hôc conflatô exercitu munitiſſimas atq; opulentiſſimas urbes uberrimamq; Regionem in deditionem redegit, unicà tantùm urbe ad extremum reſiſtente Roboretô: Ipſe verò ſtatim adventu Anglorum nunriatô inde fuſus, victoriam partam tandem circumactâ fortunâ revomuit, uti dehinc referam. Roboretum eſt urbs elegans & dives, ſplendidiſſimas inter Septentrionalis Regionis Ultoniæ urbes haud poſtrema, ut qvæ qvâdam qvaſi in peninſula inter humum uliginoſam, qvâ majori parte circumdatur inacceſſa, & flumen Logiam ſita eſt, naturâq; loci & operis induſtriâ, muris, aggere & vallo munitiſſima, antiqva memoria incolarumq; fama & hoc bello maximè ad perpetuam poſteritatis memoriam inclyta: namq; annonæ primùm gravitate, deinde fame preſſa, invictæ fidei atq; conſtantiæ erga Regem electum dedit argumentum, eaq; propter ſicut anteà ſemper bonitatis fideiq; famam meruerunt ejus cives, ità eandem hoc conſtantiæ

ſuæ

Thus, with this considerable force King James coerced many fortified and wealthy cities and bountiful regions into submission. Only Londonderry held out. James himself withdrew from Londonderry at the very moment when the advent of the English was announced and I have been told that, when the fortune of war had turned, he eventually squandered the victories he had won.

Londonderry is an elegant and rich city, certainly not second to any of the splendid towns of the northern province of Ulster. Looking like a peninsula amidst the marsh of mud by which it is enclosed, it is almost inaccessible. Moreover, the river Foyle, the environment, the produce of the locals, the city walls and their well-palisaded ramparts, the chronicles of times bygone and of the inhabitants and not least of their efforts during this war make this metropolis stand out among cities.

In spite of harsh taxation and then the pressing shortage of food during the siege, Londonderry proved its loyalty and unconquered constancy towards the chosen king. Because of this, now as before, its citizens have deserved their reputation for decency and loyalty. Thus, this same reputation of theirs was increased and made even more admirable by their constancy.

21

suæ specimine auctam & ornatiorem posteris suis reliqverunt. Jam æstivorum tempus imminebat adventante vere, atqve adversus hostem necesse erat exire; ideoq; Qvartô Idus Junii cohortes Danicæ Calneni, relictis in Ultonia hybernaculis, LVI stadia per urbem Carrigfergum retrocesserunt. Hæc urbs est nobilissima & vetustate eminens, non præaltis solùm fossis tutisq; muris cincta, sed arcem qvoqve magnam in complexu suo habet ad Vinderii fluminis ostia exstructam, qvò incolæ Scotiæ & Angliæ mercandi causa confluunt, à Fergusio Rege ibi naufrago inditum illi nomen est. Hinc Belfastum L & amplius VIII stadia iter pedibus ingressi, ab altera urbis parte tentoria instruentes, posteroq; die XXIV stadia emensi Dumbrigam pervenerunt. Huc eadem vesperâ cum Rege Wilhelmo Serenissimus Princeps Georgius appulsus, urbem Belfastum intravit; qvo cognito tota ferè nocte regio, qvacunqve fama discurrit adventus, ignibus lætitiæ fulgebat. Hic
tridu-

With the coming of the spring season and summer around the corner, the time was ripe for facing the enemy.* Thus, on 10 June, having left their winter quarters† in Ulster, Kalneyn's Danish regiment retraced their steps for about 56 furlongs through the town Carrickfergus. Carrickfergus is a pretty town and eminent in its age.‡ It is girded not only by deep moats and high walls, but it also features a formidable citadel erected on the shore of Carrickfergus Bay,** where the English and the Scottish gather for trading. Carrickfergus got its name from King Fergus whose ship was wrecked there.†† On the next day Prince Frederick's Regiment marched 50 furlongs into Belfast and proceeded through the city for another eight furlongs and pitched camp at the farther outskirts. The next day they reached Dunbrigam, then having traversed 24 furlongs.

On the same evening, King William entered Belfast together with Prince George.‡‡ Once they had been

---

* The campaigning season was approximately from May to September, where fodder for horses and draught animals might be found in the fields.

† The Danes had been in winter quarters in Co Antrim with Württemberg's HQ set up in Galgorm Castle (close to the present golf links).

‡ Carrickfergus became an inhabited town shortly after 1170, when Anglo-Norman knight John de Courcy invaded Ulster, established his headquarters in the area and built Carrickfergus Castle.

** Today Belfast Lough.

†† Carrickfergus takes its name from Irish: Carraig Fhearghais, meaning 'rock of Fergus'. In the 5/6th century, Fergus, the son of Erc of Armoy, left Ulster to form a kingdom in Scotland. Upon returning to Ulster some time afterwards, his ship ran aground on a volcanic rock by the shore, subsequently known as 'Carraig Fhearghais'.

‡‡ Prince George, 1663-1708, was the brother of Danish King Christian V and married to Princess (later Queen) Anne.

22

triduum ad qvietem militibus datum, deinde XVI ftadia per Lifnagarvum, indeq; LVI ftadia iter facientes caftra apud oppidum Meiram fixerunt, proximo die ad otium dato XVI ftadia Lorginam haud procul fpatiofo lacu Neagho diffitam, ubi Præfecti copiarum Danicarum Sereniffimorum Principum Chriftiani & Georgii cum pedeftribus fuis præfidebant, latiùs XXXII ftadia Portadunum profecti funt, ubi Baro Julius & Donepius eqvitum Præfecti noftrates, locum amœnum undiqve denfis virgultis & arboribus confitum occupârunt, urbe peragratà ab altero latere apud Regiam cohortem peditum caftra locârunt. Craftino die adjunctis his copiis ad caftra Anglorum Dondregam inter & Legocorriacum munita perventum eft; ubi obviam fibi penuriam commeatuum reperiebant; qvatriduò ibi per reqviem abfumptô, interjectoq; tempore ingens inter milites murmur, in diftributione pecuniarum ob retentum unius menfis ftipendium,

recognised, along the route which the rumour of their arrival had travelled, bonfires were lit by welcoming citizens, and fires continued burning throughout the night. Here the troops were granted three days of rest. Then they marched on for 16 furlongs through Lisburn and, having covered another 56 furlongs, they pitched camp at Moira.

The following day was off, but subsequently they marched on to Lurgan, lying only about 16 furlongs from the vast Lough Neagh. There the commanding officers of the Danish regiments of the Princes Christian and George had pitched camps and set up their headquarters. The troops continued their march for another 32 furlongs to Portadown. Here the Colonels Moritz Melchior von Donep* and Christian Juel, Baron of Rysensteen,† with their regiments of horse, had camped at a pleasant place grown with shrubbery and trees on all sides.

Having traversed the city, Prince Frederick's Regiment pitched camp among the Royal Foot Guards' companies. On the following day, when our troops had married up with the English columns, we secured the area between Dondrega‡ and Rich Hill** making reasonably good progress. However, we now faced a severe shortage of supplies.

At this moment, having spent four days of rest in this area, a huge dissatisfaction arose among the soldiers regarding their pay, since for more than a month no money had been

---

* Colonel, Moritz Melchior von Donep, Commanding Officer, 2nd Cavalry Regiment.

† Colonel, Christian Juel Baron of Rysensteen, Commanding Officer, 1st Cavalry Regiment.

‡ This unidentified place would be somewhere between Armagh and Portadown, possibly from the Irish "dùn", stronghold.

** Or Legacorry.

23

dium, exortum eſt: duobus igitur prehenſis é legione Calneni, alter eorum forte talorum jactâ, bombardarum globulis occiſus eſt, alter papicola, præcipuusq; hujus contentionis inſtigator capitis periculum evaſit. Inter qvinqve eqvites é turmis Donepii eadem de cauſa etiam prehenſos, unus Romano-Catholicus convictus cœterorum primipilaris pari bombardarum ſupplicio affectus eſt, alió in alium culpam referente, qvod in rebus adverſis ſolet fieri, cum omnes mortem metuant. Qvo facto exercitus qvadraginta fere qvinq; millium militantium & mercenariorum militum manûs L ſtadia Armacham proceſſit; Hæc urbs primarium Inſulæ locum obtinet, antiqvitate & Archiepiſcopatûs titulô inſignis, florente omni diſciplinarum genere Academiâ celebris, nulli clariſſimarum urbium, ſive opes, ſive ædes ſplendidé exſtructas reſpicias, ſecunda, muris adverſus hoſtium inſultus tutiſſimis armata, habet patentes & omnium rerum copiâ fœcundiſſi-

forthcoming. Moreover, the situation fermented almost to the brink of mutiny.* Two of the mutinous soldiers, both from Kalneyn's regiment, were caught. Having drawn lots, one of them was executed by a hand grenade, while the other – a Catholic – although being the primary instigator of this crime, escaped capital punishment. Among five horsemen from Donep's troops, caught for the same offence, one Roman Catholic was sentenced to death as was one grenadier officer.†

When this was done the allied army, a crowd of around forty-five-thousand officers and men, marched along for 50 furlongs to Armagh. This city, which is among the finest on the island, is distinguished by its considerable age and by being an archdiocese. It is famous for its university, flourishing in every discipline, and it is second to none among the most beautiful of cities. One may take pleasure in the remarkable riches of its splendidly built churches and its defences, which are fortified by the safest walls against enemy attacks, but you will also notice its most fruitful plains lying open, offering an abundance of everything.

---

* This was an abiding problem throughout the war. For further information see Kjeld Hald Galster, *Danish Troops with the Williamite Army in Ireland, 1689-91*, Dublin, Four Courts Press, 2012.

† The direct translation would be "as was the officer commanding the grenadier company, the first *maniple* of the other bombards." It is difficult to gauge what Claudianus actually means. Only the Royal Life Guards (foot guards) had a grenadier company and there is no report on the penalty having been inflicted upon an officer of either the Guards or Prince Frederick's Regiment. In this instance, as in several others, Claudianus must have been out of his depth, since there was no such subunit as a grenadier *maniple* (a *maniple* being two *centuria* i.e. companies) and no grenadiers with the cavalry.

24

diffimos campos. Lucis ab ortu ftadiis LXXX Meridiem verfus confectis, ulteriùs LVI ftadia vaftas per folitudines ibant, nulla biduano fpectata itinere domus præter unicam mille paffus Armachâ diffitam, oppidum nullum, humani cultus veftigium nullum occurrebat, undiq; vis mali telumq; neceffitatis durum urgebat milites, deficiente commeatu: ingens tamen fame fitiqve langventibus obvenit auxilium; larga enim poma, (ut vocant) caduca excuffit terra, e qvibus effoffis qvisq; pro lu‑bitu exceperit, multiq; fontes aqvæ etiam frigidiffimæ ex radicibus montium faxorumq; manantes, alios præter dulces amnes Regionem permeantes; funt verò hæc poma caduca genus leguminum humi nafcentium, præcipuumq: agricolarum cum lactis potione alimentum; Hinc autem longiori temporis intervallô commorari prohibebat feftinatio; Rex igitur inftructo ac perarmato exercitu XXXIV ftadia ad Dunkeranum contendit; Nobile erat olim

Since first light, we had covered 80 furlongs en route towards the south. Now we carried on for 56 furlongs through a vast wilderness. For two days of travel we did not see but a single house lying about one thousand paces outside Armagh. No hamlets or villages, no sign of human activity, and everywhere evil seemed to loom and the hunger spurred the soldiers on while supplies were running low.

However, nature provided for those suffering from starvation and thirst. For the Irish soil offered an abundance of vegetables. Everyone might collect and eat as much as he wanted, and there were many springs of cold and clear water flowing from the foot of the mountains running through the fields and into the rivers. Moreover, there was an apple-like[*] pod-vegetable developing in the ground, providing plentiful nourishment especially to farmers, who eat them along with milk.

But time did not allow us to remain here for long. The King continued 34 furlongs to Dundalk, where the army gathered and replenished.

---

[*] Similarly, on 15 April the chief secretary of the Danish contingent, Gerhardt Neve, found reason to praise the abundance of food and fodder. He described the potatoes as similar to *Erdäpfel*, and paid tribute to the local beer, which he found particularly good if accompanied by brandy. The expression concerning potatoes is probably due to Neve's limited knowledge of English. His letter is written in German, and *Erdäpfel* is the Austro-German word for exactly the same fruit (cf. French *pomme de terre*). Neve's letter to Harboe, in Danaher and Simms (eds), Danish forces, p. 107.

25

olim emporium maritimum omnium rerum mercaturâ incolarumq; freqventiâ admodùm florens, muris turribusqve ac splendidis ædificiis spectabile, nunc verò ab hostibus incendiô & ruinâ fœdatum atq; ad nihilum feré redactum luget. Hìc primùm pretiô emebatur obsonium post octiduanum panis & aqvæ usum, cerevisiæ autem in propinqvo emendæ nondum ulla erat facultas. Hinc LXX stadia ad arcem Clintonam & vicum Capogum Rex progressus ultima Ultoniæ intraverat. Hæc Regio Ultonia, qvæ ad septentrionem jacet, est spatiosissima regio, à latere septentrionali vasto maris interfuso Hibernici fretô à Scotia avulsa; à latere meridionali ad Connaciam & Lageniam extensa, pars Orientalis ad turbidum & procellosum mare Hibernicum excurrit, pars Occidentalis ad Oceanum Occidentalem vergit, qvadraginta viginti milliaria circuitu suô comprehendit; mira cœli temperies est & aër salubris, qvæ æstivo tempore incolas

Dundalk was once a prominent coastal town, whose market thrived from all sorts of commerce and, at that time, blossomed with a large number of residents. Then, it sported walls, towers and fine buildings, but now it has been disfigured by fire and ruin. War has reduced it nearly to a heap of debris. Here the soldiers bought fish, having now subsisted for eight days on bread and water, but there was not yet any opportunity for getting beer anywhere around.

Marching on for 70 furlongs the King then entered the farthest part of Ulster, Castle Clinton* and the village Cappoge.† Ulster, which is the northernmost province of Ireland, borders in the North and East on the Irish Sea next to Scotland. While in the South it is neighbouring the provinces of Connacht and Leinster, the western part faces up to the Western Sea. Ulster's circumference is about 40 miles. The weather is wonderful and the air healthy with frequent calm and mild showers cooling off the inhabitants in the summer. The rain is welcomed by the dry ground, which is thereby

---

* Whilst no such castle or ruin seemingly exists, the Clinton family was prominent in Louth, and this could refer to any estate.

† No such village exists today, but there are traces in other place names.

※ 26 ※

colas aurâ refrigerans lenes fæpè mitesqve imbres emittit, qvem avidè abforbet humorem ficcitas, eodemqve humore durities terræ emollitur, ardorem Solis, qvô cuncta velut igne torrentur, mitigant umbræ arborum montiumq; juga, pifces exhibent flumina, frugum pabuliq; divites funt agri, nifi qvà fylvæ vaftiores & montes afperi intercedunt; maxima pars terræ ob freqventes lacus aqvarumqve latè ftagnantium intercapedines, ob afperitatem locorum & focordiam atqve inertiam incolarum fterilis eft & tantùm non emortua. Hâc in regione olim Hibernorum habitàrunt populi ferociores qvàm cœteris in partibus Hiberniæ, Pridiè Calendas Julii Droghedam usq; L ftadiorum iter progreffi funt, ubi ad Boandum flumen radicibus montis ardui vicinum, ultrà præruptam fluminis ripam, qvà Regi omninò effet trajiciendum, magnô eqvitum peditumq; numerô Jacobus confedit; imminente verò jam vefperâ prælii Martisq; difcrimen

tolerably softened. The shades of the trees and the mountain ridges take the edge off the heat of the sun, which scorches plants and crops like fire. Rivers abound with fish; the ground is rich on fruit and vegetables, apart from where vast forests and rough mountains dominate. Here a large part of the earth is infertile and only kept alive by the great number of lakes, some with still water.[*] Because of the roughness of the terrain and the inhabitants' negligence and want of talent this region yields only little. Once, here lived a people more brutal than those in any others part of Ireland.

On 30 June, we continued our march for 50 furlongs all the way to Drogheda, where King James had taken up a position on the River Boyne near the foot of the steep hill on the far bank of the river, which the king had crossed with a great number of horse and foot.[†] However, with the hours of

---

[*] This could refer to i.a. Lough Owel, since it has been identified with the "Locherinum Stagnum", i.e. "stagnant lake" mentioned by Claudianus' source Gerald of Wales.

[†] On 29 June 1690, King James crossed the Boyne with his army and took up defensive positions on the southern bank.

27

men inire non poterant, ideò in dorſo tumuli non multis paſſibus ab urbe diſtantis, caſtra e regione hoſtibus adverſa metari Rex juſſit Hoſtis inter initia adventûs Regiorum è binis ad ripam fluminis erectis molibus tota nocte impigrè tormenta exploſit, cuj nec ſegniùs ab Anglis retorqvebatur, tandemq; occidente Sole, nè præſidiô noctis qvicqvam tentaret hoſtis, milites ad imperium exſeqvendum paratos & intentiori curâ vigiles, frænatosqve eqvos feſſoresq; accinctos adſtare mandavit. Unica illa ſupererat nox, qvæ diſcriminis eventum morabatur, remora tamen erat nulla freqventibus telis in hoſtem ingeſtis. Fluvio iſti à præ-rapida, qvâ defluit, celeritate, Boandi nomen eſt inditum, nam Boan Hibernicè eſt velox, è fontibus ſuis labens Mediam orientalem ab Ultonia abſcindit & diſcriminat, per diverſa ad varias urbes vagus & diſperſus Regionem irrigat, & multa millia paſſuum ad urbem Droghedam magno inflectitur ſtre-

D   pitu,

darkness approaching King William could not take the risk of giving battle that day. The enemy's positions were close to the city and partially placed on the top of the mound.* Thus, the King ordered the camp pitched in a straight line opposite the enemy.†

While in the evening a reconnaissance party including the royals moved as far as the river bank to get an impression of the lie of the land, the enemy fired their cannon from two field fortifications thrown up near the river. The King suffered a superficial scratch, but the English did not return the fire. After sunset, when no more could be done, King William ordered that the soldiers stand to for battle and be on guard with intense caution, horses bridled and horsemen girded.

Thus, although the enemy had fired throughout the night, at dawn the outcome of the battle was still to be awaited.

The river Boyne takes its name from the very rapidity of its current, for 'boyne' is an Irish word for 'swift.' From its spring it cuts through the landscape separating the central eastern part of the country from Ulster. It runs through various cities, leading water through the countryside and through many bends and turns and with much din many thousand

---

* In fact the Jacobite positions were mainly situated low, close to the river near Oldbridge, though an infantry reserve was held ready behind Donore Hill 150 m south of the main positions.

† In the line Mellifont Abbey-Tullyallen.

28

pitu, ubi in mare Hibernicum se ingerit. Ipsis verò Calendis Julii oriente luce flumen, qvod utriusq; nobilissimæ gentis aciem interfluebat, transire & objicere sese Hibernorum copiis Rex statuit; ideoqve exercitus priùs admovendus auxilium divinum precibus imploravit, sacris sic belli more peractis, duo cornua divisa sunt peditum, utrumq; latus eqvites tegebant; hostis hoc cognitô omnes etiam copias numerô longe superiores exposuit; itaq; signo sonituqve buccinarum tibicinumq; aciem dispositam ad transitum fluminis tentandum Rex movebat, relicto modicô ad custodiam castrorum præsidiô. Jamq; universa futuri periculi species omnium oculis obversabatur, ut qvæ animos Anglorum horrore perstrinxerat, cernentium profundum amnem, cujus natura illis hactenus fuit ignota; magnitudinem tamen discriminis virtus vicit: Duces enim periculi præsentis & maximè multitudinis hostium contemptores, Deo confisi, suaq; virtute & experta mi-

paces to the city Drogheda, whence it flows into the Irish sea.

On 1 July during sunrise, the King decided that his army should cross the river, which flowed across the front line separating the two parties, and attack the Irish troops. Before moving closer, in order to solicit God's help in the upcoming battle, religious services were held throughout the army.

While the infantry was organised in two wings,* the cavalry protected each of the flanks. When realising this, the enemy arrayed the bulk of his troops in a long row. Then, by a sign and to the sound of trumpets and flutes,† the King moved his combat units to try a crossing of the river, though with a small reserve left behind for the protection of the camp.‡ Soon, the spectacle of the whole battle scene could be seen from various vantage points. The minds of the British and their allies were bewildered from anxiety as they fixed their eyes on the river, whose characteristics had so far been unknown to them. However, trusting in God, the commanding officers, contemptuous of the present danger and the number of enemies, drove the soldiers on.

---

* Although we are well aware that the Romans used 'wings' *alae* as the term for the cavalry flank protection units, in this case 'wing' is a translation of *cornu* used as the designation for the right and left of infantry formations.

† The means for giving direction during battle were: trumpets (the bugles came later) with the cavalry, drums with the infantry and hoboes with the dragoons.

‡ Cladianus sees this from the perspective of the infantry of which he was a part. In fact a cavalry movement and crossing on the extreme right in the early hours of 1 July was the initial manœuvre of the Williamite army followed about midday by the infantry crossing in the central sector of the battle ground (vis-à-vis Oldbridge).

✿ 29 ✿

ta militum fortitudine freti, animos omnium ad subeundum ex necessitate periculum, ad gloriam & virtutis memoriam apta oratione & adhortatione permulserunt, qvi metu in fiduciam mutatô interriti omnes, corpore velut uno ex membris omnibus facto unà cum ducibus & antesignanis, qvi summo cum mentis ardore nec alacritate minore antecedebant, in flumen descenderunt, levatis super capita armis, etiamsi sine mora desuper vi telorum ab hostibus in eminenti ripa obstantibus, animo scilicet prohibendi aditum, obruerentur, haud ægrè tamen ad ipsum penetrârunt alveum, cujus altitudo cervices sinistri peditum cornu, in dextro vero summa virorum genua attingebat. Multorum miseranda erat conditio periclitantium, & præcipuus labor vagantium, cum alii humilioris staturæ ob vestigia fallentia & altitudinem aqvæ à commilitonibus procerioris corporis accedentibus sublevarentur, & sic alter alterius auxiliô profundum fluminis su-

D 2   pera-

Moreover, once immersed in the river and in the heat of battle they steadied themselves, faced the danger and fought courageously and honourably. Given appropriate encouragement, everyone discarded their fears, and with the confidence that emanates from being part of a large, monolithic body, they rushed into the river, weapons raised above their heads. The commanders and the skirmishers up front, the infantry proceeded without hesitation imbued with zeal and eagerness.

From the enemy positions on the overhanging, opposite bank, the allied soldiers were pelted with musket balls. However rough, they reached the river bed and plunged in. While the depth where the left wing units went in was considerable and the water reached the necks of the foot soldiers, on the right it merely came up to the highest part of the knee. The crossing was risky business to many, and especially to those who slipped and fell. Many soldiers were in a deplorable condition, but some of those more modestly build were lucky enough to find help with their taller fellow soldiers, who supported them on their way to the far bank.

30

peravit; alii, qvorum oculos in flumine mortis somnus oppressit, pro sepultura locum istum in qvo steterunt, pro tumbis undas habebant; aliis cum gradum fixum habere vix possent, onus armorum, ne à rapidissimis auferrentur vorticibus, erat subsidio; nec qvisqvam è suo vestigio ullum more trepidantium retulit pedem, qvippe infixa animo inhærebat pristina virtus, & id qvod erat militis spectatæ virtutis atqve animi promtioris, aut constanter exseqvi, aut strenuè mori, qvàm timide & ignave cedere præoptabant; timido tamen non licuit recedere, necessitas enim procedendi omnem acie excedendi viam præclusit; unde hostes conspectà transeuntium virtute & constantia Anglorum Danorumqve, rati de se esse actum, & animi paululùm pendere cœperunt, vociferantes: O Lord God in heaven that is Danish men, God save our live ɔ: O! Jehova Deus in cœlis, Dani sunt, Domine saluti

Those who did not succeed in crossing found their final resting place beneath the waves. Others, though, who could move only slowly found support in the weight of their equipment, which prevented them from being carried off by the rapid whirls. No one retraced his steps. Since it is an ancient military virtue, rooted in the soldier's mentality, to stand and fight rather than flee fearfully, they all either followed their comrades to the end or died in harness. Moreover, the timid are not given a chance to retire, since the throng of fighting men precludes any leaving of the battle array.

The Jacobites, having witnessed the display of virtue by those crossing and the steadiness of the Danes and the British, reckoned that they were done for. Their spirit started wavering as they cried out to God Almighty to save them from falling into the hands of the gruesome Danes.

luti nôstræ ac vitæ parce! tantum enim pavoris incuſſit intra ripam ipſis nominis Danorum terror: cum autem multo niſu in continentem evaſiſſent, mox concinnô tubarum tympanorumq; ſtrepitu ad crudelitatem exercendam datum eſt ſignum militibus, qvi incitamentis Præfectorum militumq; mutuo clamore alacritatis indice pugnantium more pulcherrimas hoſtiles copias aggrediebantur, veluti turbinum motus, qvi aridas lateri cujusdam montis imminentes arbores crebritate agitationum & concuſſionum ventorum evulſas, ipſius ſubter montis radices in vallis cavernas ita deturbat, ut truncorum ramorumqve fragoribus horrendum efficiant ſonum, & mons ipſe tandem arboribus nudetur. Sic collato pede & horribili ſonitu ac clamore dimicatum eſt, vir viro, arma armis, virtus virtuti oppoſita contendebant; nullum vulnus, diſcrimen nullum à cædibus abſterruit milites, niſi qvem pugna cum lethali vulnere, palmâ & pauſa condecorabat:

adeò

As we have seen, the mere notion of the Danes imbued the Jacobite soldiers on the river bank with profound terror.

So far the Danes had done without too much effort, but soon by the sound of trumpets and drums the soldiers were instructed to fight with no mercy, and with their fervour boosted by the shouting of generals as well as soldiers, they assaulted the enemy's finest troops. The effects were like those of a tornado, which tears down withered trees hanging from the sides of a mountain, uproots them by repeated shaking, and hurls them into the void of the valley. Likewise, the reverberations of this clash sounded like trunks and branches crashing to the ground, when the mountain is eventually stripped of its last tree.

Thus, the battle took place under horrifying noise as man encountered man, weapon rang against weapon, and courage faced courage. No wound and no killing stopped the soldiers, none but those who were adorned by the honour of a heroic death.

✿ 32 ✿

adeò enim confertim manus invicem conferuerunt, ut alius alium arietando in terram trucidaret, ipfeqve interfector ab ultore altero pari vindictæ ardore occideretur. Irâ deindè in furorem verſâ omnia velut rogi exardebant, usqve dum humus cadaverum cumulis & aggeribus intercluderetur. Dux ipſe Würtenbergicus ad exemplum fortitudinis inter primos promptiùs pugnans, in manus Hiberni militis incidit, qvi inſolenti elatus gaudio & exiſtimans Regem ſe cepiſſe, eum ſecum ducere vivum ſtatuit. Dux autem ad ſpernendum omne periculum aſſvetus, non magnitudine animi modò, ſed corporis etiam dexteritate armorumqve minîs ſtrenuè ſe defendebat, donec Centurio Regiæ cohortis Danicæ Lützovius repentè advolans à tergo hoſtem invaſerit, gladiumq; in viſcera Hiberni nihil tale metuentis capulo tenus intulerit; ſic ſpem ſæpè maximam cùm anima ſimul avidiſſimus miles amittit, at ope divina per manum Lützovii Dux inclytus pugnacis-

Little by little the fight developed into close combat, linking the fighters so narrowly that their swords became of limited use. Thus, thrusting in lieu of slashing and seeking revenge for their comrades, they killed each other one by one. As everyone was in a frenzy burning with wrath, the fighting went on until the earth was covered by dead bodies.* The Danish commander, the Duke of Württemberg, while fighting courageously in the first line, proving both muscle and audacity, was captured by an Irish soldier, who very pleased with himself, believing that he had caught the King, decided to bring him with him alive.† The Duke however, who was accustomed to scorn all kinds of danger, not only by his fighting morale, but also by his fitness and weapons proficiency, defended himself energetically, until an officer commanding a company of the Queen's Regiment, Lützow,‡ engaged the enemy. Surprisingly, this officer dashed towards the Irishman from behind and ran his sword through him right up to the hilt. In such a way even the most devoted soldier often misses an obvious opportunity along with losing his life. Thus, thanks to Lützow and by divine support the Duke

---

* It is obvious that Claudianus does not have the full picture. The battle of the Boyne was not particularly bloody (compared for instance with that of Aughrim the year after), though it might well have looked that way seen from the position of a fighting foot soldier on the ground.

† The Irish soldier believed him to be King William III.

‡ There was no such officer in the Danish contingent. However, Claudianus might have got the name slightly wrong as there was a Cornet Lüttich in the Danish 1st Cavalry Regiment.

※ 33 ※

gnaciſſimum hoſtem & fermé ineluċta-
bile malum evitavit. Poſtremó edi-
tâ cadentium magnâ hoſtium ſtrage,
paucis ad moriendum pluribus ad fugam fuit animus; ergó trans montem
non ſegniter ſed citato curſu recedentes,
qvó qvemqve devium raperet fuga, di-
ſtrahebantur, nec inſeqventem retroſpe-
ċtare victorem fugientium qvisqvam
audebat; tantus enim metus animis in-
ceſſit, ut artem pugnandi unà cum animis ſtandi remiſerint, haſtæ, gladii,
ſclopi jam ipſis erant impedimento magis qvàm tutelæ, itaqve vias omni armorum ſupelleċtili, velut hyberno tempore arborum foliis longé lateqve re-
plêrunt, additîs ad ultimum ſarcinis,
cadaveribus & ſemivivis fatigatorum &
vulneratorum corporibus. Eqvites hoſtium egregié in primordiis prælii ſe
tuebantur, deſerti autem à peditatu in
fugam ſe dedêre, omnesqve dato fugæ
ſpatiô ad præſidia urbium volitârunt,
ſicut in agris aliqvæ frugum ſpicæ emi-
nentes, reciprocô flexu hinc illinc vi
D 4 ven-

escaped a very accomplished enemy and an incredible evil.

When the carnage was about to be over, few more Jacobite soldiers wished to die, and the majority chose to abscond. Therefore, taking no unnecessary risks, the Jacobite horse retired at the gallop, going wherever they could. They were scattered and none of them dared to look back at the enemy in pursuit; for they had been struck by such great fear that they forgot about fighting in closed formations, stirrup by stirrup.

The enemy foot made a similar hasty retreat, and since pikes, swords and muskets were now more of an encumbrance than a shield, they discarded all these implements on their way. Enemy weaponry along with knapsacks, cadavers, wounded and dying covered the roads, just as the trees' leaves do in winter.

At the beginning of the battle, the enemy horse fought bravely and efficiently, but as they were deserted by the foot, they, too, abandoned the battlefield. As soon as the opportunity of retreat arose, everyone dashed for the cities. It looked as when crops in the fields are being swept by the

❊ 34 ❊

ventorum agitatæ ſpeciem undarum præbent, donec fractis ſtipulis imbelles terram propendent, reliqvæ tamen ſuperſtites capita rurſus extollunt; ità Hiberni uno devicti prælió, in contumacia ſua tamen præfractè permanſerunt; laudanda eſt etiam virtus in hoſte, Hibernorum qvidam Signifer eqvitum, ſangvine nobilis, prælió clarus, avidior gloriæ qvàm victoriæ capax, cujus nomen ſi ſciſſem, merita cum laude dediſſem, vexillum ſiniſtrâ, dextrâ gladium circumferens, non interrito modô, ſed & contumaci vultu confertos per Anglorum ordines eqveſtres ſolus irrupit, utrum ad virtutem oſtentandam, aut rerum à ſe geſtarum gerendarumqve famam aucupandam, an temerariâ potiùs confidentià id fecerit, conjecturâ non facili augurari poſſum; à cæde eum revocandi ſignum ſonitu tubæ dederunt cœteri fugati, ille autem immemor ſui omniumq; ſuorum deſperata victoriâ celebrioris nominis famam ex morte præliantis, omni fugientis incolu-

wind. Then it gives an impression of a wave-like movement until such a point when the stalks are weakened and eventually broken, hanging towards the ground.

However, the Jacobite survivors raised their heads again. The Irish had been defeated in one battle, but they remained resolute in their determination. Among the last to abandon the field was a cornet from the Irish horse, dignified by blood, valiant in combat, and more keen on glory than capable of victory. If I had known his name, I would have paid tribute to it. In his left hand he was holding his standard, in the right his sword. Not only was he undaunted, but alone and with a determined expression he attacked the closed ranks of cavalrymen forming the English front. Whether he did so to prove his valour or simply to do what had to be done, he did it by recklessness rather than assurance of the outcome. By a sound of the trumpet the others, who had already commenced their retreat, gave a sign to call him back. Nonetheless, unmindful of himself and his troop, preferring the glamour of a more distinguished name to the safety in flight, he fought on until death. Desperately he sought victory, refusing to abort

❀ 35 ❀

columitati anteferens, ab incepto defistere renuit; ad omnes igitur ictus expositus corpus & vexillum tuebatur, loricâ alia tela excipiens, corpore & armis alia vitabat; eqvi curfu praevalentis faltuqve & mira agilitate praealtas praecipitesq; foffas, qvae non capita modò peditum fed etiam cum eqvis viros poterant fuperare, faepiffime tranfiliit, qvotiescunq; continuatô fatigatum labore corpus qvâdam levaret qviete; cum verò unum tot manus peterent, vulnera excepit multa, qvorum unum mortiferum pectori infixum, haud fecus qvàm juftum erat, ad explendam animi ejus cupidinem & exftingvendum fangvinis ardorem; hôc tandem ictu percuffus caput inclinare coepit, & emiffo fpiritu exanime corpus ex eqvo defluxit. Non caret miraculo hujus diei pugna victoris: nam hoftis fi aut fuftinuiffet vincere aut debuiffet, facilé ad unum omnes potuit in ipfo fluminis tranfitu delere; larva autem illa coecitatis divinitùs objecta,

D 5   veni-

what he had begun. Thus exposed, he examined his body and standard, and took out some bullets from his breastplate while avoiding others by his manœuvres. Cantering and jumping his exquisite steed, and by superb agility, crossing mounds and hedgerows, which reached above not only the heads of foot soldiers but also horsemen, he occasionally rested, wearied from the exertion. But since the opposition was overwhelming, he sustained many wounds, of which the fatal one was to his heart. This appeased his soul's desire and brought him peace. His head dropped, and with his spirit gone his dead body fell off his horse.

King William's victory was in no way an assured matter. The enemy might just as well have destroyed the King's army during its river crossing if he had either kept on going or kept back; but the inadequate intelligence, caused by divine

❀ 36 ❀

venientibus ficut in ficcum naufragis, hoftem à ripa planè avertit, ipfo ergò in conflictu Hibernorum fex millia cæfa, paucioribus captîs; Ex parte Regis non multi defiderati funt, qvorum Fridericus Dux Scombergicus, Princeps fortiffimus, confiliô, manu promptiffimus, charus Regi & Ducibus Angliæ, vulgo militum defideratiffimus. Qvis ceffiffe hoftem hoc tempore & loco non miraretur, & cuinam gentium res ea non extremæ audaciæ videretur, nempè Regem tam facili negotiô Boandum fine ponte tranfiiffe. Poftremò, licèt mifericordia in prælio militis inter animi vitia computetur, ira tamen Regis in mifericordiam verfa eft; fatiùs enim putabat, hoftes clementiffimo animi tenore in fui obfervantiam & obfeqvium ducere, qvàm armîs & terrore; & ut clementiam ipfius & manfvetudinem non minori qvàm fortitudinem brabeo dignam deprædicees, ardentes ad perfeqvendum hoftem fuos cædibus abftinere receptuiqve canere

intervention, turned the Jacobite army into a shipwreck on the shores of the dry land, and it was swept away from the bank by King William's troops.*

In this battle about six thousand Irishmen were killed and even fewer were captured.† On the part of the King only few were missing, but among them was Marshal Frederick Duke of Schomberg, a brave prince, advisor and close associate of the King and other English leaders and universally beloved by the soldiers.

It is incredible that the enemy was so easily checked then and there, and it is noteworthy that only through an extravaganza of the utmost audacity did King William succeed in crossing the river Boyne without a bridge.

Though among military men in battle compassion is not what should be foremost on the mind, the King's determination was now turned to consideration; for he believed that the proper way to conquer was persuading the enemy by clemency into allegiance, rather than by coercion by military means. Trusting that leniency and mildness no less than strength was worthy of heavenly reward, the King ordered his men, who were keen on routing their enemies, to

---

* What actually happened was that the Williamites made a far reaching outflanking movement to the West. King James misinterpreted this as being the bulk of the hostile force, and moved most of his troops from their central position towards the Williamite crossing in the western sector, thus depriving the centre, where the main crossing actually happened, of adequate defensive strength.

† This is hardly an accurate estimate. Most sources believe the Battle of the Boyne to be not particularly bloody with about 1,500 Irish casualties dead and wounded and merely a few hundred on the Williamite side.

37

nere jussit, qvi repentè ad obseqvium cum triumpho redeuntes è certamine ad exspolienda cadavera discurrerunt; Ingens auri argentiq; pondus repertum est, corporibusqve occisorum sepeliendis Rex curam impendit. Totâ jam Ultoniâ subacta in Lageniam & Mediam Rex tetendit, eo scilicet consilio atqve animo, ut urbes maritimas, qvas Jacobus præsidiis armavit, in suam redigeret potestatem, missisq; aliqvot legionibus ad occupandam Droghedam, ipse cum reliqvis copiis XL stadia Dulekiam profectus est. Seqventi pugnam proximè die Drogheda sine labore oppugnationis capta est, eâ lege, ut captivi Reformatæ Religioni addicti è vinculis dimitterentur omnes, direptaqve bona suis restituerentur, præsidia sine armis salvo cum conductu sarta-tecta, ut ajunt, ad suos abirent. Drogheda à ponte prolixo super flumen strato sic dicta, undè & Pontena à qvibusdam vocatur, urbs est populosa, antiqvitatum reliqviis civiumqve freqventia cla-

ra,

abstain from killing. He therefore beat the retreat in order to call back those who roamed ubiquitously in the hope of pillaging the slain soldiers. Re-establishing order after the successful battle, a considerable consignment of gold and silver was found, and the King arranged for the bodies of the fallen to be buried.

As soon as all of Ulster had been conquered, a few regiments were detailed to mop up Drogheda. Together with the remainder of the army the King proceeded 40 furlongs to Duleek. He then headed for Leinster and the county of Meath with the coastal cities, which King James had equipped for defence as his primary objectives.

On the following day, Drogheda was captured in close combat though without too much effort. It was agreed that all captives adhering to the reformed religion should be released from their chains, and that stolen property was to be handed back to them. The garrison was granted safe conduct to leave and to go home to their families, though without weapons. The city of Drogheda possesses a long bridge across the river Boyne, and it is from this fact that some refer to the city by the name of "the Bridge."* It is a populous city, lying adjacent to the River Boyne and renowned for its remnants of old buildings and its great number of inhabitants. It is famous for

---

* Drogheda literally means "bridge."

38

ra, mercatu nobilis, & non fitu folùm fed opere etiam munita, naviumqve appulfu celebris, flumini Boando adjacens. Qvintô nonas Julii LVI ftadia ad Ballibrighanam Rex procedens caftra Crucem inter & Dunamoriam locavit, in itinere legati ex Dublinio ipfi occurrerunt, urbis fuæ deditionem commeatusq; & alia ineundæ pignora gratiæ offerentes pacem petiêre, gratius antiqviusq; nihil adventu eorum fuit, qvippe magni moliminis futura effet obfidio tam vaftæ ac munitæ urbis: Legatos ergò benignè in fidem fufceptos domum remifit, ipfeq; deftinata exfeqvi perrexit. Nihilò tamen minùs conftanti famà relatum eft, Regem fugitivum eâdem nocte, fimulatô novi prælii propofitô, five præfagiô fortè fati finiftrioris, five metu nè in hoftium poteftatem vivus veniret, aut certè eventuræ proditionis, qvam vitare malebat celeritate fugæ, paucis cum comitibus eqvo Dublinium petiiffe, maturiusqve mirâ indè velocitate Hibernos

its commerce and prospers not only from its location, but also because of crafts and its busy harbour.

On 3 July, the King, having advanced 56 furlongs to Balbriggan, pitched camp between the crossroads and Dunmore.*

While on his way towards Dublin, emissaries seeking peace came out from that city. They offered capitulation of their city with all its supplies and other amenities upon the army's entry. Nothing could be more convenient than this offer, since a siege of such a grand and well-protected city would have required considerable efforts. Therefore, having approved their offer in a benevolent manner, he sent the emissaries back while he himself carried on with his plans.

It was rumoured that on that very night fugitive King James with a few companions had come to Dublin on horseback with a phoney proposal for a new battle. However, he gave up the notion and left in a hurry. He might have had a foreboding of an unpleasant fate, should he fall into enemy hands, or become a victim of a treachery, which he rather wanted to escape by speedy flight.† Soon after his departure,

---

* Whilst no Dunmore exists in the area today, it was, and is, a very common place name, meaning "great fort."

† In reality James abandoned his army and the Irish and fled to France, blaming his people for the defeat.

❀ 39 ❀

nos urbe relictâ ad castellum Duncanense se recepisse, eoq; Jacobum ipsum concubiâ nocte pervenisse: interrogatum autem ab excubiis, qvis esset, Jacobum Regem adesse respondisse, voce hac ad Præfectum delatâ, Rex in arcem receptus omnia de prælii infelicitate copiarumqve strage suarum narravit, mox navigiolô conscensô Galliam passis velis petiit; hoc prudentiæ erat consilium: nam post acceptum ictum demùm circumspicere, præpostera cautio est. Unô die ad reqviem datô, bis mille passus ad Svorsam & indè XL stadia Dublinium versus Rex cum exercitu profectus est; ipse postero die cum cœteris Ducibus exercitum in armis stantem lustravit. Post bidui spatium ob defectum his in locis pabuli & frumenti atqve aliarum rerum egestatem mille passus ad Dublinium progressi sunt, & altera ab urbis parte mille passus apud castellum Drumnochum, qvia pingvius ibi erat solum, castra locârunt, biduô stativa ibi habebant, interea

with the city left behind, James' party retired to Castle Duncan, where they arrived in the first hour of sleep,* and as the guards had asked who was there, James merely replied that the King was present. When this had been brought to the commander, King James was received into the castle and told everything about the hapless battle and of the destruction of his troops. Leaving Ireland he embarked in a small vessel and sought France under full sails. This action was a prudent one, for looking around for threats when one has already taken a blow is a precaution taken too late.

When one day had been spent resting, King William advanced with his army two thousand paces to Swords and then another 40 furlongs towards Dublin. On the following day, together with the other commanders, he reviewed the army standing ready for inspection.

After a period of two days, the army proceeded a thousand paces because of shortage of food and fodder and other supplies in the area. And on they went for a further thousand paces to Drumnochum Castle,† since the earth was more fertile there. They pitched camp and they remained stationary

---

* The Battle of the Boyne had been of immense psychological and strategic importance as it opened the way to Dublin and contributed to James abandoning Ireland and his subsequent voyage back to France. The Irish, however, were less forgiving than Claudianus. After King James' flight, the leading tiers of Irish society did not feel obligated to remain loyal to their king, who had, in many respects, behaved in a disgraceful and selfish manner having abandoned his troops and his people as soon as he saw no further personal advantage in staying and fighting – thus his nickname *Séamus an chaca*, "James the shit."

† Whilst unidentified, it is possible that this refers to a fortification nearby or in Drimnagh, since dismantled.

40

terea commeatus largè ex oppido cives adduxerunt, qvi etiam Anglos intrà mœnia urbis exceperunt lætabundi, urbe omni tunc temporis præsidiô nudatâ. Hæc urbs metropolis est totius Hiberniæ, sedes Præfecti Regionis, qvem titulô Pro-regis ornatum Rex Anglorum eòdem mittit, in palude fundamenta ejus validas super arborum moles & lignorum strues, qvæ tanqvàm fulcra totum onus sustinent, demissa sunt atqve structa, qvippe hic locus nigra aqvarum profunditate primò erat palustris, amplitudinis ratione suæ & magnitudine reliqvas urbes omnes vincit, gloriâ opibusqve aucta ob freqventia ex diversis orbis terrarum partibus commercia mercatorum eò undiqve confluentium; sicut trito Politicis dici solet proverbiô: Ubi Imperator, ibi Roma; non mirabili modò situ naturaq; loci, mœnibus, suburbiis, armis & inhabitantium multitudine insignis, verùm arce etiam

suâ

for two days. In the meantime, Dublin was declared an open city and the citizens even welcomed the English within their defensive walls, providing them with abundant supplies.

This city is the capital of Ireland and the seat of its regional governor, who is appointed by the English King and designated as Viceroy.* While the city is founded in the middle of a swamp, it rests upon a huge pile of trees and wooden waste. Like the posts supporting the weight of a bed, the material has been dumped in the water and piled up in what used to be a marshy, black pool of water.† Thus, by its configuration, its size and its grandeur this metropolis stands out in comparison with all other Irish cities. It has gradually increased its glory and riches by lively commerce with various parts of the world and by tradesmen from everywhere gathering here.

A proverb frequently quoted by politicians goes: "Where the Emperor is, Rome is." Similarly, this city is not only distinguished by its situation and nature of the place, walls, suburbs, weapons and multitude of inhabitants; but is just as

---

* However, at the time the Viceroy was frequently referred to as "the Lord Deputy."

† Thus the city's name Dubh Linn/Dublin, which means "dark pool," a reference to the place where Rivers Liffey and Poddle meet.

41

suâ & Archiepiſcopali ſede maximé conſpicua, eximiâ templorum magnificentiâ ornata, qvæ ut operum ~~magni~~ magnitudine ità architecturæ artificio non mediocriter aſpicientium oculos oblectant; illuſtri Academiâ, ubi artium omnia ſcientiarumqve ſtudia florent, decorata, adeò ut Muſarum domicilium, literarum decus atqve doctiſſimorum virorum emporium dici poſſit, lætis atqve amœniſſimis agris diſpoſita, fructuum varietate fœcunda, fluvioqve nobili interfluente, qvem Liffium appellant accolæ, memorabilis, Liffius flumen flexuoſo Mediam meatu percurrens, leni modicoqve aqvarum defluxu é fontibus ſuis circa mœnia Dubliniæ ſegnes ſemper aqvas ducit, niſi imbre & nimbis repentinis aut vento procelloſô ad vehementiorem curſum urgetur, & ſic ſæpè immeabilis eſt; etenim cum Oceanus ſtata vice exæſtuans ſævire ventis cœperit, & retrò flumen urgere, turbidum limum arenamqve multam fluctibus

remarkable because of its castle and very much so for its archdiocese. Its cathedral is amazing by its splendour and ornamented by decorative architecture, which catches the spectators' eyes. It is provided with an eminent university,* where the studies of all branches of art and science flourish to such an extent that it is fair to call it the abode of the Muses. It is the shrine of the humanities and the venue of erudite men, surrounded as it is by bountiful and pleasant fields. Moreover, the city is productive by a variety of manufacture, and worth remembering for its prominent waterway, which the inhabitants call the Liffey. By its smooth and moderate outpouring, river Liffey follows a winding course while flowing gently through County Meath, and leading leisurely flowing water from its springs around the walls of Dublin, unless, of course, rain and unexpected thunder or boisterous winds force it to a more violent course. Thus, the Liffey is often impassable, for when the ocean foams up and begins to rage with high winds driving the river back, the sea introduces into the estuary mud and sand to such an extent that ships

---

* Trinity College Dublin. This university was established in 1592 as a small group of Dublin citizens obtained a charter from Queen Elizabeth incorporating Coláiste na Tríonóide/Trinity College, formally known as the "College of the Holy and Undivided Trinity of Queen Elizabeth near Dublin."

42

bus & aqvarum concursu subindé evomit mare vicinum, adeò ut navigia ob cumulatæ arenæ acervum sæpè impedita per arctiorem alveum ad interiora urbis penetrare non possint; hæc autem facies rerum asperitasqve loci interdum cum ventis simul ità mutatur, ut per multa stadia navium patiens sit fluvius; verùm enimverò intra ostia maris pisces alit, & velut in gremio suo alimenta accolis parat, multa riparum amœnitate obumbrata, interjacentibus sparsim nonnullis nobilium castris & oppidis, colendis agris & alendis, herbis nuspiam alia regio est aptior, qvicqvid enim alluit fluvius jucundis floribus vestiens, & integros, qvos limpidô permeat alluviô, campos svavissimis odoribus complent. Jamqve tota belli moles ultrà LXIV stadia serpsit, iteruinq; oriente luce totidem stadiis absumptis apud castellum Mortonum & Kilcullinbrigam consedit. Hinc XL stadia ad Kilruschiam iter fecit exercitus, freqventiq; itinerum molestiâ ac tumultu de-

often cannot make their way through the remaining narrow channel into the interior of the city's harbour. However, this is no permanent challenge, because when the weather changes the estuary is again cleared for navigation.

Moreover, the roads of Dublin sustain fishing and furnish the city dwellers with nourishment. The surroundings of the river Liffey's bed are more generous with herbs than most other places, its banks are delightfully shaded, there are towns and noblemen's castles scattered around, and the fields are neatly cultivated and easily maintained thanks to the river's course. The untouched plains are covered with sweet flowers and filled by pleasant smells.

The main force of the war-machine had already moved 64 furlongs further, and, having during sunrise covered a similar distance, it settled anew near Castle Morton and Kilcullen.* From here the army made a journey of 4.5 miles to Kilrush,† where one day of rest was granted to the men who had been

---

* Although written as Kilcoole by Claudianus, Kilcullen makes more sense in the context, and it is probable that Claudianus simply confused Kilcoole and Killcullen (the latter being spelled Kelcolen at the time).

† Near modern Kilberry in county Kildare, and can be found on 17th century maps.

※ 43 ※

tu defeſſis ſpatium unius diei ad qvietem datum eſt. Deindè XL ſtadia ad caſtellum Dormotum & inde ſub lucem XL ſtadia Catherlogiam caſtra moverunt. Catherlogia eſt urbs ampla, variarum opum dives, ſuperbis ædificiis freqvens, caſtellô & ampliſſimo murorum ambitu benè munita, nomen Brigum habet flumen urbem præterfluens. Poſtera die XL ſtadia ad Loughlinbrigam & ulterius XXIV ſtadia ad Wellas; hinc matutino tempore XXIV ſtadia Gouranum, & ultra XL ſtadia ad Bennisbrigam ſunt profecti. Seqventi die ad reqviem datô XL ſtadia ad pontem Thomæpolis & ampliùs tria millia paſſuum procedentes caſtra apud Igrinam fixerunt. Lageniâ jam in deditionem redactâ, in Regionem, qvam Momoniam appellant, Rex toto cum exercitu venit. Lagenia Regio ab ortu unum latus Angliæ proximum ad *littus* maris Hibernici expandit, ab occaſu à Connacia abſcinditur alterum latus interfluente flumine Senô; à Septentrio-

E   ne

worn out by the frequent trouble and disturbance of the marches.

On and on we went: 40 furlongs to Castledermot while the sun was still out, thereupon 40 furlongs to new camps at Carlow. Carlow abound with commodities, rich in many respects. It sports elegant buildings and is well protected by a well-kept ring of walls. The river flowing before the city bears the name of Barrow.

On the following day we covered 40 furlongs to Leighlinbridge and 24 furlongs further to Wells.[*] In the morning, the army marched 24 furlongs from there to Gowran, and another 40 furlongs to Bennetsbridge. After one day of rest, we proceeded 40 furlongs to the bridge in Thomastown, and three thousand paces more, pitching camp in Igrin.[†]

As soon as Leinster, too, had been brought to capitulation, the King marched with the whole army into the province, which the Irish call Munster. The province of Leinster borders on the eastern side, which is the one closest to England on the Irish Sea; in the West its border with Connacht is delineated by the River Shannon, to the North lies the county of Louth,

---

[*] Not to be confused with the more well-known Wells east of here.

[†] The place cannot be located on any modern map of Ireland.

44

ne comitatum Loudiæ, & à meridie Momoniam respicit, circuitus ejus ducenta septuaginta milliaria Anglicana comprehendit; cœlum ibi serenum & mitissimum est, terra nec acerrimis solis ardoribus uritur, nec vehementissimo frigore aut siccitate statas ad temporum vices constringitur, sed multarum umbrâ arborum & proceritate variisqve inclytis amnibus amœna, qvi ex rupibus placidum per campos iter præbent, qvorumqve adspectu maximé gaudent accolæ, eaqve uti Angliæ propior, ità agris & oppidis cultior, frugum ditissima sunt arva, pecorum pascua prata, & flumina piscibus abundantia, carne, butyro, caseo, lacte, aliarum copiâ rerum & omni commeatu adeò affluens, ut ubertas hujus terræ non indigenas modò retineat, sed & advenas invitet alendos; ingens eqvorum multitudo alitur, qvos Hobbies incolæ vocant, qvi molli ac rotundo incessu suos glomerant gressus, ungulasq; qvasi in numerum colligunt, moribus ac

and to the South it borders on the Province of Munster. Its circumference amounts to 270 thousand English feet; the sky there is peaceful and the climate is mild. The earth's surface is neither scorched by the heat of the sun nor plagued by drought, nor is it bound by extreme frost. The landscape is pleasant with the shade of many tall trees and with rivers which run a gentle course out of the cliffs and through the plains – a sight which the dwellers very much enjoy. The closer to England, the more cultivated are the fields and cities.

The rivers are abundant with fish and the ploughed lands are rich on crops and grazing pastures for cattle. There is an abundance of meat, butter, cheese, milk, and plentiful stocks of other commodities. The province overflows with any kind of nourishment, so that the richness of the earth not only maintains the indigenous, but also allows foreigners to be fed. They breed lots of horses, which the inhabitants call "hobbies."[*] These move by a soft and rolling stride, and contract their hooves as in rhythm. The inhabitants of Leinster

---

[*] Hobby/hobbies is an archaic word for a small horse(s).

45

ac virtutibus honeſtis ſunt incolæ nobiliores. Duodecimo Calendarum Auguſti die recto curſu qvi in Watterfordiam ducebat abruptô, iter flexuoſum per LXXII ſtadiorum circuitum ad Carrigiam nullo ponte ſuper flumen Svirium Watterfordiæ ſtratô direxerunt, ad Corcagiam qvoqve præcipua erat intentio Anglorum, triduô ibi ſtativa Rex habebat ob exſpectationem deditionis urbis Watterfordiæ, eandemqve ad expugnandam qvasdam eò legiones miſit; oppidani ergò ne obſeſſorum inexorabiles redderent animos in ſe vi & virtute devictos, deditione ſpontanea clementiam & pacem poſcebant, qvibus in fidem acceptis urbem intactam & nulla direptionis injuriâ multatam victor reliqvit. Hæc urbs Watterfordia Epiſcopali ſede ornata, parvum qvondam prædonum fuit habitaculum à piratis Norvegicis qvadraginta ſex ſtadia ab ore maritimo conditum, mirum qvantum nunc temporis auctum, opibus & freqventi mercatu no-

E 2   bili-

are known for their respectable living.

On 21 July we made a diversion; having given up on the right course that led straight to Waterford, we moved by a loop of 72 furlongs to Carrick [on Suir], as there was no bridge across the river Suir in Waterford. Initially, the English had wished then to move on to Cork, but since they awaited the capitulation of the city of Waterford, the King pitched camp and remained there for three days, dispatching a few regiments to urge the city to surrender. Thus, persuaded by the besiegers' steadfast resolve and obvious supremacy, the locals asked urgently for clemency and peace since they had capitulated out of free will. Accepting this, the Williamite victors left the city intact, not punished by any injury of pillage.[*] Waterford, being an Episcopal see, was once a small enclave of Norwegian pirates. It is situated 46 furlongs from the estuary of river Suir. It is amazing how much it has been enlarged over time, how it became prosperous by its resources

---

[*] At the time there were strict rules for surrendering a city. If the besieger was strong enough to make a breach in the walls wide enough to allow a carriage to pass through, the commandant might capitulate honourably, and the garrison would be allowed to march out with colours flying, music playing and burning matches (either one, two or all of these depending of the degree of bravery displayed). If under such circumstances the garrison refused to capitulate, the attacker might sack the city.

46

bilitatum, commoda navium ſtatione in celebre excreverit emporium, omni vetuſtæ honore claritatis memorabile, per fluminis Svirii littus effuſum. Svirius autem fluvius in tres alveos ſciſſus eſt, qvorum alter Brigus, alter Neorus, ultimus Svirius, qvi tergeminæ ſorores ab incolis dicuntur, iidemq; fluvii ex montibus Bladinis oriuntur, & qvò longius manant meridiem verſus, eò anguſtius inter ſe ſpatium terræ relinqvunt. Svirius horum maximus eſt, Seno fere naturâ compar, ſed magnitudine impar, longo varias tractu urbes præterfluens, ſc: Durleam, Caſſiliam, Clonmellam, Carrigiam & Watterfordiam, ubi Neorus & Brigus eum latè augent, qvos velut comites in uno receptos ampliùs ſecum devehens, vaſtis fluctibus per oſtia in mare Vergivium ſe evolvit; fluminis ripæ imminentibus collibus & objectis rupibus cinctæ, arces, oppida & nemora freqventia qvoqve littoribus ſunt juncta. Capta urbe Watterfordiâ Rex ipſe in Angliam reverſus

and frequent trade, and, due to a fine harbour, it has developed into a notable emporium.

Obviously, lying here on the river Suir, Waterford is renowned for all this. The river is a fusion of three smaller ones,* of which the first is Barrow, the second Nore, and the last Suir. The locals call them "The Three Sisters." They all rise out of the Bloom Mountains, and the longer they flow towards the South, the narrower the strip of land they leave behind between them. Suir is the greatest of these three rivers, by its nature almost comparable to River Shannon, although dissimilar with regard to magnitude, flowing round a number of cities. Its route leads past Thurles, Cashel, Clonmel, Carrick, and Waterford, where the Nore and the Barrow greatly increase it.

Travelling on more forcefully as it has received these tributaries, the Suir swells by vast waves as it enters its estuary in southern Ireland. The banks of the river are characterised by high hills and steep cliffs, castles and small towns, and at the sea-shore there are numerous shaded meadows.

When the allied army had taken Waterford, the King himself returned to England.†

---

* What is actually happening is that these three rivers merge in the Suir estuary.

† On 26 July 1690, King William left the army with the intention of returning to England to meet the perceived threat of an imminent French seaborne invasion. Eventually, this menace turned out to be non-existent and the king remained in Ireland for two more months.

47

versus est. Sextô Calendas Augusti XLVIII stadia procedebant; hinc iterùm sub lucis ortum seqventis bis mille passus Clonmellam, emporium magnum opibus & muris fortissimis valens, & à præmissis nuper occupatum; indè XLVIII stadia longiùs tendebant; Inseqventi die XXXVI stadia motis ad Goldenbrigam castris, eâ in sede spatiô ferè octidui constiterunt. Octavô Idus ejusdem mensis XLVI stadia Dunoghilum, hinc rursus maturiùs LXXII stadia Cahironlisham sunt profecti, ubi cuncta sedecim abhinc stadiis circumqvaqve vicina recenti fumantia incendiô triste dederunt spectaculum, raptim enim tectis acervisqve frumenti flammas hostes injecerant. Qvanta ergò fuerit eorundem invidia, furor & ferocitas, hinc facili conjecturâ æstimari potest; quippe miseranda villarum direptione, obviarum urbium agrorumqve vastatione non contenti, etiam in Dominos, liberos, servos, templa, sepulchra & funera ipsa demortuorum infe-

E 3   stiùs

On 27 July, our troops proceeded 48 furlongs and, during sunrise next morning, another 2000 paces to Clonmel, a huge and splendid emporium with excellent defensive walls, which had recently been occupied by our advance guard. Then we went another 48 furlongs and, on the following day, we pitched camp at Goldenbridge,* 36 furlongs on. Here we remained for about eight days.

On 6 August we proceeded 46 furlongs to Donohil,† and from there 72 more furlongs to Caherconlish, where the army assembled. At a distance of about 16 furlongs smoke appeared. This was a gloomy sight, apparently caused by the enemy having wilfully torched roofs and crops. One can easily guess how such experiences caused our soldiers' fury and boosted their ferocity. They were angered by the meaningless sack of houses, the rambling destruction of defenceless cities and fields, and even more by the outrageous cruelty towards yeomen, masters, servants, churches and graveyards – this was indeed atrocious.

---

* Today the village is simply known as Golden.

† Not to be confused with the better-known Dunhill.

❊ 48 ❊

ftius fæviebant; O! crudelem & immanem tyrannidem! qvam reflectere non potuit ipforum magnitudo fcelerum, non parentum lacrymæ ac lamentatio, nec qviritantium qverela ac vociferatio; nec minor erat atrocitas Anglorum Danorumqve ad ulcifcendas injurias, utpote qvi urbes hoftium & vicos exfpoliabant, virginibus & fœminis qvid victoribus collibuerit perpeffis, qvæcunqve hoftium adierint naufragia igne ferroq; fœdabant, adeo ut fignum nullum, veftigium reftaret nullum, neqve qvidqvam itineris effet armis intactum; nihil aliud eft fperandum tempore belli & publicarum calamitatum: tum enim, cum armis fævitur, in hoftibus eft exftincta omnis mifericordiæ fcintilla, & corda manusqve eorum mirabili humanæ cœdis fangvinisqve & urbium devaftationis aviditate flagrant: Sunt teftes loca in folitudinem Bellonæ furiis redacta, teftes erunt ipfa dirutarum urbium rudera & ruinæ, teftis erit Hibernia tota, Poftero die ad reqvi-

Neither the scale of the Williamite warfare in Ireland nor tears and grief of the bereaved could in any way justify such atrocities. However, the actions of the English and the Danes, who wanted to revenge the injuries, were no less gruesome. They too committed crimes, ransacking the enemy's cities and villages. Maidens and women had to put up with whatever pleased the conquering army. By fire and by the sword they damaged what was left belonging to the enemy, and this was done to such an extent that little evidence of human civilisation remained.

Thus, very little was left for the soldiers' subsistence. In wartime and political strife, however, this is not unexpected; for when one's own survival depends on weapons, any sympathy with the enemy seems to vanish, and hearts and hands focus on the subjugation of the opposition and devastation of enemy property.* The wasted land, the damaged buildings, the ruins, and all of Ireland bear testimony to this.

---

* It is surprising, but the Jacobites committed numerous atrocities, especially against the larger country estates, in the land they would have considered their own. This might have been partly due to the fact that many land owners were actually Protestants loyal to Britain. "Not only rapparees, but regular Jacobite forces as well, were at large and active in the hinterland of Williamite territory. According to Württemberg's information, the duke of Berwick had burned twelve towns and numerous castles in the counties of Cork and Tipperary... The Williamite supreme command threatened to burn Jacobite prisoners alive, including officers, if it did not stop." (Kjeld Hald Galster, *Danish Troops*, pp. 161-2).

※ 49 ※

reqviem datô, Anglorum decem millium peditum manus fub ductu Ducis Duglaffi ad occupandam Athlonem præmiffa, obftante verò loci naturâ, irrito labore rediit. His itaqve adjunctis XL ftadia Limmericum adverfus hoftes dumeta inter & fepimenta ante urbem delitefcentes funt progreffi, vix primum impetum fuftinentes hoftes è latebris fuis cefferunt, qvorum tergis intra moenia urbis fe recipientium inhærentes Dani, molem meridiem verfus extra urbem jactam occupârunt. Eo in conflictu hoftem repellendi virtus Gallorum egregia Proteftantium & vigor unius legionis Anglorum clariffimè emicuit; inde hoftes multam tormentorum vim ab urbis ipfius moenibus toto tempore pomeridiano Anglis intorferunt, qvibus ad occafum usqve Solis binis tantùm tormentis minoribus remenfum eft. Deindè haud procul ab urbis muris locatîs, ubicunq; tutò & commodum fieri poterat, caftrîs, milites more ufitato ad neceffaria vitæ ex

E 4   pro-

After a day's recuperation, under the command of Lieutenant General Douglas, a detachment of ten thousand men of the English infantry was dispatched in order to seize Athlone. However, the fortifications as well as the environment of this city prohibited conquest by a military formation this size, and they withdrew having achieved nothing.* Rejoining the main force of the army, covering a distance of 40 furlongs, they advanced on Limerick, where the enemy had concentrated.

While the Williamites lay hidden in the shrubbery and hedgerows outside the city, having barely yet come into contact with the enemy, the Jacobites abandoned their positions. The Danes, pursuing those withdrawing, seized the fortification situated south of the city.† In this initial clash the French Huguenots‡ gave a fine example of their offensive fighting spirit and, similarly, particularly one English

---

* Claudianus' account of this disposition seems slightly simplified, as various other sources reveal that on Wednesday 9 July, William divided his army sending Lieutenant-General Douglas with a relatively small detachment of three regiments of horse, two of dragoons and ten of foot towards Athlone. Douglas' expedition achieved nothing as far as the operational tasks were concerned and, in obvious contravention of the king's proclamation guaranteeing the civilians protection and promising a peaceful existence, it turned into an extravaganza of profligate looting. Douglas' orders forbidding these outrages seemed utterly ineffective probably because neither was the soldiery controlled nor did their commander possess the will to apply sanctions adequately. cf. Kjeld Hald Galster, *Danish Troops*, pp. 138-9.

† Following severe fighting, the force now constituting the first line – the Danes on the left, Bellasis' vanguard at the centre and the Dutch Blue Guards on the right – managed to drive back the enemy to Singland Ridge east of the city. Although in the western sector an old redoubt dominated this place providing an excellent defensive position, repeated assaults by Württemberg's troops succeeded in forcing the Jacobites out. cf. Kjeld Hald Galster, *Danish Troops*, p. 141.

‡ Apart from four regiments of Huguenots there were individual Huguenot officers in many units. One of them was the commander of Danish horse Major General Suzannet Marquess de la Forest.

50

proximis vicis ferenda difcurrentes, varios pecorum greges ad caftra retulerunt. Ortâ luce turmæ eqvitum qvædam cum Anglis dimachis flumen Senum tranfierunt, qvos imitabantur qvatuor legiones peditum, animô hoftem ad pugnam provocandi, fi qvis viritim dimicare auderet, at hoftis in patentibus campis nusqvam obvius erat, nam alii in urbis ipfius, in Gallovadiæ alii, alii in Athlonis provinciarumqve cuftodiam majori firmandam præfidiô erant difpofiti, alii in Connaciam, infulam ubi totius regionis opes direptionibus congeftas, magnamqve pecorum vim coactam effe fama prodidit; fitu autem loci exploratô redierunt præmiffi, & toto die utrinq; tormenta bolidesqve igniarias evomuerunt, adeo ut biduô e univerfis Anglorum copiis decem fint defiderati, qvindecim vulneratis; Tribunus militiæ Waltherus per mamillam finiftram fclopô transfixus paucos poft dies ictu defunctus eft. Poftera die continua tormentorum displofio audieba-

regiment performed brilliantly.

In the afternoon, the enemy seemed to have steadied himself and delivered a heavy and well-aimed gunfire from the city walls against the English, who responded, though merely with their smaller field pieces.

Then, while the Williamite army was engaged in pitching its camps at a safe distance from the city walls, the enemy, not surprisingly, roamed the countryside in order to gather the supplies required for sustaining life of man and beast, bringing back flocks of cattle to his own camps.

At sunrise the next morning, troops[*] of allied cavalry as well as English dragoons[†] crossed the river Shannon. Dismounted, the latter appeared as if they were four regiments of foot. Their plan was to probe and see if the enemy was willing to give battle. However, in the open field the opposition was nowhere to be seen. As it turned out, in order to strengthen their defence the enemy had redeployed his forces, with a large garrison in Limerick itself, some troops in Galway, others still in Athlone, and some spread out across the province of Connacht. It was rumoured that the whole region had been stripped of resources, and the supplies thus concentrated where the Jacobite forces needed them. However, the troops detailed for the probing manœuvre returned as soon as they had surveyed the area.

For two days, incessantly, mortars of both sides hurled red hot balls onto the positions of their opposition. Among the English ten soldiers were killed and fifteen wounded. Colonel

---

[*] Although, today, a "troop" is a subdivision of a tank regiment including three to four tanks, in 1690 it was rather a company of horse. In combat two troops would combine to form a squadron, six troops constituting a cavalry regiment.

[†] At the time dragoons could fight either mounted or on foot, though mostly the animals were used for transport only while the actual combat happened dismounted.

🟊 51 🟊

diebatur, & magna erat cœterarum ad obsidionem urbis machinarum exspectatio, materies etiam ex sylvis ad oppugnationem vehebatur. Intempesta verò nocte ingens inter hostium & Regis milites aborta est perturbatio, illis campanas pulsantibus oppugnationem, his ad sonitum campanarum eruptionem adesse ratis; causa erat hujus erroris, qvòd in cuniculorum accessibus tela solitò infestiora cum illis committerentur, hinc pavore qvasi è somno excitati oppidani ad defensionem se accinxerunt, Angli autem ad sonum æris campani ingentem sustulerunt clamorem, vociferantes: Now ring Pater Peter to masse, go to church ye Popish rogues, ɔ: Jam pulsat ad missam Pater Petrus, petite templum vos scelerati Papistæ; Qvæ verba contumeliosa dirô qvasi malignoqve vulnere pectora oppidanorum magnoperè affecerunt. Interim tormenta qvædam & alia belli præparato-

E 5   ria

Walther,* being pierced by a bullet through the left side of his thorax, died after a few days.

While on the following day one could hear continued rumbling of the guns, the Williamite army anxiously awaited the arrival of additional siege train, guns and ammunition to be used for softening up the city's defenders. Materials for the siege and assault were now being gathered from afar and expected to arrive at any moment.

During a night of much commotion, however, huge confusion had arisen among the soldiers of the enemy as well as with those of King William. While the former were striking the alarm bells, the latter mistakenly believed that a Jacobite sally was in the offing. The reason for this misinterpretation was that the defenders were applying more dangerous explosive charges than those that were normally used in the approaches to the mines. Thus, the citizens awoken from their sleep feared what was afoot, and readied themselves for defence.

In the meantime, the English made considerable noise trying to ridicule the opposing Catholics, calling them 'wicked papists' and suggesting they take refuge in their churches. This insult very much affected the hearts and minds of the townsfolk.

At this moment, it was announced that a supply column

---

* Colonel Hans Georg Walther was Lieutenant General Württemberg's adjutant general.

52

ria in via esse adqve castra properare nunciabatur, bina minorum unà cum ingenti rerum copiâ militarium sub medium noctis incautiùs turbaverant prædones hostium, è proximis montibus ac sylvis catervatim prorumpentes, cæsisq; custodum plerisqve parùm vigilibus, deqve sua nimiùm securis salute, plaustra panibus & instrumentis aggeres ad egerendos necessariis onusta subjectô igne cremârunt; illis verò ad prædam discurrentibus supervenerunt eqvites & velites, ut vocantur, Draconici, hostis audaciam passim impunè vagantis & prædæ inhiantis strenuè ulciscentes, illi autem haud segniùs refugientes, qvàm erumpentes, ad primum nostratium adventum pleriqve in speluncas suas & montem omni abjecta cunctatione se receperunt, reliqvam latronum partem pecudum more præ se agentes victores unà cum novem balistis & qvinq; mortariis ad castra reduxerunt. Mireris furiosos hosce & flagitiosissimos latrones, qvorum magna
in

with the anxiously awaited ordnance and other sinews of war was on its way to the Williamite camp. However, bringing such a vast amount of military equipment* in the middle of the night, the supply column had accidentally roused the enemy's suspicion. The logistics people and their guards were hardly as alert as the situation would seem to have required, and not at all concerned about their safety. Actually, they were fast asleep when suddenly a large formation of Jacobite troops and rapparees debouched from the nearest mountains and forests. A great many guards were slain, and wagons loaded with bread, ammunition, and engineering tools were set on fire.†

While the Jacobite assailants were heading from all directions for possible booty, our cavalrymen and dragoons intervened to revenge the enemy's brazenness. The assailants, however, then fled no slower than they had come, and many of them retired to their caves in the mountains as soon as they realised the advent of our reinforcements. The Williamite

---

* Apart from siege guns, there were munitions, food stuff, tin boats, cart wheels etc.

† This was a major setback for the Williamite army, since the loss of this ordnance and equipment prevented them from executing the siege successfully before the end of the 1690 campaigning season. Jacobite General Patrick Sarsfield had picked a body of more than 500 men and left Limerick on Sunday 10 August. He advanced cautiously to Killaloe, but finding the bridge there held in force by the enemy, he passed on and crossed the Shannon at Ballyvally. Thence, guided by a rapparee chief named Hogan, the party turned into the deep gorges of the Silver Mine Mountains, where it stayed all Monday. At 3 a.m. on the following morning Sarsfield's party surprised the convoy at Ballyneety some 16 km from Limerick. The guards were killed or taken prisoners, and three standards, the eight eighteen- and twenty-four-pounder guns, five mortars, eighteen tin pontoons and 200 wagons loaded with ammunition and supplies, were captured. The siege artillery was now spiked, and the other supplies including 5,500 kg of powder, 3,000 cannonballs, large quantities of match, grenades and carcasses and three days supply of bread were collected and destroyed. Galster, Danish Troops, pp. 145-46.

※ 53 ※

in ea regione copia eft, aufos é fcopulis'&
montibus fuis contra milites prodire,
folitos aliás in plana defcendere, rabie
velut qvadam toto ex ore emicante,
cum enim prætereuntem aut viatorem
in itinere qvendam viderint, fpe prædæ
audent fubindè inopinato impetu, animo crudeli, horrido corporis habitu
vifuqve & vultu torvô procurrere ad
obvium qvemq; interficiendum. Hi
prædones indigenæ relictis vicorum agrorumq; fedibus, fpecus in denfis fylvis atqve paluftribus virgultis deviisqve
montibus foderunt, difficiles aditu, in
qvos fe ac conjuges & liberos condiderant, fed captivos vario cruciatus fuppliciorumqve genere Angli mactârunt,
cruce & rotâ alios, alios fractione & diftractioné membrorum. Sub vefperam
materies militi dabatur molibus faciendis, è qvibus tela ingeri in urbem poterant. Noctu ex obfeffa urbe bis infeftis armis eruptione factâ pugnatum
eft, multa autem ftrage & vulneribus
confectos, cedentibus cœteris, Danorum
cohor-

survivors brought back the captured rapparees to the camp, leading them in front like cattle, together with nine mortars and five pieces of siege guns.

The rapparees are a large crowd of savage robbers and partisans spread all over this region. They hide in cliffs and mountains where they constitute a permanent menace to the soldiers. Frequently they descend onto the plains, while at other times they break forth surprisingly taking on with great ferocity any one standing in their way. They regard travellers and the occasional passer-by as their natural prey, they fall upon them surprisingly and with no mercy, and they do not hesitate to kill whoever might dare to oppose them.

Together with their spouses and children, these local robbers have settled in dense forests, boggy terrain, and secluded mountains, which are difficult to access.

The captured rapparees were chastised by the English, each by a different way of torture and punishment. Some were hanged, others broken on the wheel, others still had their limbs stretched.

In the evening, field fortifications were thrown up in order to facilitate the emplacement of batteries from which bombs and grenades might be lobbed into town. During the night the enemy twice sallied out of the occupied city, and we engaged them in close combat. The Danish companies repelled the assaults, dislodging the destabilised hostile troops.

❊ 54 ❊

cohortes retroëgerunt, caufa harum excurfionum erat, qvòd acceffibus apertis fortalitium qvoddam ante urbem exftructum Angli feliciter expugnàrunt. Poftera die plauftra pulveri pyrió & glandibus onufta Watterfordiâ in caftra venerunt; Eademq; nocte obfeffi vehementem audentes eruptionem ftrenuè fecerunt, qvos Dani fortiter repulerunt, etiam nunc à fociis deferti. Lucis fub ortum alia extra munimenta urbis moles haud multo cum difpendio occupata eft, duobus ex cohorte Calneni lethaliter vulneratis, qvorum alter ex vulnere in antecedenti nocturna dimicatione manu amputatâ, alter in oppugnatione hujus molis globô per cranium transfixus obiit: Infeqventi die imperante in fuggeftu tormentorum Duce Duglaffô media ferè nocte ignis bis urbi injectus eft, qvem ad inhibendum, nè locum amplius daret flamma, hoftis volitabat. Oriente luce fub imperio Ducis Würtenbergici bombos ignivomos è capite molis tormentorum
tectis

One reason for the success of the night's encounters was that, once the approaches had been cleared, the English assaulted and took the small fort lying south of the city walls.

On the following day, a wagons column coming up from Waterford, heavily loaded with cannonballs* and gunpowder, was received in the Williamite camp. In the following night the Jacobite garrison sallied out with considerable force. However, the Danes, at the moment fighting alone, repelled them effectively.

During sunrise, various field fortifications outside the city walls were captured with limited effort, though two soldiers of Kalneyn's regiment were fatally wounded. One died from his wound, having his hand cut off in the night's battle, the other from having been shot through while storming the enemy fortifications.

The day after, under the leadership of Lieutenant General Douglas, who commanded from the gun line, fire was hurled into the city twice. The enemy did his best to contain the blazing fire, trying to prevent its spread to an even larger area.

At sunrise, under Lieutenant General Württemberg's

---

* Possibly 18 and 24 pounds balls and carcasses (incendiary bombs) used by the siege artillery.

55

tectis urbis injecerunt, ignis celeriter conceptus ab obseſſis posteà ſub medium noctis exstinctus est. Nono decimo die ab inchoata obſidione milites, qvi in acceſſibus erant, alacres & tunc temporis avidi certamimis gloriævé loricas expugnârunt, qvibus feliciter qvidem occupatis, proruptum ingentis operis murum furiali impetu ardentibus velut oculis inſiliebant; tum impigrè ac ſummis viribus jam eminus jam cominus decertatum est, & in vallo magna erat strages, hostium enim alii omne telorum genus grandinis in modum largaqve qvoq; tormenta é muris turribusqve urbis excuſſerant, alii ingentis magnitudinis ſaxis per mœnium prona devolutis capita militantium proterebant, multos etiam gladió impulſos ac duris contis præcipitârunt. Hic oppugnantibus ad ſeſe tuendos & hostibus ad inceſſendum ingens incitamentum, ideoqve primùm triumphus, mox trepidatio, dehinc fuga; cum enim egregia edita pugnâ, Dani defenſioni

command, we lobbed incendiary bombs onto the city's houses from salients in the trenches. Although the fire made considerable impact on those under siege, it was effectively extinguished at about midnight.

On the 19th day since the beginning of the siege, the soldiers, who were present in the approaches, were now keen on battle and glory. Thus, from the trenches, which they had dug over the previous days and nights, they now attacked over the top. They sprang forth energetically in order to make an attack on the wall, which the defenders had so skilfully constructed. The ensuing clash was fought with untiring vigour, both at a distance and close quarters. And in the positions there was a massacre as the enemy discharged a hail-storm of bullets and plentiful grape-shot, too, from the walls and towers of the city. Moreover, numerous large stones were rolled out from the curtain wall, crushing the heads of the assailants – even those who had already been pierced by swords or pikes.

For assailants as well as for the defenders there was an obvious motivation to fight and conquer, because, if they did not, panic and rout would ensue.

But as the besieged Jacobites resisted doggedly, and since their commanders were up to the task, the Danes' assault was

❊ 56 ❊

sionis impotes, virtute obsessorum pertinacissimè resistentium & vigilantiâ Prætoris loci illius denuò essent ab urbe repulsi, arma tamen non omittebant omnes, donec multo sangvine effuso multisqve vulneribus confecti, pauci integri remeare cogerentur; Ex legione Celsitudinis Regiæ Serenissimi Principis Friderici, Tribunus ipse Calnenus sclopò per gulam trajectus, amissô naturali colore pallescere cœpit & animam Deo reddere, cujus corpus promiscuas inter cadaverum strues à Decurione (jam verò Centurionis honore & officiô aucto) Hartmanno extractum, proximi adstantes in castra retulerunt, funus ejus ad Clonmellam magnificé elatum est; Tesserarius Wittinghoffius globô plumbeô interfectus est; Ordinis Ductor nomine Formholtus Wittinghoffius, Centuriones Brochdorfius & Muschevallus, tres Optiones, totidem vexilliferi saucii, centum circiter & qvinqvaginta milites cæsi ac vulnerati sunt, ut de cœteris copiis taceam,

repelled by the tenacity of the defenders.

However, they did not abandon their weapons, and it was not until they had been completely worn down by intense bloodletting and many casualties that the few who were still unscathed were forced to retire.*

Colonel Kalneyn, the commanding officer of Prince Frederick's Regiment, was himself pierced through the throat by a bullet. He turned pale while losing his natural colour and his soul returned to God. Sergeant Harmann, who is now a captain, managed to drag the colonel's body out of a pile of dead bodies. He was given a dignified and splendid burial in Clonmel.

A duty officer, Major Vittinghof, was killed by a lead bullet. A company sergeant major by the name Formholt Witinghoff, the Captains Brockdorf and Münschefall, three lieutenants and just as many ensigns were injured. Moreover, about one hundred and fifty soldiers were also among the killed or wounded. I shall not comment on the casualties of other units as I am not sufficiently well-informed as to these.†

---

* While the grenadiers routed the Irish into Irish Town, the Danes managed to reach the counterscarp where they secured a lodgement on the covered way, which however, was so close to the walls that showers of stones and musket shots made the position untenable. Lieutenant-Colonel Erffa forced his way through the breach with his unit, the Funen Infantry Regiment, but since no support was forthcoming he was obliged to retire to the approaches. Württemberg then attempted an attack with Prince Frederick's and one English regiment, but they were forced to abort the attempt with considerable losses. Having fought for three hours the Williamites were obliged to retreat. Galster, *Danish Troops*, p. 148.

† Major Vittinghof was the OC (Officer Commanding) A Coy, Captains Brockdorf and Münschfall the OCs of C and E Coys respectively.

57

ceam, earum jacturæ ignarus; at credibile est, ex parte hostium licét numero incerto nec paucos cecidisse. Tum hæsitâsse videbatur perpetua ista felicitas, splendorqve fortunæ atrâ velut nube obfuscatus fuisse; alacritas etiam illa, qvæ paulo ante milites tot rerum prosperarum fiduciâ plenos ad pugnam accendit, jam in desperatione cœpit debilitari. Vix aliud remedium apparebat, qvàm obsidionem solvere, dubii ergò Duces & suspensi, & perseverarentnè, an propositô abirent tam irritô, satis incerti, fatigati tamen statuerunt ab obsidionis perseverantia in aliud usqve commodius tempus desistere; qvippè exigua spes potiundæ urbis eô tempore supererat, & obsidionem diuturniorem magno sibi esse credebant impedimento in cœteris, qvæ constituerant, expediundis; Maxima vero causa ipsius retrogressus erat metus cuniculorum, qvibus suffossa mœnia, non omnes tantum Protestantes urbis captivi, sed ipsi etiam expugnantes vi pulveris subjecti in
aërem

But I believe that it is credible that, on the part of the enemy, although the number of casualties is uncertain, only few of them died. In war, luck is rarely lasting and chance can go either way. When great losses are sustained, the soldiers' fighting spirit sags.

The situation being as it was, there was hardly other remedy than to raise the siege. The commanders were uncertain of whether they should persist or abandon the project, which seemed increasingly hopeless. Eventually, it was decided to quit the siege and wait for a more promising opportunity.

The campaigning season was drawing to its close, and there was little probability that a long-lasting siege would yield any positive outcome. Moreover, it was of paramount importance to disengage the besieging troops safely, and the fear that the Jacobite defenders might have undermined the walls and approaches seemed worth taking seriously. Many Protestants being held captive in the city, as well as the men assaulting, risked being obliterated by the explosive force of the powder, should the defenders choose to ignite it.*

---

* Moreover, Sarsfield's successful raid had postponed the siege and the campaigning season was drawing to its close. The weather deteriorated and within weeks there would be a serious dearth of fodder for the animals as well as supplies for the men.

✺ 58 ✺

aërem levarentur. Tum demum Pridie Calendarum Septembris solutâ obsidione XL stadia ad Cahironlisham remensi sunt, ubi biduum constiterant. Limericum urbs speciem insulæ præbet, nam castello, muris, præaltis fossis & munitissimo non modo ingentis operis vallô, sed flumine etiam Senô qvasi coronâ cingitur, crebrisqve fluctibus compages mœnium atqve munimenta urbis verberantur. Hæc urbs est Episcopatûs titulô insignis, habet suburbium ponte lapideo conjunctum, latisqve aqvarum fossis ac fortissimis mœnibus cinctum, adeò ut inexpugnabilis videatur, qvadringenta octuaginta stadia ab Oceano Vergivio & aditu fluminis Seni, qvò Connaciam & Momoniam intramus, dissita est, maritimô Anglorum commerciô dives, qvippe flumen est navigiorum adeò capax, ut naves onerariæ mœnibus urbis applicentur. Deinde LVI stadia ad Culliniam castra movebant, triduo ad otium dato ulteriùs XXXII stadia Tipperariam ibant, ubi

octi-

Eventually the siege was raised, and on 31 August* the Williamite army retraced their steps, marching the 40 furlongs back to Caherconlish, where they rested for two days.

At first sight the city of Limerick appears to be an island, with a small citadel lying behind secure walls and a very deep moat. Thus, the city lies safely within the skilfully constructed battlements, and its defensive qualities are increased by the fact that it is enveloped by the river Shannon, forming a crown-like figure† round the city, its waves permanently lapping the joints of the defensive walls. The city has an Episcopal residence; joined by a stone bridge, there is a suburb‡ that is similarly enveloped by strong defensive walls, wide ditches making it look impregnable.** Limerick lies about 40-80 furlongs from the sea in the south-western part of Ireland at the mouth of the river Shannon, by which one may enter the provinces Connacht and Munster. It has a lively trade with England because the Shannon is navigable, allowing merchant-vessels to moor at the city's defensive walls.

Subsequently, the army moved its camp 56 furlongs to Cullen, and after three days' of rest, it carried on for 32

---

* King William decided, on 29th August, to raise the siege.

† English Town, being the largest part of the city of Limerick at the time, was an island set amidst the dual prongs of the Shannon.

‡ Probably, Claudianus means Irish Town.

** The so-called English and Irish towns were connected with a bridge. Irish town was not a suburb but an integral part of Limerick.

❈ 59 ❈

octiduô stativa habuerunt. Posteà LXXII. stadia contendebant Cahirum, ibi novem dies Dux militibus ad qvietem dederat. Dehinc longius XL stadia Glaheinum & LXIV stadia Kilvortham profecti sunt. Seqventi die XL stadia Rathcormochiam tendunt. Sextô Calendas Octobris LXXX stadia Corcagiam adire festinantes, qvam à parte septentrionali obsidio clauserunt. Angli nuper ex Anglia sub ductu Ducis Marlbourgii advecti, castrîs à parte urbis meridionali munitîs, è mole à se jactâ in urbem tormenta ingesserunt. Postridie ad pacis conditiones ferendas ex urbe missus est caduceator, sed ubi de pace non convenit, placuit certamen. Post tridui obsidium reciprocantibus aqvis per lutum cœnumqve fluminis ad summa genua transeuntes urbem fortiter expugnârunt, mox secuta est deditio, occupata itaqve urbe ad direptionem provolabat miles, sed sub pœna capitis inhibuit Dux, ut ne qvis ullas ædes invaderet civium, data tamen præ-
F   dæ

furlongs to Tipperary, where we pitched camp and stayed for eight days. And on we went; we carried on for 72 furlongs to Caher. Here the general granted the troops a nine day break.

From Caher the army continued 40 furlongs further to Clogheen and 64 furlongs to Kilworth. The next day, they marched 40 furlongs towards Rathcormack. On 26 September we hurried 80 furlongs to Cork, which we cordoned off from the north. Under General Marlborough's command, English reinforcements had been shipped recently from England. These brought in extra cannon, pitched camp south of the city, and began laying siege there.

On the following day the city beat a parley in order to set up articles of peace. However, since it did not come to any agreement, strife persisted. After three days of siege, traversing during ebb as well as flow through the mud and dirt of the river, the Williamite troops boldly assaulted. Soon surrender followed and, when the city had thus been duly occupied, a soldier ran forth in order to pillage. However, the general prohibited this and, under the peril of capital punishment, he forbade soldiers to invade any civic premises,

60

dæ funt qvædam tecta Papiftarum, & captivos diligenti aſſervari cuftodia juſſit; tam facilé in poteſtate Regis redacta eſt munitiſſima illa per fluvii Saurani littus effuſa Corcagia. Urbs ea fatis amœna eſt, & ſedes Epiſcopalis, caſtelló exiguo, muris turribusq; munita, unius tantùm plateæ longitudine extenſa, copià negotiatorum adventuqve advenarum & navium ſtationibus maximè celebris, magna munimenta urbis eſt flumen Sauranus mœnia præterfluens breviſſimo qvidem curſu, ſed latiſſimis oſtiis. Ipſis Calendîs Octobris urbe peragratâ XXXII ſtadia emenſi ſunt, iterumqve ſub lucis ortum XLVIII ſtadia Kinſaliam & circuitum ter millium paſſuum ad obſidendum Novum Caſtellum ſeu Arcem Carolinam perrexerunt, ad qvorum adventum vicinia locorum omnis luctuoſo velut incendio ardebat, & turpi ruinà deformabatur. Noctu vero Vetus Caſtellum in edita rupe trans flumen ſitum ad occupandum emiſſus eſt Legatus

apart from houses belonging to papists, which were released for general looting. Moreover, he ordered that captives were to be kept in thorough custody.

Thus, with limited effort the fairly well-defended city of Cork was brought to submission, and the King's power was extended throughout the lands on the shores of River Suck.* Cork is agreeably pleasant; it has an Episcopal residence and it is overlooked by a small castle, walls, and towers. There is only one street cutting lengthwise through the city, which is very famous for its many merchants, the traffic by foreigners, and the piers of its harbour. The river Suck greatly adds to the effectiveness of the city's defences as it flows past its walls. Though it has quite a narrow course where it passes Cork, it has a very wide mouth.†

On 1 October, when the city had been traversed, the troops travelled 32 furlongs more and once again, during sunrise, 48 furlongs to Kinsale. They performed an outflanking movement of three thousand paces in order to lay siege to the new castle or 'Charles Fort.'‡

As we went, we saw the whole countryside was on fire, obviously in a process of being reduced to a depressing heap of rubble. During the night, however, Major General von

---

* Claudianus writes "per fluvii Saurani" (on the river Suck), which must be due to a limited knowledge of Irish geography. The waterway traversing Cork is river Lee.

† Again, Claudianus writes Sauranus, though, obviously, he means "Luuius" (river Lee).

‡ On the opposite side of the inlet lay the old "James Fort."

※ 61 ※

tus Imperatorius Tettovius vir claritate rerum bellicarum magnificus, qvi tota nocte per XXXII ſtadiorum circuitum exigua peditum manu comitante iter faciens, prima luce flumine Buvindâ trajectô in conſpectu hoſtis erat, & mox arcem mœnibus ſtrenue tranſcenſis, victor fine ſangvine ſuorum, & ne uno qvidem deſideratô ingrediebatur immani cum hoſtium contuſione ac tumultu magis qvàm prælio; nam ex peregrinis militibus tanta ipſis incuſſa fuerat formido, ut hoſtes primum impetum non ſuſtinerent, ſed potius ſpes ſalutis erat in fuga omnis. Nec felicior in mari qvàm in terra fuga, multi enim fugientium abjectis armîs in flumen humeris tenus ſe immiſerunt, gradûs verò firmi impotes ingenti brachiorum pulſu plauſuqve in profundum ruebant, ut qvaſſatæ naves in præalta aqva, modò ſuper ipſas allevantes undas, modò ſuperfuſis diverberatisqve fluctibus immerſi, innoxii tamen feſtinandô flumen transnaverunt; partim in ſcaphas

F 2 hoc

Tettau, one of the two deputy commanders, was ordered to occupy Old Castle – James' Fort – lying on the steep cliff on the opposite side of the river.* Major General von Tettau was a magnificent man much acclaimed for his achievements in previous wars. During the preceding night he had, accompanied by a small infantry detachment, completed a tough cross-country march of 32 furlongs.

At first light, von Tettau crossed the river Bandon and deployed his troops before the enemy fort. With no further ado, he assaulted the stronghold almost instantly and scaled its defensive walls. Victorious, as he then was, he had achieved a breakthrough neither having spilt too much of his soldiers' blood nor with any wish to do so. The Williamites' surprising appearance in James' Fort caused considerable confusion among the enemies, and the resulting disorder seemed even greater than in an open battle. Fear of the foreign soldiers was pervasive with the defenders; so much terror had been induced that they could not even withstand the first strike. Thus, their only hope seemed to be one of salvation by running away.

However, the endeavours to escape were unsuccessful on the water as well as on the dry land. Many of those trying to take flight discarded their weapons and plunged into the neck-deep river. However, not being able to control their steps, they tumbled into the wet abyss, while their beating and clasping their arms made them sound and look like boats tossed on deep water – soon borne on their billows, soon immersed in the waves. Nonetheless, some of the fugitives, who had leapt into small dinghies prepared for that sort of contingency, came towards the English forces on the far side

---

* Major General von Tettau with 300 Danish and 300 English musketeers and the Danish Guards' company of grenadiers was detailed to accomplish the task; and at 10 a.m. the following morning they set out to cross the river Bandon out of sight of the occupants.

62

hoc ad ipsum præparatas defilientes in manus Anglorum venerunt; partim sexaginta circiter ex præfidio arcis primô impetu hauriebantur incendiô, qvod celeriter conceptum erat ex pila qvadam ignita, qvæ intrà vallum in dolium pulvere nitratô confertum improvifè cadebat; partim ipfô in caftello in captivitatem arrepti funt. Prætor arcis in vallo, ut fama vulgaverat, à Vicario Tribuni Eppingero fclopô occifus eft, fic eodem, qvô obfeffum eft die, captum eft Vetus Caftellum. Interjectô tempore mirum in modum è mole meridiem verfus erectâ octo tormentis in muros Novi Caftelli fæviebant Dani; fiqvidem moles Anglorum in Orientem nondum perfecta, indies magis magisqve crefcens eminebat; hic cœfus eft é legione Cimbrica Ordinis Ductor Patterbornius in acceffus defcendens. Poft qvatuordecim dierum obfidium de legibus pacis confultare cœperunt obfeffi, qvibus petentibus venia ad ignofcendum data eft,

eâ

of the river, where they were promptly apprehended by the English.

In the first assault on James' Fort, a crowd of about sixty men were driven out of their positions on the battlements by fire. Others still were taken prisoner at the wall close by. A captain was rumoured killed at his command post on the parapet by a bullet from Brigadier Eppinger's troops. Soon after, the keep was hit by an incendiary bomb, coincidentally striking exactly where the gun-powder was stored. Thus, the Old Castle – James' Fort – was captured on the very same day it was assaulted.[*]

Days later, from a gun line facing south, the Danes strafed the walls of New Castle – Charles' Fort – with eight cannon. It was here that Sergeant-Major Paderborn of the Jutland Regiment was killed while he was trying to descend into the passages leading towards the fort. Although the English trenches east of the fort had not yet been finished – they improved by the day – they were already rather remarkable. After a fortnight's siege, the besiegers began to discuss how to phrase the articles of surrender. Pardon should be given to all those who sought it, allowing them to leave unconstrained

---

[*] The old fort was taken with the loss of only 23 Danish and 30 English dead or wounded. Forty-six guns were taken.

※ 63 ※

ea lege, ut tantô impedimentorum sarcinarumqve onere, qvantum humeris & paucis cifiis, clitellariisq; eqvis vehi poterat, tibiarum tympanorumqve cantu fignisq; erectis per ruinam & foramen mœnium arcis effent egreffuri; cœtera omnia magnâ copia congefta hoftes fummo cum mœrore reliqverunt, ingens qvoqve vini & commeatûs in arce copia reperiebatur. Exeuntibus igitur per proruptum murum Hibernorum cohortibus, præfidium Anglorum per portam arcis introductum eft. Decimo qvintô Calendas Decembris XLVIII ftadia à Kinfalia retrovadebant. Kinfalia eft vetus civitas, exigua qvidem & ignobilis, belli hujus rabie admodùm deformata, pro nautis verò ad Indiam aliasqve mundi partes navigantibus recreandi cauſâ omni commeatuum copiâ celebris, commodum majorum navium corporibus acceffum præbens, duobus fortiffimis caftellis ad oftia maris munita, infrà rupes præaltas ad littus fluminis Buvindæ

F 3   urbs

through the ruined passages of the fort, bringing along with them all their baggage.

As the Williamite troops gained access to the castle they discovered a huge stock of supplies. The Jacobite soldiers left it all with great sadness because it was a considerable store of wine and nourishments that they had thus to relinquish.[*] While the companies of Irish troops filed out through the breached wall, English reinforcements were brought in through the castle's main gate.

On 17 November, we retraced our steps 48 furlongs to Kinsale.[†] Kinsale is an old community, small and not very well known. Although it has been severely damaged by the calamities of this war, it has been known by sailors bound for India and other overseas destinations. Over the years many such seafaring men have been fed here by the town's rich supply of nourishments. Kinsale's roads are cut in between high cliffs on the shores of the river Bandon's estuary. The harbour gives reasonably easy access for large ships and it is secured by two strong[‡] castles on either side of the river mouth.

---

[*] The spoils of included 94 guns, of which 34 were of brass, and various other goods such as "1,000 barrels of beef, forty tuns of Claret, a great quantity of sack, brandy and strong beer." Galster, *Danish Troops*, p. 158.

[†] Claudianus is wrong. 48 furlongs is c. 10km. However, there is only about 4km between Charles Fort and the Town of Kinsale.

[‡] Only Charles' Fort was in good defensive condition. James' Fort was derelict.

64

urbs cavata jacet. Transacta nocte ulteriùs XXXII stadia Corcagiam euntes extra muros urbis castra fixerunt. Hinc sub lucis ortum singulæ copiæ, hyeme jam instante, ad hyberna destinata processerunt: Legio Celsitudinis Regiæ Principis Friderici cum Regia cohorte Danorum peditum comitante LXXX stadia Rathcormochiam contendit. Indè prima luce ad Castellum Leonis XVI & Tallagum LXIV, Lismoram XXIV, Capperqvinam XVI & longiùs VIII stadia Saltabrigam ad littus dissitam fluminis Dabronæ, Capperqvinam & Lismoram præcurrentis, & longissimo in Jagoliam excursu sese in mare evolventis, processit: CXXVIII stadia fuêre iter unius diei, ibi posterô die milites itineris magnitudine defessi stativa habuerunt. Deindè Dungarvanum LXIV stadiorum iter progressi & inseqventi die LXIV stadia ad Kilmathomam emensi sunt. Hinc XCVI stadia Watterfordiam, ubi & in urbe & in Regione Momonia distributa sunt singulis
hospi-

Next morning, we marched 32 furlongs on to Cork, where we pitched camp outside the city walls. During sunrise, since winter was already near, the various regiments proceeded from there to their individual winter quarters.

Together with a company of Danish royal foot,* Prince Frederick's Regiment covered 80 furlongs, thus reaching Rathcormac. At first light, we set out, marching 16 furlongs to Castle Lion, 64 furlongs to Tallum, 24 furlongs to Lismore, 16 furlongs to Cappoquin and 8 furlongs further on to Salterbridge, which lies near the river Blackwater. The Blackwater passes Cappoquin and Lismore and, by a very long excursion, it flows into the sea at Youghal.

During the following day's trek we covered 128 furlongs. Tired from the long march, we then pitched camp for one night. Then, we continued our march 64 furlongs to Dungarvan and, on the next day, we covered another 64 furlongs to Kilmacthomas. From here we continued 96 furlongs to Waterford. In this city, as well as at various other places in the Province of Munster, we were all billeted.

---

* Regia cohorte Danorum = The Royal Life Guards.

65

hospitia. Momoniæ Regionis amplissimæ sunt termini: à Meridie mare Vergivium habet, à Septentrione ad partem Connaciæ inclinat, ab Oriente Lageniam prospicit, ab Occidente Oceano Occidentali alluitur, ambitus ejus qvadringenta & qvadraginta milliaria Anglicana complectitur. Cœli temperies adeò benigna, temperata & salubris est, ut nulla alia hâc regione salubrior habeatur; tempus diurnum non intolerabili æstu ac calore Solis fervens, neqve frigore brumæ gelidum est; magna Regionis pars nudis collibus, vastis solitudinibus & montibus asperis sterilis est atqve inculta, arbores etiam habet umbriferas, præaltas sylvas rupesq; invias adspectu tristes, valles tamen, qvæ undiqve jugis montium & ambientibus ceu munitissimo vallo cinguntur nemoribus, sunt agris & pascuis lætis fertilissimæ, ut pro rei copia seminum fruges nutriat pingve vallis solum, & prata pabulô exornet, passim pecorum oviumq; greges videntur errantes, mul-

F 4   ti

The delineation of the Province of Munster is the following: to the South is the Celtic Sea, to the North it borders on a part of Connacht, to the East lies Leinster, and to the West the Atlantic Ocean. Munster's circumference is forty thousand times forty thousand English feet. The climate is benign, temperate, and healthy, and there is hardly another region as pleasant as this. The day temperature is neither intolerably hot from the rays of the sun in summer, nor is it freezing during the winter. A large part of the province is infertile and unfarmed. There are bleak hills, vast wastelands, and rough mountains. Moreover, there are trees giving shade, extensive, tall forests, and impassable cliffs which are dismal to look at. The valleys though, which are enveloped by chains of mountains and copses, are fertile with plentiful fields and pastures. They furnish the meadows with crops and grass, and there are roaming herds of sheep and cattle to be seen all around.

※ 66 ※

ti fontes crebris diftingventibus rivis agros fylvasq; alunt, amnes pifcibus uberrimi, terra qvoqve lanæ ferax, indè plerisq; funt veftes, incolæ nemorum & fylvarum difperfis habitant tuguriis. Intereà temporis nihil prædicatione dignum aut memorabile geftum eft, felecta modò manus è copiis Celfitudinis Regiæ Sereniffimi Principis Friderici ad caftellum Duncani per flumen Svirium munitum præfidiô tenendum profecta eft, cujus poft fingulos menfes per vices reditura; Dux etiam Würtenbergicus menfe Decembri cum expedita mille militum manu Limericum verfus iter fecit, qvò cœteri Duces Angliæ cum copiis fuis ad duodecim millia virorum undiq; contrahendis ad intercludendos à commeatu hoftes, & ad deditionem compellendos fe conferrent, fed poft tres hebdomades re infecta rediit.

Hìc

Fields and forests are nourished by the countless springs and streams. The rivers provide abundant supplies of fish, the earth is fertile, and the grazing sheep provide wool for clothing. People living in the valleys and forests dwell in dispersed cottages.

There is not much worth mentioning concerning the time in winter quarters, though Prince Frederick's Regiment detailed a task force for guard duties in a forward covering position at Duncan Castle. They went there by the river Suir and were relieved every month.

In December, Lieutenant General Württemberg launched a raid towards Limerick with a combined force of a thousand men. En route, he married up with some English generals, together with their troops, in order to amass twelve thousand men on all sides so as to cut off the enemy from his food supply and to concentrate in order to force the enemy to capitulation.* After three weeks, however, they returned without having accomplished their goal.

---

* The operational aim for the winter was to deprive the Jacobites of access to provisions and so the harbours and the conquered territory (which was the source of fodder for the animals and food for the soldiers), had to be controlled effectively. Moreover, effective control was required in order to provide security for civilians and troops alike. Thus, General Ginkel launched a major sweep through the southern and central parts of the island. County Kerry was mopped up in December 1690 as Major-General von Tettau moved towards Killarny with two battalions. As he advanced, 1,000 British foot joined him pushing the enemy forces north before them towards Ross. After the fall of a small redoubt, as no siege ordnance was available, the attack ground to a halt in front of a Ross Castle. The Williamite forces managed to drive the enemy further north towards and across the Shannon. However, they did not manage to outflank him and prevent the opponent from escaping. Although the aim was not fully met, the attrition of the Jacobites and the rapparees as well as the moral benefits of keeping troops employed in successful operations reaped considerable benefits. Galster, *Danish Troops*, pp. 164-65.

❊ 67 ❊

Hìc finis rerum geſtarum ſiſtitur Anni Præteriti; Faveat Numen, ut opto, Novo!

Agitur jam Annus æræ Chriſtianæ MDCXCImus, cum Sexto Nonas Martii legioni Celſitudinis Regiæ Sereniſſimi Principis Friderici, locó Calneni in oppugnatione Limerici occiſi præfectus eſt Fridericus Munchgardus anteà Vicarius Tribuni Regiæ cohortis peditum Danorum, qvi paucos poſt dies ad alia hybernacula in proximis villis copias ſuas eduxit; Tribunus ipſe Munchgardus cum córporis ſui cuſtodibus in arcem Caroghmoram LXIV ſtadia Watterfordiâ diſtantem hyemavit. Aluit nos tota hac hyeme ſpes ampla, offerentes Hibernis æqviſſimas pacis conditiones, ut univerſalem amneſtiam amplecterentur, & ad ſinceræ concordiæ petitionem ſuiqve deditionem animos applicarent, duro neceſſitatis fræ-

This marks the end of the actions of last year; May the Divine Will, as I hope, smile upon the one to come!

The 1691st year of the Christian Era was already in progress when, on 2 March in the place of Colonel Kalneyn, who had been killed during the assault on Limerick, Lieutenant Colonel Frederick Munchgaard was appointed commanding officer of Prince Frederick's Regiment, having previously been the deputy commander of the Royal Life Guards. After a few days, Munchgaard led his troops out of their various winter-quarters in the neighbouring villages.* In his rôle as deputy commander of the Royal Life Guards, Munchgaard, had spent the winter together with his guardsmen in the fortified position at Curachmore, 64 furlongs from Waterford.

Through the whole winter we had a great expectation for the immediate future. The Irish had been offered favourable terms of peace – namely that they might enjoy universal amnesty if agreeing to the request of sincere union and surrender – and the hard constraints of necessity might persuade them to accept.

---

* Munchgaard had been acting CO of the Royal Life Guards, as the nominal commander had been and remained Lt Gen Württemberg, who was too busy commanding the entire Danish force to also take personal command of the Life Guards.

❊ 68 ❊

no cohibiti; sed ad consilium neq; tam salutare, neqve ad imperium aut leges pacis admittendas flecti potuerunt, qvin potiùs benevolentissimos amicitiæ nodos omnes incidentes in extimam rabiem furoremqve sese converterint. Postremò allatô è Gallia Officialium, Machinatorum armorum, pulveris nitrati, glandium, vini, farinæ, tritici, totiusqve belli instrumentorum & apparatus, aliarumq; rerum ad bellum continuandum subsidiô spiritus sibi altiores sumpserunt; ecqvis verò crederet obstinatæ tantam mentis feritatem, tantamqve vim morbi tabis adinstar pestilentissimæ illos infimæ sortis homunciones sed seditiosos corripuisse, qvorum mens densissimis rebellionis tenebris adeò erat involuta, ut pacis & libertatis radios non suspexerint; itaqve de integro, qvicqvid militum contrahere potuerit, coëgit Jacobus & tandem robur qvadraginta millium pugnantium, qvorum eqvites septies mille numerabat, eduxit, reliqvis urbibus
Lime-

However, they could be persuaded neither to agree to this favourable solution nor to recognise the vital importance of the rightful laws. More and more stubborn was their refusal to accept the proposed conditions of alliance. After all, they found hope for themselves as France provided support sending cannon, gunpowder, ammunition, wine, flour, wheat and various instruments of war and military equipment, as well as other necessities for continuing the conflict.

The Irish demonstrated such an unbelievable fierceness of their stubborn minds and such lack of judgement that they did not realise the benefits of peace and liberty. They appeared the scum of the earth – tough and rebellious. Their behaviour drove them towards their own assured annihilation because their minds were enveloped by the darkness of rebellion.

Once again, King James* summoned whatever military forces he could conjure up, and eventually he took onwards his choice troops of forty thousand men, of which the cavalry numbered seven thousand. The cities remaining on Jacobite

---

* Claudianus may not have been aware that James had fled Ireland shortly after his defeat on the Boyne in the summer of 1690 and never returned. During 1691, the Jacobite forces were under the command of the duke of Berwick, Tyrconnel, St Ruth and, finally, Sarsfield.

✱ 69 ✱

Limerico, Athloniâ, Gallovadiâ aliisqve caſtellis præſidiô firmatis, qvapropter nec minor belli præparatio ex parte Anglorum ad maturam usq; expeditionem facta eſt; Omnibus igitur jam paratis, campisqve tantâ graminis copia veſtitis, qvanta opus eſſet exercitui, ſub exitum menſis Maji in unum undiqve evocatas ex diſtantibus hybernaculis copias Anglicanas, & ad Molingariam manum ſedecim millium virorum cum ingentibus machinis bellicis contraxit Dux Baro Ginkelius; Dux autem Würtenbergicus Nonô Calendas Junii Watterſordiâ cum legione Regia peditum, cuj præerat, Caroghmoriam iter fecit; hinc maturius additâ legione, qvam Munchgardus ducebat, primò per invia montium & inculta viarum XXIV ſtadia ad Rathgomughiam, & longius XL ſtadia Clonmellam emenſus eſt, impedimentorum verò cuſtodes XXIV ſtadia — Carrigiam & ultrà LXIV ſtadia Clonmellam ibant, ubi reliqva vis Danici peditatûs & tres eqvitum

hands – Limerick, Athlone, Galway, and a few more fortified places – were yet again reinforced and prepared for dogged defence. Because of the Jacobite endeavours to strengthen their position, the English, too, engaged in enhanced preparations for conducting a successful campaign.

Thus, by the last days of May, when everyone had again prepared for action and the plains were covered with as much grass as the army required for feeding its beasts, Lieutenant General Baron Ginkel concentrated the allied troops summoned from their widely dispersed winter-quarters, and detailed to Mullingar a task force of sixteen thousand men together with siege guns.

However, on 24 May, Lieutenant General Württemberg together with the Royal Life Guards, of which he was, officially, the commanding officer, marched from Waterford to Curachmore. Here, most opportunely, Munchgaard's regiment married up and we then traversed many miles of heavy-going mountainous terrain and irregular roads, 24 furlongs to Rathcormack, and another 40 furlongs to Clonmel. However, the detachment guarding the baggage train went 24 furlongs further to Carrick and another 64 furlongs onwards to Clonmel, where they joined the remainder of the Danish foot and three squadrons of horse. At this time, the Queen's

❊ 70 ❊

tum turmæ hisce se adjunxerunt, exceptis legionibus Reginæ & Principis Georgii, qvorum illa Clonmellam, hæc Watterfordiam præsidiis firmandi gratiâ relicta est, Triduo ibi continuo extracto LXIV stadia Cassiliam procedebant; hic sub vesperam adjunctis cœteris legionibus Belgicis & Gallicis unaqve Anglorum, proximo die XL stadia ad urbem Sanctam Crucem, hinc longius XXIV stadia Thurleam iter ingressi sunt, in ea sede ad qvintum diem substiterunt. Deinde LXIV stadia ad castellum Kilnesheahanum, iterumqve cum prima luce LXIV ad Rosgreaham contenderunt, ibi unius tantùm diei spatium stativa habebant. Proxima die LXIV stadia ad Biram castra moverunt, qvam urbem hac hyeme obsidione cinxit hostium septem millium armatorum manus, at in arce centum & qvadraginta milites præsidiarii fuerunt, qvi hostem, licet urbs & arx ignobiles & exiguo fortalitiô essent munitæ, ad discessum coëgerant. Inde
LXIV

and Prince George's Regiments had also arrived. The former was then stationed in Clonmel, the latter in Waterford, in order to strengthen the defence of these cities.

Having stayed there for three days, we marched 64 furlongs to Cashel. In the evening, some Belgian[*] and French units, as well as one English, joined the regiments which were already here, and on the next day they advanced to the town of Holycross and then 24 furlongs further to Thurles. Here we stayed for five days. Then we marched 64 furlongs to Castle Killoskehane and again, setting out at sun-rise, 64 furlongs to Roscrea. There we camped for a single day.

On the following day we moved our camp 64 furlongs to Birr, a town which had been under siege the whole winter by a band of seven thousand armed enemy soldiers. However, within the walls one hundred and forty defenders had held out and, eventually, the enemy cordon broke up, even though the city and its castle were not particularly impressive.

---

[*] Although the country did not exist at the time, the designation "Belgium/Belgians" was used of some parts of northern France and its inhabitants.

※ 71 ※

LXIV ftadia Balliboiam pervenit agmen, jam duodecim peditum legionibus totidemqve eqvitum turmis, qvinqve leviter armatorum eqvitum, five Draconariorum, turmîs conftans. Hoc in itinere ingens vis latronum extremis fub montis radicibus in palude qvadam confpecta eft, locô nempe à natura inacceſſô. Occafo Sole emiſſus ducentorum militum delectus rediit inanis. Qvatriduum eôdem locô ad qvietem militi datum eft. Intereà feptimô Idus Junii Ballimoriam copias fuas moverat Dux Ginkelius, qvam urbem unà cum fortalitio qvodam ab hofte in palude extra urbem per totam brumam erecto atqve munito, poft obfidium viginti qvatuor horarum tormentorum pulfu mugituq; occupavit, nam totum præfidium feptingentorum pecuniâ conductorum militum manu, & qvadringentorum catervâ latronum conftans ultrò fe dedit. Cecidêre Hibernorum, qvorum numerum victores inire potuerunt, centum & qvin-
qva-

A column then arrived from Ballyboy, which is 64 furlongs away from here. It comprised twelve regiments of foot, as many troops of horse, and five troops of lightly armed horsemen – the so-called dragoons.

These days, a large crowd of rapparees was observed at the foothill of a mountain. The adjacent terrain was a quagmire making the place almost inaccessible. Thus, a detachment of two-hundred men, which was detailed at sunset, returned empty-handed. At Birr the soldiers were granted four days of rest.

On 7 June, Lieutenant General Ginkel moved his troops to Ballymore. His guns having rumbled throughout a twenty-four hour siege, he then occupied the town and its fortress. The fort was situated in a bog outside the town, where the whole garrison had held out throughout the entire winter. It was garrisoned by seven hundred soldiers who had taken the King's shilling,* and a mass of four hundred rapparees, all of whom now surrendered voluntarily. As far as the victors could count, one hundred and fifty Irishmen had died.

---

* The King's Shilling was the popular expression for being recruited by an army recruiter, because an enlistment bounty was then handed over to the prospective soldier. At King Charles II's time it was 5 s., so probably it was much the same under James.

※ 72 ※

qvaginta, reliqvos omnes captivos Molingariam & Dublinium Dux mifit, conjuges verò liberosqve ducentos circiter alimentô tridui datô Athloniam devehendos tradidit, qvòd hoftibus non placuit tantam inutilium turbam buccarum excipere alendam. Anglorum fedecim funt defiderati. Deinde relictâ Balliboiâ LXXX ftadia Ballicomeram & ad caftellum usqve Ballifarcelum penetrabant, qvod facibus injectîs, né eò refugium feu afylum hoftis haberet, combufferunt. Hinc fub ortum lucis XLVIII ftadia per virgulta & invias paludes ad caftellum Niewtonum & longiùs ftadia XL Streamftoniam emenfi, omnia vafta atqve fine ullo aut raro humani cultûs veftigio intuebantur. Qvatriduo ibi exactô, primùm XVI ftadia, inde additîs in itinere fedecim millium Anglorum copiis, fub Duce Ginkelio ad occupandam Ballimoriam qvæ præmiffæ fuerant, XL ftadia ad tranfitum Ballimonæ pervenerunt. Decimo tertio Calendas Julii XL ftadia
Athlo-

The surviving captives were dispatched to Mullingar and Dublin, save for two hundred women and children who were send off to Athlone, having been given three days of nourishment. There was obviously no proclivity for feeding enemy civilians who did not serve the Williamite cause. Sixteen Englishmen were missing.

Having left Ballyboy the troops marched 80 furlongs towards Ballicumber and further still to Castle Ballifarcelum,* which they burned down. The place was torched on purpose to prevent the enemy from seeking refuge in the buildings. Then, at sunrise the army set out on a march of 48 furlongs traversing shrubbery and bogs to Castle Newtown and from there 40 additional furlongs to Streamstown. What they saw was a wasteland hardly marked by any trace of human culture.

We stayed for four days in that place, whereupon we marched 16 furlongs. Being then joined by an advance guard of 16,000 English troops under Lieutenant General Ginkel, who had just been occupying Ballymore, we pressed ahead 40 furlongs to the passage of Ballymona.†

---

* This unknown location – not surprisingly given that is was destroyed at this time – was in all probability formed of two words, the first being "Baile" (homestead).

† This unknown location could either have had the name of *Baile Mòna*, just as the modern Ballymoney in Ulster, or *Bealach Mòna* - literally a passage in the peat land, rather than a town.

73

Athloniam feftinabant; tunc temporis frontem exercitûs obtinuit Regia peditum Legio Danorum mille paffus ab urbe cum hofte præliantium; hoftis verò virtute horum maximè perterritus fugam intendit: Ideoqve trepidatione hoftium compertâ ad fuos recurrentium, tergis ftrenué inhærebant Dani, diffipatosqve in montem usq; urbi vicinum infeqvebantur ; jugô autem montis occupatô, foffas qvibus hoftiles eruptiones prohiberentur, ad viam egerere, & moles è qvibus tela & tormenta in urbem ingeri poterant, educere cœperunt: toto die ac noɛte crebrò ab utraq; parte explofa funt tormenta. Sub occafum Solis dum ad vices Regiæ legionis permutandas in acceffus defcendit legio Celfitudinis Regiæ Principis Friderici, militis cujusdam è cohorte Schilderi Centurionis finiftrum latus globo plumbeo adeò affligebatur, ut né ad evellendum qvidem globum fufficeret dextra, cumqve fieri non poffet, ut fine corporis interitu detraheretur,
eo

On 19 June we hastened 40 furlongs to Athlone. The Royal Life Guards, marching as advance party, made contact and then attacked the enemy's covering force about a thousand feet from the city. The enemy, however, thoroughly frightened by the Danes' courage, tried to escape. Therefore, realising the enemy's panic as he was running away, the Danes kept contact and routed the dispersed Jacobites towards a mountain in the vicinity of the city. When the summit of the mountain had been taken, we started to dig trenches around the city, so that enemy sallies could be checked before they might spread out onto the roads. From our gun positions, we lobbed bombs into the town. Day and night the cannon fired constantly from both sides.

At sunset, the Royal Life Guards was to be relieved in place by Prince Frederick's Regiment. As we moved in to take over, a soldier from the company of Captain von Schiller[*] was hit in his left side by a hand grenade. He could not remove the grenade with his right hand, as such action

---

[*] Captain von Schiller was the officer commanding F Company.

74

eo vulnere exſpiravit; alius etiam e cohorte prætoria Munchgardi per frontem globô trajectus animam exhalavit. Hæc urbs Athlonia ſitu naturaqve loci ferè inexpugnabilis eſt, & clauſtrum Connaciæ, ad flumen Senum poſita, cujus fluminis latitudo centum & triginta paſſus apud urbem occupat; eſt civitas biceps & vetuſtate eminens, ab interveniente flumine tenuiqve fluctuum placiditate in duas partes, in urbem ſcilicet citrà & ultrà Senum abſcinditur. Urbem citrà flumen nemine hoſtium reſiſtente decurſu præteriti anni Dughlaſſus occupavit; alteram partem huic ponte lapideo annexam, qvia munitiſſimo caſtello, vallo, ſudibus, foſſis ingentiq; qvaſi loricâ erat circundata, eam ad occupandam cum decem millibus paucisq; tormentis invalidus, voti non compos intactam reliqvit, partemqve citrà flumen captam atqve incolis vacuam vi & incendio delevit; at hoc anno utramq; urbem firmiſſimis munimentis majoriq; præſidio hoſtis firmârat;

would cause his death. Thus, he expired as a result of his wound. Another man from, one of Lieutenant Colonel Munchgaard's company, died having been hit in the face by a grenade.

The city of Athlone is almost impregnable because of its natural location. Lying on the River Shannon, it forms a protection to the province Connacht. Close to the city the river is 130 feet wide. Athlone is outstanding by its old age. It is divided in two by the intervening river and its modest waves.* Thus, there is a town on the nearer side of the river and one on the farther side.

The previous year, Lieutenant General Douglas had occupied the city on the nearer side of the river without enemy resistance. The farther part, which was connected to the nearer by a stone-bridge, was enveloped by a wall, stakes, and trenches, and thus looked like an enormous cuirass.† Unable to occupy the whole city with his ten thousand soldiers and cannon, he did not achieve his purpose. He therefore left the farther part intact, while the part on the nearer side of the river, which had been captured, and emptied of its inhabitants, he demolished by force and fire. This year, the enemy had secured both cities by very strong fortifications and an improved defence.

---

* The two parts of the city on either side of the river, commonly designated "English Town" and "Irish Town."

† On Wednesday 9 July 1690, William had divided his army sending Lieutenant-General Douglas with a relatively small detachment of three regiments of horse, two of dragoons and ten of foot towards Athlone. He himself had taken the bulk of the forces westwards from Dublin in the direction of Limerick, which then had become the projected rendezvous with Douglas.

※ 75 ※

rat; præsidium enim qvod urbem citrà flumen diffitam tenebat, ad septingentos milites numeratur, de præsidio autem ab altera fluminis parte judicium ferre nisi incertum non poffumus, qvippe hoftes longiffimé per totum fluminis litus effusi, huc illùc & ubicunqve ulla fuerat transeundi rima, præaltis foffibus & aggeribus præsidiô bené munitis se circumvallârunt. Prætereà poné urbem radicibus ipsisqve montium jugis inhærens sub tentoriis & frondeis cæspititiisq; tabernaculis Jacobi exercitus delituit, qvi ad qvadraginta octo ftadiorum circuitum transitus omnes introitusq; fluminis præsidiis obsidebat, ut nobis nuspiam transeundi effet facultas, sic non sine ingenti belli difcrimine hoftem & arcem aditu difficillimam submovere, aut flumen Senum transire neceffum nobis erat. Senus vel Sinnus fluvius inclytus eft, & omnium, qvæ in maria Regno Hibernico vicina profluunt, fluminum ampliffimus atq; profundiffimus; fons ejus & origo é
G   mon-

The defenders, who held the town on the nearer side of the river, numbered about seven hundred soldiers. As to the defence on the other side of the river, we cannot be precise since, of course, the enemy, having been spread far and wide on the bank of the river, had hid himself in deep trenches and behind palisades.

Moreover, beyond the city the Jacobite army occupied assembly areas in the foothills of the mountains, where the soldiers were accommodated in tents and wooden shelters. From these outposts they placed demolition guards at all river crossings and entrances in a radius of 48 furlongs, so that there was nowhere for us to get across. It was thus necessary for us to engage the enemy and force our entry into the fortified town as a preliminary to crossing the river Shannon.

The Shannon is famous, and of all the rivers flowing into the oceans around the Kingdom of Ireland, this is the largest

76

monte Therneo excurrens per Subjectam delabitur terram, crebris subinde flexibus per diversa curvatus varias insulas ac lacus molitur, circumjectosqve rigat campos, partim ob cumulos tenacissimi sabuli & saxorum, per qvæ fluvius procurrit, asperitatem, sexaginta qvatuor circiter stadia apud urbem Kelleloam navium impatiens est, inde violentior intra ripas suas ad Limericum decurrens, ubi duo itinera velut dispensatis fractisq; aqvis aperiens urbem intercipit, & per decursum qvadraginta octo stadiorum infra urbem renascitur, flexumqve suum in unum alveum recipit, & ingenti aqvarum murmure ac vastissimô tractu præruptas Patricii rupes interruens, Occasum versus in mare Occidentale se effundit. Jam crebris arietibus saxorum compage laxatâ munimenta defecerant, & rima muri nullo prorsus vallô aggerato adeò ampla & ingens facta erat, ut viginti seu plures militum per istam ordine transire possent. Deinde oppugnationem audere

and deepest. Its source being in the Cuilcagh Mountain,* it flows through the adjacent landscape. Bending with many turns, it creates small islands and lakes and it inundates the surrounding plains. Because of piles of sharp gravel and jagged rocks, over a distance of 64 furlongs, which the river has to flow before reaching the town Killaloe, it is not navigable. Then running fiercely between its banks to Limerick, where it envelops the city opening two waterways – one with smoothly flowing water, one with rapids – which, after a downward course of 48 furlongs, merge into one large trough beyond the city. With an audible hum the water passes a vast tract and continues across the rocks into the Western-Sea.

Because of the Williamites' intensive use of battering rams the joints of Athlone's walls began to come unstuck, and a breach materialised wide enough to allow that twenty or more soldiers could march through it line abreast. The

---

* For unknown reasons, Claudianus refers to it as "Therneus."

77

dere à Ducibus decretum eft, qvem in finem qvatuor legiones, qvas inter legio Regiæ Celf: Sereniffimi Principis Friderici unà cum trecentis Pilanis magnoqve eorum numerô, qvi ad arborum ramorumqve fafces comportandos & ad labores erant deftinati mandantur. At hoftes propofitô Anglorum compertô, trans pontem lapideum ad alteram urbem fe conferunt præmuniendam, opportunitatibus loci freti fe fortiter defendebant, vexillum album per rimam urbis erigentes, ex palis figere fepem atqve in urbe ipfa fortalitiorum abrupta multa facere cœperunt. Horâ fextâ pomeridiana initium factum eft oppugnationis. Pilani primo muris confcenfis globos igniferos hoftibus injecerunt, mox per foramina muri ovantes in civitatem penetrârunt; Hoftes verò, cum exiguam fcloporum vim fub principia pugnæ difplofiffent, celeriter per pontem lapideum alteram in urbis partem pedem retulerunt, omnibus fuis propugnaculis derelictis. Tan-

G 2   tus

commanders now decided to launch an attack for which four regiments were assigned, among them Prince Frederick's Regiment together with three hundred more infantrymen and a great number of workmen, who were tasked with collecting branches for fascines. However, when the defenders realised the designs of the English, they established a defensive position near the stone-bridge in order to protect Irish Town, lying on the Connacht side of the Shannon.*

Knowing the advantages of their defensive position the Jacobites defended themselves vigorously raising a white flag† through a gap in the city wall. They began building palisades from poles and in the city centre they manufactured additional ascents to the redoubts.

At six in the afternoon we launched the assault. The infantry, having climbed the walls, threw incendiary hand grenades at the enemy and, while cheering, soon penetrated through the breaches in the wall into English Town. However, since the enemies had dispersed the limited firepower of their guns during the beginning of the battle, they quickly realised the need to withdraw across the stone bridge into Irish Town and thus desert their defences.

---

* In order to prolong the war and to create the best possible conditions for an eventual peace settlement, the Jacobites were expected to act defensively. Underscoring this assumption, the fortifications of Limerick and Athlone were repaired and expanded, and with the castles of Ballymore, Nenagh and Ross still constituting pockets of Jacobite resistance, the Irish stood a good chance of holding the defensive line on the Shannon. Galster, *Danish Forces*, p. 171.

† This was hardly a sign of imminent surrender, but rather the French flag, which was a white cloth adorned with *fleurs-de-lys*.

78

tus fuit iste conflictus, ut ingens multitudo ex desperata istius urbis tutela in arcem concesserit, alii ferro & plumbo perierunt, alii imminente necessitate in flumen se præcipitârunt levato capite, submerso autem corpore expansis brachiis pedibusqve ranarum natantium ritu, omni arte pro salute natantes, cum vero madefactæ vestes tranare prohiberent, & ad obnitendum nihil superesset virium, morbo qvasi magno & insanabili hydropis animam efflârunt undis absorpti, cœteri summo natatûs labore impendentia littoris virgulta & arundines complexi semivivi tandem emerserunt. Qvantùm sangvinis ex hostium parte effusum est, existimari non potest, qvippe ad pontem lapideum maxima clades est commissa, plurimosqve rapidior unda subduxit, ideoq; de numero cæsorum certiores non sumus facti; unus ordinis Ductor lethaliter vulneratus cum sex militibus gregariis captus est: à parte Anglorum minùs qvàm qvinqvaginta desiderati sunt atqve

Indeed, this battle was so intense that the enemies abandoned their defensive positions in English Town, taking cover behind the ramparts on the far bank. While in the process of withdrawing some were killed by the sword or by bullets; others panicked, throwing themselves into the river. With only their heads above water and the remainder of their bodies submerged, trying desperately to save themselves, they swam with arms and feet expanded like frogs. However, since their wet clothes hampered swimming and too little strength remained, many gave up and were quickly devoured by the waves. Those who managed to cross in spite of the pains from swimming finally came out of the water merely half-alive, groping for the overhanging bushes and reeds on the shore.

We can hardly estimate how much enemy blood was spilt. Severe damage had been done to the stone bridge and a great many soldiers on or near the bridge had been carried off by a fast surge. For this reason we are not adequately informed on the casualty figures. One sergeant-major was fatally injured when he was captured by six privates.

On the part of the English less than fifty were missing and

※ 79 ※

qve fauciati, fauciorum verò in numero fuerunt Legatus Imperatorius Maccajus, Prætor Stufardus, è legione Celf: Regiæ Principis Friderici qvatuor milites gregarii faucii, Centurio Baro Uflenius tempore antemeridiano in tumulo urbi vicino per latus colli ictu fclopi faucius eft, nullo tamen vitæ difcrimine. Multus in eadem pugna Dux Würtenbergicus fuit, ubi laudatiffimi Herois eximia virtus & in fubeundis periculis conftantia emicuit, talem enim fe præftitit, ut non erubefceret inferiora militis gregarii opera præftare, atqve adeò nulli fecundum exiftere, in laboribus exantlandis impigrum fe gerere, ftrenui & militis & Ducis officia exfeqvens; nam incredibili mentis ardore accenfus, medius inter contertiffima hoftium tela unà cum legione Celf: Regiæ Principis Friderici murum proruptum perfregit, ignaris cœteris Ducibus, & ad victoriam & hoftem profligandum plurimùm tam opere qvàm exemplô confulit. Magna Du-

very few were wounded. Amongst the wounded officers were Major General Mackay and Judge Advocate Stuffard. From Prince Frederick's Regiment four soldiers were wounded, and in the mid-morning's combat Captain, Baron Ueffeln[*] was injured in the side of his neck. He was hit by the blast from a gun, although with no fatal outcome.

In this same mêlée Lieutenant General Württemberg showed extraordinary valour. This most distinguished hero, who would yield to no danger, proved himself such a bold character that he made the private soldiers' efforts pale beside him. He excelled in soldierly merit as well as in fulfilling the duties of a lieutenant general, and he carried on to the end of battle in spite of his physical exertion. While being kindled by incredible zeal, in the midst of the enemy's hail of well-aimed bullets, and together with Prince Frederick's Regiment, he broke through the wall unnoticed by the other allied commanders. Thus, he contributed to the victory and the defeat of the enemy as much by his effort as by his example.

---

[*] Captain Johan Mauritz Baron von Ueffeln was the officer commanding D Company.

❀ 80 ❀

Duces Anglorum fubibat admiratio, qvòd tantam periculi aleam & in tam afpero urbis aggrediendæ negotio discrimen ipfe inclytiffimus Heros inire vellet; Ob hoc qvidem multorum reprehenfiones perpeffus, qvi audaciùs fe periculis objicere illum dicerent, qvàm deceret Imperatorem, cujus confiliô potiùs qvàm manu res geri deberet: At non eo inficias, Imperatoris confilium, militum manum in bello expofci, fed incidunt tempora, cum vel maximè Imperator ipfe in hoftes irruere, primum fe illis opponere debeat, cum fcilicet laborat exercitus, ut ad invictum robur & virtutem acerrimè fic milites excitentur. Itaqve captâ, non absqve virtute magna & jactura perexigua, citrà flumen urbe ab incolis defertâ, ad ripam fluvii & in urbem varias moles ramorum fafcibus, terrâ & faxis adverfus caftellum trans flumen diffitum exaggerabant, ut validiora hoftium munimenta opprimerent. Qvocircà undecimô Calendarum Julii in arcem

There was, of course, general admiration of Württemberg's achievement among the English generals. Everyone was impressed that the eminent commander would personally risk so great hazards under so adverse conditions while assaulting a city. However, because of his obviously reckless action, Württemberg had to face much criticism. It was mentioned that he exposed himself unnecessarily to more danger than was reasonable for a person in high command. Many complained that it would have made better sense to follow the common plan approved in the war counsel than going ahead alone.

However, no one should tarnish his reputation. The war council's decisions put the soldiers in harm's way, but times do occur when a commander must personally lead an assault on the enemy's positions. Under such circumstances the commander must place himself at the front of his array. While the army fights as one body, it is no more than reasonable that the general should take upon himself to instil courage and fighting spirit in the soldiers by his own example.

Athlone's English Town was captured with limited attrition on the Williamite side. English Town, i.e. the city on the nearer side of the river, was deserted by its inhabitants and the English soon advanced to the bank of the river. There they stockpiled large quantities of field fortification equipment and fascines, pouring earth and rocks into the river opposite the castle so as to facilitate an attack on the enemy's far side positions.

81

cem & mœnia è tormentis majoribus bellicis, injectisqve malleolis sæviebant. Eodem tempore ad vires, qvæ ibi sub adventum Anglorum consederant, copias suas qvoqve admovebant Dux de St. Ruth & Sarsfeldius, adeò ut totum hostium robur qvadraginta millia eqvitum peditumqve attigisse constans fuerit opinio, transitùs ergò fluminis & expugnatio arcis eo majori cum discrimine & jactura erat conjuncta. Post exacto qvinto die tormentorum & maximè arietum pulsu adeò perfectum est opus, ut non arx modò acerbissimo concideret incendio conflagrata, atqve in lapidum cumulum proruta, sed omnes ædes etiam deletæ & funditùs essent eversæ, munimenta hostium sic diruta, ut triginta ab utroqve pontis latere rectâ fronte per foramina valli transire possent. Hostes interdum dejecta mœnia raptim saxorum arborumqve strue & cumulis ex humo aggerata refecerant, qvæ ad impedienda curam omnem & operam Angli contule-

G 4

Therefore, on 21 June heavy siege artillery shelled the battlements with grenades and incendiary bombs.

Simultaneously with the English preliminary actions, the Marquess de St. Ruth[*] and Sarsfield joined their defending troops such that it was fair to say that the Williamites now faced the bulk of the opposing force. The Jacobite opponent was about forty thousand horse and foot, for which reason fording the river Shannon and assaulting the fortified city of Athlone might now be estimated as a high-risk operation.

When the fifth day was over, the preparatory work was done to such an extent that by pounding from the gun line and by applying rams the walls began to crumble. Not only were the battlements shattered and turned into a heap of stone, but all the churches, too, were obliterated and levelled to the ground. The enemy's defences were flattened to such an extent that from across the bridge thirty men could pass through the breach line abreast.

Nonetheless, the enemy managed to repair the damage done to their defensive walls. With stones and trees, which had been torn down during the bombardment, they hastily piled up material from the ground. Thus, the defenders succeeded in re-establishing their defences enough to hamper severely the English attempts at assault.

---

[*] St Ruth was the *nom de guerre* of *Lieutenant-Général* Charles Chalemont Marquess de Saint Ruhe, 1650-91.

82

tulerunt, at intempesta nocte non solum pontem lapideum, qvatenus ab hoste non abscissus erat, occupabant, sed etiam lignis, plancis trabibusqve illi reparando impositis ibi inhærebant. Deinde omnia sine magno discrimine flumen trajiciendi inierunt consilia, nam invium atq; inaccessum in id temporis flumen se prodidit; Sed qvoniam occulta saxa aqvis subesse ostendebant variis locis unde repercussæ, & in oppugnatione urbis citrà fluvium dissitæ qvidam hostium à læva pontis parte per flumen fugâ salutem qværentes conspiciebantur; idem igitur fluminis vadum tentare decretum est, cujus rei explorandæ gratiâ Olaus Normannus è cohorte Regia Danica Pilanorum Decurio, Metator Gizeus è turmis Develii Magistri eqvitum, & eqves qvidam è turmis Legati Imperatorii la Foresti, qvanta esset altitudo fluminis explorare ac Ducibus nunciare jussi. Hi loricâ subter tunica galeaqve armati, utraq; manu hastam amplexi ad ruinam valli
sub

During the night, however, not only did the Williamites take possession of the stone bridge, which the enemy had not been able to demolish completely, but they also laid hands on fire-wood, slabs and timber for its restoration. Then, having the worst hazards laid behind them, they began planning for fording the river. At the time, the river appeared both impassable and difficult for troops to approach.

However, the recoiling waves revealed that in several places stones lay hidden under the surface. Moreover, during the assault on English Town on the near side of the river, a group of enemy soldiers had been observed from the left side of the bridge, while they were seeking safety by trying to cross the river. It was decided, therefore, to try and find the same shallow of the river where the Jacobites had managed to cross. To find the place and explore how deep the river was and to inform the commanders, Olav Normann, a section commander* of the Royal Danish Life Guards, Surveyor Gizeus of 2nd-in-command Lieutenant Dewitz's company of horse, and a certain cavalryman from the unit of the deputy commander, de la Forest, were selected.† Carrying helmets and wearing body armour in the form of leather cuirasses underneath their tunics, and having a pike in each hand these men ventured into the river.

---

* Claudianus apparently knows little about military organisation. "Olaus Normannus" is described as a *"decurio."* However, although at the time these designations existed, companies were not subdivided into platoons and sections.

† Dewitz, by Claudianus mentioned as Magister [deputy cavalry commander] Develius, might have been either Lieutenant Friederich von Dewitz, 2i/C of C Troop or Lieutenant Franz Joachim von Dewitz, 2i/C of D Troop, both 2nd Cavalry Regiment. Major General de la Forest was the cavalry commander and one of two deputy commanders of the entire Danish expeditionary force (the other one being Major General Tettau).

83

sub tegmine & tutelâ Anglorum per flumen penetrârunt, haftis fuis & à dextra & à læva fluminis vadum tentantes, qvanqvàm grandinis in modum confertis globorum ictibus peterentur, obfervatâ loci qvalitate, tantùm non omninò incolumes redierunt omnes, periculum opinione minùs adeffe nunciantes. Normannus per furam fclopô faucius decem Guineas, ut vocant, à Duce Ginkelio accepit. Gizeus fine vulnere redux duodecim Guinearum munere donatus, & promiffo vexilliferi eqveftris honore & officio auctus eft. Eqves verò per malam vulneratus & tribus in cataphracta ictibus fcloporum fignatus, decem Guinearum donô fublevatus eft. Altitudinem fluminis ad fpatium fedecim militum fimul transeuntium fumma æqvare genua vix poffe judicârunt exploratores. Hinc ab utroqve lapidei latere pontis navalem fuper flumen, qvô miles effet trajiciendus, pontem componere decretum eft, ut prima luce expugnationem ar-

G 5   cis

While being covered by the English they managed to get to the derelict wall across the river probing with their pikes the depth both from the right and left banks of the river. Although they were harassed by frequent grenade impacts, they managed to explore the conditions on the spot and most of them returned safely.* Upon their return, they informed about their observations, estimating that in their opinion the risks crossing would be negligible.

Normann, injured by a bullet through the calf of his leg, received ten guineas from General Ginkel. Gizeus, who returned without a wound, was given a gift of twelve guineas and promised the substantial rank of cornet.† Additionally, a horseman, injured through his jaw and hit by three gun blows to his armour, was given ten guineas as recompense. The scouts estimated that the water would barely reach above the knees of the soldiers if the river were entered by columns of sixteen men abreast. It was decided that on both sides of the stone bridge, boat bridges be built to facilitate the soldiers' crossing so that they might assault the defensive positions at first light.

---

* Claudianus' words on this achievement are opaque, though it is fair to assume that what he meant was that those who were not too seriously injured did in fact return.

† According to the establishment found in the Danish State Archives Gizeus (Latinised name) was not known as an officer. However, he was promised promotion to the rank of a cornet, but we do not know if he actually lived long enough to get it. His Danish name might have been Geese or Gise.

❀ 84 ❀

cis inirent. Interim tormentis atqve pyrobolis noctu dieqve multò atrociùs qvàm aut in Limericum urbem, aut in arcem Carolinam, aut in urbem paucos ante dies captam fævitum eft. Sole occidente advenit transfuga, at mediam fub noctem ponti lapideo inhærentes incubantesqve excubitores Anglorum ab hoftibus repellebantur, cæfisqve ex legione Melonieri, Centurione Pilanorum, duobus Optionibus, qvadraginta Pilanis, pontem nocte proximè priori flumini impofitum hoftes impetuofè excurrentes abfciderunt; Vicarius Tribuni Willerfius, Optio Tappermontanus & fex milites gregarii è legione Regia fuper hoc opere & conflictu funt vulnerati, at oppugnatione in feqventem diem decretâ, duo Legati Imperatorii, vulgò Generales Majores, duo Prætores, qvinqve legionum Præfecti, totidemqve Vicarii, Ordinis Ductores, Centuriones, Optiones, Vexilliferi, viri minoris auctoritatis fecundum proportionem, octingenti Pilani,

In the meantime, preparatory fire with grenades and carcasses was laid over Irish Town. This preparation was far heavier than those against either Limerick or Charles' Fort, or against Athlone's English Town, which had been taken a few days earlier.

At sun-set an enemy deserter arrived.* In the middle of the night, the English posts who were watching and securing the stone bridge were driven away by the enemy, and from Melonier's regiment a captain, two lieutenants, and forty soldiers were killed. At night the enemy made a sally and violently cut off the bridge. Captain Lieutenant Willersius, Lieutenant Tappermontanus,† and six common soldiers from the Royal Life Guards were wounded during this skirmish. However, when, on the following day, an attack had been agreed upon, two lieutenant generals or simple major generals, two brigadiers, five commanding officers, and as many deputy commanders, sergeants major, company commanders, lieutenants, ensigns, men of lesser authority,

---

* It is unclear why Claudianus mentions the deserter in this context. It is likely that this deserter has given some useful intelligence, but Claudianus does not explain.

† There were no such officers with the Royal Life Guards. The name Tappermontanus might easily have been a Latinised version of someone by the name of...berg or bjerg (common Danish surname suffixes). The name Willersius is not known from the Danish establishment and might be the name of a gentleman volunteer or an NCO having been promoted to substantial officer rank. The name may or may not be a Latinisation of Wille, Willers or Villiers.

※ 85 ※

lani, duo millia fclopetariorum, atqve adeò ingens operariorum & ramos fafcesq; vectantium numerus emittitur. Poſtero die convenerunt deſtinati flumen Senum transnaturi, fed inexplicabili difficultatum nodo impliciti hic tanqvàm ad Sirenios qvosdam fcopulos hærere tempus jubebat, nam nec pontones, qvibus in trajiciendo flumine locô pontium uterentur, nec aliæ machinæ maturé fatis erant in procinctu. Itaqve die ad vefperam inclinante, & temporis oportunitate deſtituti qvieverunt; accedebat & cœli & ventorum injuria, Zephyrô reflante, & fulphureos pulverum fumos in oculos oppugnatorum revomituro. Poſtremò jam hùc & illùc advolans fubindè numerofus hoſtium exercitus, jam ipfam fluminis ripam obfidens terribilem rerum faciem noſtratibus obvertit, ut per tot naturæ rerumqve obſtacula extremam velut belli aleam temerariô qvafi qvodam aufu viderentur fubituri, qva de caufa diſtractô in aliud commodius tempus
certa-

eight hundred soldiers, two thousand gun-men,* and just as great a number of workmen for gathering branches for fascines were dispatched.

On the following day they were marshalled for the crossing of the river Shannon. However, they were stuck here for too long as if among the rocks of the Sirens, entangled, as they were, in a complex of difficulties. For neither the pontoons, which were necessary for constructing the boat bridges, nor the other logistics required for the river-crossing had arrived. With the twilight approaching they had to abandon the enterprise, and so instead they found time to rest.

More troubles materialised from the sky as a western breeze blew sulphurous gunpowder fumes into the eyes of those poised for assault.

Moreover, the numerous Jacobite troops, now moving around, now in positions on the river bank, presented a frightening sight to the Williamite soldiers. However, in order to give the impression that now the moment had come for the final push, now an audacious attempt to cross was in the offing, the Williamites tried to deceive the enemy by a false call to arms, hoping thereby to cause confusion among the defenders.

---

* It is difficult to fathom what Claudianus actually means. There were not that many gunners in the Williamite army, but the Latin word is indeed *sclopetariorum*, which means one who handles grenades and bombs. We might therefore interpret this as covering all ordnance personnel – artillery as well as artillery and engineering logistics.

86

certamine, fimulatæ tantum tranfitionis & falfæ ad arma vocationis certiffimæqve trepidationis opinionem hoftibus præbebant; namqve Anglos voluntariâ fugâ retrocedentes, ob altitudinem fluminis ac magnitudinem difcriminis hanc oppugnationis aleam experiri minime aufos augurabantur Hiberni, lætiq; omine eô ad epulas & convivia fefe mutuò invitabant. Milites verò animofi ægré jam contineri poterant, qvin citiori curfu ad arma cum hofte conferenda proruiffent, qvisq; tædiô comperendinationis longioris Hibernos fugare & vallum confcendere ad immortalem virtutis fuæ famam & nobilitatem confeqvendam anhelabat, & qvod vulgò maximé Danis militibus in ore fuit, ægré fe conferre, qvòd tam longum temporis fpatium Duces darent hoftibus, qvorum numerus in fingulos dies crefcebat, qvos protinus dejectis mœnibus aggreffuri fuiffent, virtus enim elata tarda non admittit molimina, & gaudet victoria duris, clamabant; tanta
cupi-

The Irish troops, though, imagined that as the English had endeavoured, unsuccessfully, to cross and then turned back, they would hardly persevere. Rather, it was reckoned, they would acknowledge how deep the river was and the immense hazard of a crossing operation. Elated therefore, the Irish regaled themselves with a lavish banquet.

Although the Williamite soldiers were fearless, they were persistently prone to sickness, because remaining for an extended period in the same wet and cold place with too little food was detrimental to their health. They had not pressed ahead on a speedier course to engage in battle, and they grew impatient from the continuous delay. All of them wished to scale the walls and rout the Irish defenders in order to achieve everlasting praise of their high merit.

That was the reason why the Danish soldiers worried that they might eventually surrender to sickness, because the commanders allowed the enemies too much time, while the number of sick soldiers grew by the day. Thus, they carried on with breaching defensive walls hoping that by their endeavours and persistence victory might ensue.

※ 87 ※

cupido animis incessit militum discriminis tentandi, ut Duces admirati sint etiam mortem tanta animi magnitudine appetere milites & oppetere. Sub lucis ortu seqventis rursus convenerunt Duces, animô ut à læva per flumen & à dextra per pontem lapideum, primô in impetu simul restaurandum, penetrarent; hoc autem tantô actum est silentiô, ut non prius qvàm appetente meridie ad flumen admoverentur ad imperata facienda prompti, ferentes secum trabes, plancas, fasces ramorum, aliasqve machinas ad pervium ac reparabilem pontem faciendum, nec pertrepidus erat hostis cognitô Anglorum adventu, qvippè cum dies in vesperam declinaret, nec minor qvàm pridie tempestatis violentia adversa, & nulli pontones flumini essent impositi, neq; pons pervius, nihil mali exspectavit, ad transeundum tamen omnia erant parata. Sub vesperam horâ sextâ datum est signum irruptionis campanulâ qvâdam è templo urbis citrà flumen

Obviously the Williamites had a great desire of reaching the culmination point of this contest. The soldiers' zeal was kindled by their aspiration, and the commanders were rightly proud of their troops' dogged efforts in the face of death.

At sunrise the following morning, the generals met again to discuss the way ahead. They believed that it would be possible to penetrate the defences on the left by fording the river there and on the right by crossing the stone bridge, though this would have to be repaired first. Preparations for this were carried out in profound silence, and not until noon had they moved close enough to the river to execute the operation. They carried with them planks, fascines and other engineering equipment for mending the bridge.

The enemy was not too worried by the movements of the English, since they expected no immediate danger. The day was waning, the weather was as atrocious as the day before, no pontoons had been brought forward and the bridge, therefore, was not passable. However, everything was now ready for the Williamites' crossing operation.

At six in the afternoon,* a small boy signalled from the church tower in English Town that the advance should commence.

---

* Moving forward at 6 p.m. the attack column managed to pacify the opposition to an extent permitting the workmen to place on the damaged bridge planks sufficient to allow a second column to rush across. Irish Town fell into Williamite hands within the next hour. Apparently, the attack had gone in exactly at the weakest point, which was guarded by a regiment of raw recruits under O'Gara. This regiment soon bolted and its place was taken by MacMahon's regiment, who reacted in the same ineffectual manner. Galster, *Danish Troops*, p. 182.

❀ 88 ❀

men confitæ, mox à lævis compofito ordine per flumen movebantur Dani & externi milites fingulis è legionibus qvinqvaginta felecti; Ordo hujus agminis talis erat, unus Optio, unus Vexillifer, duo viri minoris auctoritatis cum qvindecim Pilanis & qvibusdam volonibus, duo Centuriones, duo Optiones, duo Signiferi & qvinqvaginta Pilani; Unus Tribunus, unus Vicarius Tribuni, unus Ordinis Ductor, fex Centuriones totidemqve Optiones & Vexilliferi cum ducentis Pilanorum, qvibus duo machinarum artifices adjuncti funt. Poft Legatus militiæ Imperatorius Tettovius, Prætor Melonierus, Tribunus Munchgardus, unus Ordinis Ductor, fex Centuriones, duodecim Optiones, fex Signiferi cum trecentis Danis. Centurio Bilitzius cum centum & triginta duobus operariis, unus Tribunus cum fexcentis militibus, duodecim Centuriones, viginti qvatuor Optiones, duodecim Signiferi, frons lævi cornu hæc erat. Dextrum verò cornu
Anglo-

Immediately on this signal, the left wing stood to for the river crossing. It was spearheaded by an advance party of Danish and foreign soldiers, individually selected from fifty different regiments. The organisation of the advance party was one lieutenant, one ensign, two non-commissioned officers together with fifteen soldiers, and some volunteers.[*] Then followed the main force of the left wing front line: two captains, two lieutenants, two ensigns and fifty soldiers; one general, one brigadier, one sergeant major, six captains, and just as many lieutenants and ensigns together with two hundred soldiers, to whom two artillery experts were attached. Subsequently went Tettau, the major general commanding the infantry, Brigadier Melonier, Lieutenant Colonel Munchgaard, one sergeant major, six captains, twelve lieutenants, and six ensigns together with three hundred Danish soldiers. Captain Bilitzius[†] together with one hundred and thirty-two workmen, one major general together with six hundred soldiers, twelve captains, twenty-four lieutenants, twelve ensigns.

---

[*] At the time, "volunteers" were persons hoping for a commission but not yet on the army's pay role.

[†] Probably Captain Blitz, OC of E Company, the Zealand Regiment.

※ 89 ※

Anglorum Legato Imperatorio Maccajô & Prætori Principi Darmſtadico ad tuendum datum eſt, ejusdem agminis ordo erat talis, qvalis lævi cornu; ſeparatim in ſubſidiis ad arcem obtinendam ſtetit Vicarius Tribuni Rubinus ex legione Darmſtadici cum qvadringentis militibus. Inſtructo igitur hoc modô agmine per flumen Senum ruebant Duces atqve Principes, qvi ſolitâ vincendi felicitate confiſi animos militum gloriæ, laudis ac virtutis ſtimulis concitaverant, ſed ingens globorum telorumqve hoſtilium nimbus eos undiqve operuit, haud magnâ tamen jacturâ, nam à lævo cornu flumen tranſeuntium duo tantùm milites ictu hoſtium necabantur, paucîs ſaucîs. Nihil interim per omne id tempus neglectum fuit crudelitatis è tormentis & mortariis globis ignivomîs ingeſtis. Rupturæ verò valli appropinqvantes cum ingenti victoriæ ſpe tripudiantium inſtar pilulas igneas levi manuum agitatione ità immiſerunt Pilani, ut vehemen-

Major General Mackay commanded the English right wing with Brigadier the Prince of Darmstadt as his deputy. The battle order of this part of the array was such that, within it, its left wing was composed of Captain Lieutenant Ruben of Darmstadt's regiment, together with four hundred soldiers who were poised to assault the walls. Then, as the units had been instructed, the commanders ordered the charge across the river Shannon. They were confident of their luck and, stimulated by the splendour and high calibre of their soldiers, they were convinced that they would triumph.

However, the Williamites were met with a shower of hostile grenades and bullets. Nonetheless, the casualties were few, as from the left wing of those crossing the river only two soldiers were killed and even fewer were wounded. The whole panoply of gun and mortar ammunition was brought to bear, incendiary bombs included. Approaching the damaged fortification, hoping for victory, the infantrymen lobbed hand grenades over the wall. The violent blasts of the grenades terrified the Irish.

❊ 90 ❊

mentiffimâ globorum vi & fragore perterriti Hiberni, vix primum fuftinuerint impetum, & initiô qvidem refiftentes, fed mox turbati pedem ex alio in alium aggerem alacriter retulerint, breviffimoqve poft temporis intervallô omnibus fuis munimentis & propugnaculis expulfi fugam capefferint; qvibus rurfûs præfidiô firmatîs, crebros tormentorum fcloporumqve ictus hoftibus fugitivis intorferunt urbis caftelliqve tanta celeritate potiti victores. Qvivis in præliando & flumen penetrando militum fuerit fervor, à nullo magis qvàm ab ipfo hoc belli difcrimen experto & oculato tefte exprimi poteft. Hoftes etiam in munitiffimo aggere caftrenfi alteri arcis parti obverfo fe abdiderunt, ubi cruentiùs dimicatum eft, donec exindè pulfi fugatiqve auxilium ab inermibus petere pedibus cogerentur. Agmen aliud hoftile tribus infigne candidîs vexillîs in molem arci vicinam fe contulit, eâdem excedere nolens, fed ob freqven-

Claudianus' Account

Although having withstood the initial assault, the Irish soon panicked and withdrew from the walls. Having thus been driven out of their primary defence line, shortly after, they abandoned their positions entirely.

As soon as the defences had been taken, the Williamite artillery fire was shifted onto the fleeing enemy, on whom the victors inflicted numerous casualties. The capture of Irish Town and its defences had happened with great swiftness. The fury that possessed the fighting and fording soldiers can only be realised by one who has personally witnessed the action.

Some enemies entrenched themselves in a redoubt, where they fought stubbornly until eventually they were driven out and routed. Another enemy force marked with three white colours rallied to a gun in the vicinity of the redoubt, unwilling to abandon the field.

91

qventes è mœnibus arcis excuſſos globorum ictus non tutum nocturnâ ſe fugâ ſubduxit. Alii ex foſſis & aggeribus utrinqve fluminis ripam cuſtodientibus æq; furtivâ exeuntes celeritate, ſubſidiô aucti in eosdem novo ſe condiderunt ardore, ſed à vi tormentorum intuti per paludem in proximas ſe cavernas receperunt. Qvi aggeri à dextris erecto præſidebant, ex eodem nocturnis adjuti tenebris clandeſtinô ſe egreſſu ſubduxerunt. Qvid qvæſo admiratione, qvidqve prædicatione virtutis dignius exiſtere potuit? qvàm eôdem momento, qvô hoſtes ſuis inſtructâ acie ſubveniendi cauſâ è jugis montium deſcenderunt, victoriâ & arce potiri; Nam, cùm Anglos è mœnibus arcis & urbis valido tormentorum intonantes fragore, magnamqve ſuorum partem in loca remotiora recurrentium ſpectâſſent, ſteterunt, ut impulſæ ſegetes aqvilonibus, formidine attoniti, ſtupentesqve nec progredi nec conſidere auſi. Hoc modo Senum fluvium

H tran-

However, the position being untenable, the defenders withdrew, although flight in the darkness was a risky business. Some were sneaking out for pilfering, others, eager to get away while covered by darkness, retreated hastily from the trenches, ramparts and parapets on the river bank. They tried to hide, but cover from the gunfire was nowhere to be found, so they retired through the bogs to some nearby caves.

At this very moment a turning point was reached. The enemies now descended from the mountain ridges in order to support their fleeing comrades. However, having conquered the town and its defences, the English guns were now hauled into positions on the walls of the fort and, opening up from there, forced many Jacobites to places even more remote. The Williamite troops stood their ground, and the enemy soldiers fell like crops in a field struck by winds. They were stupefied by terror, daring neither to advance nor to stay. What admiration and what worthier merit can exist?

❋ 92 ❋

transitu difficillimum & impervium, ut ferebatur, felici auspicio transierunt Angli, qvi primò urbem, deindè flumen & postremò arcem illam munitissimam in conspectu hostis validissimi in suam redegerunt potestatem. A parte Anglorum centum circiter sunt tam cæsi qvàm vulnerati; mortuorum in numero erant Vicarius Tribuni Rubinus è legione Principis Darmstadici, & Optio Wülfernus è legione Cimbrica; Sauciorum verò è legione Regia Danica Weddelius Centurio Pilanorum pilis ferreis igneisq; pugnantium, Centurio Loggesus, Optio Langeus è cohortibus Cimbricis, Optio Kaasius ex legione Serenissimi Principis Friderici. Jacturæ hostium certum non possumus numerum inire, qvorum tamen strages magna creditur: nam tormenta & pyroboli multum incommodi ac detrimenti hostibus intulerunt, magnamqve partem etiam in arce ex vulneribus acceptis mortem obiisse rumor divulgavit; alii capti, qvos inter Legatus Impera-

By the success of this operation the English had managed to cross the river Shannon, which was both difficult and dangerous to pass. They took the fords, the whole of Athlone, and finally Irish Town's strong defences into their possession before the eyes of the toughest of enemies.

On the English side about a hundred men were killed or wounded. Among the dead were Captain Lieutenant Ruben of Prince Darmstadt's Regiment and Lieutenant Wulfen[*] from the Jutland Regiment. Among the wounded were Captain Wedell of the Royal Life Guards' infantry, Captain des Loges and Second Lieutenant Lange of the Jutland Company, Lieutenant Kaas from Prince Frederick's Regiment.[†]

We cannot gauge the precise number of enemy casualties, but we believe that they must have been severe, for grenades and mortar bombs had certainly caused much harm. Moreover, a rumour spread among the people that also a great many of the wounded who had been taken into the fort had subsequently died.

Amongst the captured Jacobites was Major General Maghfeld of Scottish nationality,[‡] together with several other

---

[*] Of F Company, the Jutland Regt.

[†] Claudianus is rather imprecise at this juncture: Captain Wedell was officer commanding F Company of the Jutland Regiment, Captain des Loges was officer commanding E Company, Lange was of E Company of the Jutland Regiment and Kaas was actually ensign Koss of B Company, Prince Frederick's Regiment.

[‡] This general cannot be found in *King James' Irish Army List*. There is a site near Vienna called Marchfeld, which might have given its name to an international warrior, but this cannot be substantiated within this context.

※ 93 ※

peratorius Maghfeldius natione Scotus cum pluribus aliis auctoritatis magnæ viris: ex noftratibus captus eft nemo: Sex tormenta cum duobus mortariis in arce reperiebantur. Numerus autem tormentorum ad Athlonem conftabat, Sex mortariis ignivomîs, qvadraginta duobus tormentîs, novem qvæ viginti qvatuor, decem qvæ octodecim, decem qvæ duodecim, tredecim qvæ fex libras ejaculabantur. Hæc tam inopinata & fubitanea Athloniæ oppugnatio ac captivitas ipfis hoftibus abfurda erat atqve ignota, inprimis Duci copiarum Gallicarum de St. Ruth, qvi ipfo tempore omnes Duces Hibernorum & Præfectos fummi Ordinis, in arcem qvandam triginta duo ftadia à caftris fuis diftantem ad epulas invitatos magnificô excepit conviviô, nullô, qvi imperium loco abfentium teneret, in caftris relictô. Ille hac re cognitâ unà cum convivis vario animi motu & cordis ftupore fluctuari cœpit, modò fuum, modò Ducum confilium, fed

H 2   nimi-

men of great authority.

None of our men were captured by the enemy. Six guns together with two mortars were found in the fort. Some ordnance, however, was left in Athlone: six fire-spitting mortars, 42 guns, nine twenty-four-pounders, ten eighteen-pounders, ten twelve-pounders, and 13 six-pounders.

The unforeseen suddenness of the capture of Athlone was rather a surprise to the enemies and especially to their French captain general, St Ruth. Ignorant of what was afoot, he had summoned all the Irish generals and lesser commanders to regale them with a magnificent feast in a castle 32 furlong away. In the meantime, no one of any decisive authority had been left in the camps at Athlone.

As soon as St Ruth realised that not all was well, he and his guests got apprehensive, though by this time their minds were baffled and a certain bodily numbness had set in. Soon they all started to reconsider their dispositions, though it was now too late.

❊ 94 ❊

nimium feró expendere, fic aërem fama per captivos & fugitivos ftrenué percurrit. De hac tam gloriofa victoria maximæ Deo tota per caftra reddebantur gratiarum actiones. Sub crepufculum ejusdem vefperæ ad triumphandum extrà caftra eductus atqve in aciem ordinatiffimam diftributus eft totus Anglorum exercitus, feftoqve tormentorum ac fcloporum fonô, concinnô tubicinum & tympaniftarum clangoré iterum atq; tértium ritu militari repetito, alios præter ignes feftivos, qvorum fplendores totam illuftrârunt noctem, milites qvoqve ingenti clamore ac lætitiâ, Vivat Rex Wilhelmus, ter vociferandô triumphum agebant. Nocte intempeftâ caftra fua ipfis montium jugis, qvibus confederant, impofitâ fugâ hoftes fubduxerunt, centum & viginta ftadia, qvantùm maximé poterant feftinantes, funt emenfi, magis fortaffe nocturni timoris, aut iftius fubiti terroris, qvô animi totius

exer-

Soon gossip was spread by captives and fugitives. The Williamites had won a glorious victory, and great gratitude to God was shown in all of their camps.

At sunset of this night, in order to celebrate the victory, the English army was on parade in well-ordered battle formation. They dressed the ranks to the festive sounds of guns, trumpets and drums, which were repeated for a second and a third time as by military tradition. Moreover, the whole night the splendour of fireworks lit the sky.

The soldiers raised their voices for three loud cheers of joy, crying out: "Long Live King William."

In a stormy night, the enemy struck camp, leaving the mountain ridges where they had stayed. Retreating, they covered post haste 120 furlongs, probably more due to the fear of night and the terror that paralysed the army's morale

❋ 95 ❋

exercitus erant impliciti, qvàm inſtantis periculi cauſâ. Intrà octiduum reparata ac reſarcita ſunt arcis mœnia; relictis deindé in ea præſidiis. Sextô Iduum Julii in Regionem, qvæ appellatur Connacia, movebatur exercitus, pars per pontem lapideum, pars per pontem navalem flumini impoſitum tranſibat: trajecto flumine Seno XL ſtadia Kilcaſſiliam profecti ſunt; Dux ipſe Anglicanus cum cœteris Præfectis ſummæ authoritatis mille paſſus ultrà Ballinaſloënſem tranſitum luſtrandi ergò loci ſeceſſit. Oriente luce longiùs XL ſtadia Ballinaſloenſem progreſſi apud Roſcomonam & amnem Suchum caſtra fixerunt. Duces intereà in montem Knochdonum in comitatu Gallovadiæ ſitum ſe receperunt, cujus é vertice milites hoſtium ſtationarios, qvingentos paſſus à caſtris Hibernorum in monte Corballienſi excubias agentes videbant, qvi ſub adventu Anglorum in Liſcappal-Iſkerum bis mille paſſus à Ballinaſloënſi diſſitum retrò fugerunt.

H 3

than because of any specific danger.

Within eight days, Athlone's walls were repaired and improved and a garrison of English troops was left behind to secure the town.

On 10 July, the whole army crossed the Shannon into the region of Connacht, a part went across by the stone bridge, another by a pontoon crossing. Having crossed the river, they went 40 furlongs to Kilcashel.

The English supreme commander,* together with the key generals, advanced a thousand feet beyond Ballinasloe in order to inspect the location. Next morning, the main force, having now covered 40 furlongs towards Ballinasloe, pitched camp close to Roscommon on the river Suck. In the meantime, the commanders mounted the hill Knochdon† in the county of Galway, from the top of which they saw a detachment of enemy soldiers. This detachment appeared to be posted on the hill Garbally,‡ 500 feet from the Irish camp. However, as soon as they saw the English approaching they fled to Liscappul-Eskerkeel, some two thousand feet from Ballinasloe.

---

* At this juncture Lieutenant General Godard de Ginkel.

† Although Claudianus mentions several mountains in this passage, these are merely hills. Knochdon is possibly the modern Knockroe.

‡ It seems logical that the Williamites would observe the Jacobites from Garbally in modern Ballinasloe. However this hill is called "Corballiensis" by Claudianus, who later mentions a "Garballaugh" as well. Either Claudianus accidently utilised both the latinised and non-latinised spelling of the same place name, or Corballiensis is another place entirely. There is in fact another Garbally to the northwest of the battlefield, though it seems too far away to be likely.

※ 96 ※

runt. Qvo comperto in verticem montis cujusdam Corballienſis Duces aſcendebant, ad ſitum & copias Hibernorum, qvantæ eſſent, ſpeculandas, qvæ ad Aghrimum caſtellum triginta circiter duo ſtadia à Ballinaſloënſi diſtans erant effuſæ, longitudine ſedecim ſtadiorum à templo Kilcommodonæ in dextra, & ad locum lævæ partis, qvem incolæ Gurtnoporiam vocant. Ad lævam erat rivus peranguſtus, ab utroqve latere clivi, colles paludesqve minores, cui proxima vaſta & ampliſſima palus colore rubra, ad finem paludis erat extructum munitiſſimum caſtellum nomine Aghrimum itineri imminens, qvod ad caſtra hoſtium ferebat: planitiem hanc limoſam in latitudinem mille paſſus diffuſam nec arbores nec virgulta operiebant, ſed omnis liberum oculorum proſpectum ac faciem regionis præbuit, ferè tamen inopportuna explicandis copiis, eqviti ineqvitabilis, & pediti prorſus invia inacceſſaqve erat ob alium prope caſtellum oberran-

Having observed this, the commanders climbed the hill at Garbally in order to reconnoitre the position and gauge the number of Irish troops. These appeared to be positioned on the ground close to Castle Aughrim, thirty-two furlongs from Ballinasloe and at a distance of 16 furlongs from the Church at Kilcommadan on the right,* and to a place on the left side which the inhabitants call Gortnahorna. To the left was a very narrow river;† on both sides there were hills, high grounds, and minor bogs, close to which was an ample and wide swamp, red in colour. At the end of the swamp was a very strong castle by the name of Aughrim, overlooking the way which led to the enemy camps.

Neither trees nor bushes covered this muddy plain that extended a thousand feet across. Nonetheless, at first sight the area appeared completely unsuited for the troops to operate in. It seemed impassable to horse as well as to infantry. It was certainly difficult to negotiate since another small rivulet ran near the castle.‡

---

* Seen from the Williamites' position this would actually be on the left.

† Tristaun River.

‡ Melehan River.

❊ 97 ❊

errantem rivulum, qvi è fcatebris terræ exfiliens, & obliqvo curfu fundum permanans uliginofum, cuncta & circumqvaq; vicina loca in paludem redigit ad dextrum usqve hoftium cornu, ubi alius erat tranfitus, Urafchree dictus, utrinqve afperis præaltus ripis. Hoftes autem tentoria ramosqve arborum abfcondentes flexuofa editiffimi juga montis incoluerunt, cujus latus & radices haud procul à ripa paludis, foffis, molibus, tormentis ac operibus obfeptas præfidiisq; bene præmunitas ipfi tenebant, adeò ut afperum iftius loci ingenium & iniqvitas hoftem aggrediendi nuspiam ullum transgreffus aditum reliqviffe, fed potius Duces à prælio tunc temporis abfterrere poffe videretur; nullum alium fibi locum aptiorem ad ineundum cum hoftibus prælium cenfebant Hiberni; Qvartô itaqve Idus Julii horâ fexta matutina, impedimentis cum præfidio relictis, & implorato Dei auxilio, cum tertium indè, ficut præceptum erat, fignum tubâ miles

Springing from the earth and cutting through the moist ground by a twisted course, this rivulet makes the adjacent terrain a marsh. On the enemy's right wing, there is another defile called Urraghry. It is very steep on both sides with rough banks.

The enemy, however, had positioned himself on the ridge of the hill, and he had covered his tents with branches from trees.[*] The sides and foot of the hill lay not too far from the edge of the bog, peppered with trenches, mounds, hedges, and guns. This layout made the area impassable, providing the enemy with excellent defensive options. However, it might seem that the taxing structure of the place and the opposition offered left the enemy no room for manœuvre; rather should it have discouraged his commanders from battle at that time.[†] Though, the Irish thought that no other place was more suitable for them to engage in combat with the enemy.

On 12 July at six o'clock in the morning, when the baggage had been left behind at a well-guarded location, and when the assistance of God had been asked for, the soldiers received for the third time a trumpet signal for advance, just

---

[*] This is pure speculation on the part of Claudianus. In fact the Jacobite camp could not be seen from the east as it lay concealed behind (west of) Kilcommadan Hill.

[†] The private soldier Claudianus is remiss as to tactical and operational knowledge. For the Jacobites this was indeed a perfect defensive position. It could not be outflanked and the bog and rivers made excellent natural obstacles at which to stop and annihilate the opposition. Had the Jacobite commander, St Ruth, not been struck by a cannonball at the crucial moment the outcome might very well have been a different one.

98

les acceperat, itineri fimul paratus & prælio, ftrenuè nebulofis involutus tenebris procedebat, pedites per pontem, eqvites & dimachæ Angli & Galli per vadum fuprà pontem, eqvites autem Germani & Dani duo vada infra templum trajiciebant, additô mandatô, ut, cùm tranfiiffent, in aciem ordinatiffimam feipfos inftruerent, id qvod apud agros Garballienfes, Rathboienfes & Dunlovienfes factum eft. Hoc modô compofitis ac perarmatis militibus, qvoniam adhuc cœlum fpiffa obfcurabat nebula, qvæ lucem profpectumqve oculis ambulantium ademit, eodem in loco ad meridiem usqve qvies data eft. Jam verò difcuffâ fub meridianum tempus fenfim caligine lux liqvidior hoftem aperiebat, qvare cum figno propius accedendi datô, Dux progredi milites juffit, ipfe aciem antecedebat ad hoftilem ordinem profpiciendum, fed compertum habens qvosdam ante caftra in collibus excubantes procubitores, eos ad repellendos
expe-

as had been agreed. And just as they stood ready to move and fight, a heavy mist descended covering the Williamite army's advance.*

The foot on the bridge,† the English and French horse, and dragoons moved through the shallow above the bridge. The German and Danish horse crossed two streams below Templepark with the added order that, when they had come across, they were to draw themselves up into a well-ordered battle-array. This subsequently happened in the lands of Garbally, Rath Bawn and Dunlo.‡ Even though the soldiers had been organised and fully equipped for combat, since a thick dark cloud** still darkened the sky, obscuring their vision, rest was given until noon where they stood.

At midday, therefore, as soon as the mist had gradually lifted and the clear daylight revealed the enemy, the signal was given to resume the advance. While the commander ordered the soldiers to move on, he himself led the array in order to gain a first-hand impression of the enemy positions. Observing that a number of men were posted in the high grounds in front of the camp, he sent out a detachment to

---

* During the morning and large parts of that day a heavy fog prevailed.

† Tristaun Bridge.

‡ All found in modern Ballinasloe, and in Claudianus known as Garballaugh, Rathboienses, and Dunloe.

** It was heavy fog.

※ 99 ※

expeditam emifit manum; illi cognitô
emiſſorum adventu de colle in collem
ad qvatuor ſtadiorum intervallum à
caſtris ſuis citô gradu aufugerunt.
Hinc Duci è loco tumuloſo data eſt oc-
caſio, modo ante memorato tota hoſtium caſtra ſpeculandi, qvæ tempore
antemeridianô denſiſſimas propter ne-
bularum tenebras circa montem effu-
ſas aciei oculorum ablata fuerant & ab-
ſcondita. Hoſtes adventantem pro-
piùs Anglorum aciem animadverten-
tes, copias ſuas arreptîs haud ſegniter
armîs ante caſtra ſua eduxerunt, ingenti tormentorum fragore ex monte Kilcommodonæ tonantes, ſed extra teli
jactum utraq; acies ſtetit. intereà tranſitum à dextra ſitum ſatisqve militibus
munitum occupare opus eſſe Dux animo volvens, ad id negotium exſeqvendum Magiſtrum eqvitum è turmis Da-
nicis cum ſedecim eqvis præmiſit, qvibus celerrimè ducenti dimachæ expe-
diti è turmis Alberti Cunninghami ſub-
venerunt, qvi foveas & aggeres qvos-

H 5 dam

drive them in. However, having detected the approach of the detachment, they escaped quickly, moving from hill to hill to a distance of four furlongs from their camp. Now, the commander got the opportunity to explore from one of the hills most of the enemy positions, which before noon had been obscured by the dark clouds covering the hills.

Observing the English battle-array closing in, the enemy speedily positioned his troops. At the same time he opened up from his gun line at Kilcommadan Hill, but both lines of the Williamites were well beyond their reach.

In the meantime, the captain general found it necessary to occupy a pass, which was situated to the right and effectively held by enemy soldiers. Thus, he sent the general of horse of the Danish contingent together with sixteen squadrons to execute the affair.* These were quite quickly reinforced by two-hundred dragoons detailed from the regiment of Albert Cunningham,† who now seized the decisive points near the

---

* Claudianus, who was with Prince Frederick's Regiment on the left wing of the allied force, possibly means the right of that part of the Williamite array. This can be corroborated by other sources and tallies with the fact that the Enniskillen Regiment was indeed moved from right to left to support de la Forest.

† The Enniskillen Regiment.

100

dam propè anguſtias aditûs occupârunt; hi virtute enitente hoſtem mollitiâ animi velitantem ad ſuffugium qvoddam removerunt, qvò hoſtis periculum ſuorum comperiens expeditam miſit manum ſuis ſuppetias laturam. Dux hôc cognitô, Prætorem Eppingerum confeſtim ſuis cum leviter armatis terga Hibernorum inter & caſtra clàm circuire juſſit, callidum hoc ſtratagema felici reſpondiſſet eventui, nî maturé nimis hoſti innotuiſſet, qvi recentes ſubindè cohortes numeroqve plures & validiores ad profligendos levioris armaturæ eqvites Anglorum emiſit. His ſe oppoſuit delecta manus è turmis Comitis Portlandici eqveſtribus, qvi concitatis ad curſum eqvis, in hoſtem proruentes pugnam intrà unius horæ trans rivum dextrum Hibernorum cornu præterfluentem ingenti cum turbamento regredi globos velitantium coegerunt, ſine magna Anglorum jactura, licét hoſtes per omne id tempus ſumma vi reſiſtentes crebros tormentorum

narrowest part of the pass. This force quickly managed to dislodge the enemy, who fought a delaying action in order to reach a refuge. In response to this set-back the enemy sent forth a detachment in support of those retreating. Realising this, the commander immediately ordered Brigadier Eppinger, together with his light dragoons,[*] secretly to outflank the Irish position. This shrewd manœuvre might have been successful had it not been detected by the enemy, who reacted by detailing a number of fresh companies in order to check the lightly armed English dragoons. These, however, were engaged by a task force of the Earl of Portland's dragoon regiment.[†] Charging at the gallop,[‡] in less than one hour the English dragoons brushed off the enemy. Although the enemy resisted with great vigour this time, the English moved ahead against the enemy across the river flowing by the right wing of the Irish. The battle caused much commotion, a lot of guns being discharged, but it inflicted little damage upon the English.

---

[*] Eppinger's (Dutch) Dragoon Regiment.

[†] Willem Bentick, Earl of Portland's (Dutch) dragoons.

[‡] Claudianus is probably either exaggerating or unaware of cavalry tactics. At the time, cavalry normally charged at fast trot, while charging at the gallop was not to be introduced until the Swedish King Charles XII reformed the battlefield tactics. Galster, *Danish Troops*, p. 73.

❈ 101 ❈

torum ictus extorferint. Dux confpectâ confuforum tam incompofitâ hoftium fugâ impetum in dextrum eorum cornu facere decernens, fimulat fe revocaturum ex finiftro copias in dextrum cornu, iterumqve dextrum Anglorum cornu in lævum hoftis converfurum, ut hoc ftratagemate univerfa hoftilis acies implicata peffundaretur. Acies autem hoc modô ftetit, finiftram alam peregrinis maximè & auxiliariis conftantem militibus, Dux Würtenbergicus vir ardentis fpiritus & bellicis operibus affvetus tuebatur; huic proximi ftabant Legati Imperatorii Tettovius, la Foreftus, Naffovius, Holtzapelius, fui qvisqve agminis Duces. Dextrum cornu tenebant Legati Imperatorii Maccajus, Talmashus, Ravignius generofis fpiritibus abundantes; cornuaqve Ducem ipfum Ginkelium virum rerum claritate bellicarum excellentem in medium acceperant, qvi aciem ubiq; eqvo circumiens, pro acumine ingenii fagacia afpiravit confilia,

Seeing the disordered flight of the confused enemy, the general decided to make a holding attack on their right wing and, at the same time, move troops from his own left wing onto the right. Subsequently, the English right wing might turn the Irish left, thus enveloping, and eventually annihilating, the enemy array completely.

The Williamite left wing, which was mainly composed of foreign and auxiliary troops, was commanded by the Duke of Württemberg, a man with a fervent spirit and extensive experience with warfare. Next to him were his deputies the Major Generals Tettau, de la Forest, Nassau and Holtzappel, each of whom was a column commander. Brimful of fighting spirit, deputy commanders, Major Generals Mackay, Talmach, and Ruvigny held the right wing.[*]

Lieutenant General Ginkel had established his command post in the centre. He was a magnificent man of high merits in war. As he toured his combat formations on horse-back, he ascertained that his plans were correctly perceived and stored

---

[*] This is imprecise: The three were commanders on the right wing of Ginkel's overall battle formation (not the right of Württemberg's left wing): Mackay was a commander of the 1st line, Talamach and Ruvigny of the 2nd.

※ 102 ※

lia, cornua laborantia, ubi neceſſitas flagitabat, ſubſidiis firmavit, omnesqve curas explorandi, qvid ubiq; hoſtis ageret, intendit. Dimidiatâ horâ qvintâ, cum jam dies in veſperam inclinaret, ſe cornu ſiniſtrum movebat, triſti qvidem progreſſûs ſpectaculô, cum pedites difficillimam paludem permeandô, rati ſe terram firmam ingreſſuros, in cœnum autem & lutum gramine atqve ceſpite obductum inciderint, cumq; alterum pedem è limo educerent corpus allevaturi, alterô vel utroqve pede jam ad genua usqve, jam lumborum tenus demergebantur, ſummô tamen corporis niſu & conatu per paludem penetrantes, in aggeres hoſtium peditibus præmunitos perſultando irruerunt, licèt obſtaculum hoc loci perdifficile hoſti opportunum, & certamen ab Hibernis uſitato more acriùs per turmas inprimis eqvitum Comitis Gallovadici & legionem Regiam pedeſtrem committeretur, ardentiſſimo tamen pectore hoſtem invaſerunt externi Anglorum

on the officers' minds. Where necessary, he strengthened the wings of the battle formation, and he turned his attention to every bit of intelligence on the enemy's dispositions.

At half-past four in the afternoon, as the day was waning, the left wing carried on. Indeed, it was heavy going as the infantry traversed a vast bog, hoping that they could negotiate it safely. They were severely hampered by the mud and morass, which was covered by grass and turf.[*] They constantly had to use their bodily force to extricate themselves from the quagmire. As soon as they had drawn out one foot, the other foot, or both feet, sank even deeper; sometimes to the knees – occasionally even to their loins. By exertion of the greatest efforts, though, they managed through the bog and attacked the enemy soldiers' positions.

This was a very difficult terrain, which certainly favoured the enemy's defensive struggle. The Irish – and in particular the troops of the Earl of Gallway's Horse[†] and the Royal Regiment[‡] – commenced the engagement even more energetically than they used to. Nonetheless, the allied soldiers of the English coalition assaulted the enemy, who did

---

[*] This bog was in front of the Williamite centre – not the left wing.

[†] The Jacobite order-of-battle at Aughrim does not include such a regiment. The unit that Claudianus mentions is Lord Galmoy's Cavalry Regiment, which ranks 4th in the Jacobite hierarchy after the two troops of Lifeguards and Tyrconnel's own regiment. Its commanding officer was Colonel Piers (also spelt Pierce) Butler, 3rd Viscount Galmoy.

[‡] King James' Foot Guards.

✵ 103 ✵

rum milites, qvi sine ullo retrocessu inter se mutuò certabant, animô pares, manu prompti, in id unicè intenti, ut aut pulcherrimô victoriæ brabeô aut morte decora laudis & gloriæ conseqverentur immortalitatem: variam inde & difficilem certaminis aleam tentantes hostem retrocedere cogebant. Mox arte & consiliô Ducis vis eqvitatûs maxima hostilis à sinistro ad dextrum cornu avertebatur, scitum qvidem stratagema, multum tamen indignationis legionibus Earsii, Herberti & Foulkii attulit. Dextrum cornu Anglorum insigni peditum, dimacharum eqvitumq; constans robore, aditum angustum ad castellum Aghrimum eximiâ qvoqve virtute transeundo oppugnavit; cœterùm angustia loci, in qvo hæc pugna hærebat, junctis viribus transire non patiebatur, nam iter vix binos capiebat armatos, qva de causa eqvitum bini simul locum istum uliginosum penetrabant, strenuo ac celeri eqvorum saltu, fulmina hostium fre-
qven-

not yield. With fine morale they fought bravely and efficiently, undoubtedly hoping to achieve enduring fame by either a splendid victory or a glorious death.

The Williamites, however, pressed on, accepting the risk of a frontal assault through which they forced the enemy to retreat. Subsequently, thanks to our commander's proficiency and fortitude, across the front from the left wing to the right, the greatest part of the enemy's cavalry was repulsed. However, this encounter inflicted considerable losses upon the regiments of Erle,* Herbert, and Foulkes.

The English right wing, comprising infantry, dragoons, and cavalry of eminent combat power, attacked the narrow passage leading to Castle Aughrim. They moved ahead with amazing courage. However, the constriction of the passage, through which the attackers had to advance, did not allow movements by larger units. The passage was hardly wide enough for two armed soldiers at a time. Therefore, two troops of horse had to move along the edge of the bog. Laboriously, they worked their way forward as fast as the horses could shift their hooves, accompanied by the recurrent

---

* In this engagement Colonel Thomas Erle was taken prisoner, but managed to escape.

✤ 104 ✤

qventia fine infigni tamen detrimento excipientes, donec continentem paludi vicinam occupâſſent, ubi ordinem explicantes lineam formârunt, & progreſſi in convallem arɟidæ foſſæ ſub mœnibus caſtelli ſe illatebrârunt. Ingens in medio Anglorum hæſit periculum, cum media acies & copiarum reliqviæ ſtrenuâ qvidem at impavidâ audaciâ atqᵢ temeritate flexuoſos foſſarum ambitus hoſtilium aggrederentur, ſed propter inopiam eqvitum ſubito hoſtium inſultu circumventi, ad labra paludis pedem referre cogerentur; aſpera qvidem res & facile militum animos debilitatura, niſi ſolitum vincendi robur exarſiſſet: mox igitur excitatis adventantium ad auxilium eqvitum ſtridore, qvi hoſtem diſtrictis gladiis adoriebantur, & pari cornu ſiniſtri eqvitatûs ſtrenuitate, redit in præcordia virtus & concitatiùs creſcens animoſitas, ut animos ex pavore recipientes ſtrenuè circumactîs in prælium redirent pedibus, ferociori qvàm anteâ pugnandi

per-

flashes of the enemy fire, but with limited harm done to them. They advanced until they were able to occupy a position at the far edge of the bog where they formed up into line abreast. They carried on towards a sheltered dry moat, allowing them to hide themselves below the castle walls.

The English centre was a dangerous place. Meandering their way fearlessly and boldly across the ground, the Williamite centre troops reached the forward line enemy troops,* they realised that, in the absence of horse and suddenly surrounded by enemies, they had to order the retreat to the rearward edge of the bog.

The situation seemed hopeless and might easily have paralysed the soldiers' minds had not their many accomplished victories imbued them with an unwavering morale. Soon – with the welcome sound of horses coming to their rescue, attacking the enemy with swords drawn – virtue returned to them and the fighting spirit grew more violent.† Presently, they recovered from their fear and returned to the battle. When the infantry had turned around they counterattacked, fighting more ferocious than at any previous moment.

---

* "FLET" in modern military parlance.

† Claudianus account becomes confusing as there is no clear distinction between centre and right wing. In the centre – the bog being impassable to cavalry – the infantry fought alone. The cavalry easing the pressure on the centre was on the left of the right wing i.e. on the northern edge of the bog.

105

pertinaciâ, & vario ac difficili succeſſu, donec hoſtes fugâ in juga montis ſe receperint palmæ paulò antè ſperatæ deſertores. Erant aſſiduæ hæ velitationes ceu præludia maximi inſtantis prælii, cujus de exitu ſpes adhuc fluctuabat. Jam verò ipſo in jugo montis permixti eqvites cum eqvitatu, pedites cum peditatu; manus conſerentes mactandô, conſectando, virosqve Marti victimando; jam haſtarum gladiorumqve impulſu & ſclopetorum ictu per ordines omnes erat ſtrages, paſſim horrenda fulminum ſpecies continuô cum tormentorum ſcloporumqve tonitru ac fragore adeò gerebatur, ut præ armorum & ignium fulgore ipſa montis juga ardere & flammas Ætnæ inſtar evomere viderentur, convallibus ipſis fumô undiqvaqve repletîs. Præliantibus jam pavor & miſericordia, ſed nec ira, nec rabies deerat, ingens terror omnisqve crudelitatis habitus ſpectantes ubiqve movebat, & qvem qvisqve locum præliando ceperat,

Success was not assured and the outcome unpredictable, until such a time when the enemy abandoned the field and withdrew to the mountain ridges, letting go of the victory they had expected a little earlier.

As an overture to the final and decisive moment of this battle, ubiquitous clashes continued. Predictions of a successful conclusion had until now been uncertain. On the ridge of the mountain close combat was already in progress; horsemen against horsemen, and foot soldiers against foot soldiers, tried their hands in maiming, slaying and sacrificing men to Mars.

Soon, by the shock of pikes and swords and by the blows of guns, a showdown occurred among all the lines. This was indeed a ghastly spectacle of lights flashing in every direction, continuously accompanied by the thunder and crashing of the guns and howitzers. Because of the brightness of muzzle flashes the mountain ridges looked as if they were burning. Guns emitted flames like an eruption of Mount Aetna,[*] and everywhere the defended valleys were full of smoke.

Soon anxiety turned to fury, replacing compassion. Great terror and the materialisation of every kind of cruelty met spectators wherever they turned their eyes. The spot, on which the individual soldier fought in this battle, he defended

---

[*] i.e. Mount Etna.

106

rat, fortiter defendebat vivus, amissâ autem animâ corpore non inhonestè nec miserè tegebat; sanè illis mors non fuit misera, qvibus nec aditus ad mortem erat miser. Spe instantis victoriæ avidissima qvisqve devorabat, & initiô pugnæ æqvali fortunæ afflatu pariqve periculô, sed honestate & causâ, ideoqve successu & eventu impari utebatur: Nec tamen in armis neqve in vegeta militantium juventute illius spes erat potiundæ, sed in Deo Ter Optimo Maximo, cujus dextra principium & finem victoriæ obtinet, datq; cuicunqve placuerit. Exacto tempore non benè multo sub ipsum diei crepusculum è collibus montis retrocedentes fugam capessere cœperunt eqvestres hostium ordines, derelicto ad internecionem peditatu; pedites autem ab eqvitatu deserti, hastam, ut ajunt, abjecerunt, & signa deserentes in pedes se conjecerunt, tum horribile in campis patentissimis spectaculum! fugientium terga insectantibus Anglis, aqvilarum more aves in
præ-

bravely as long as he was alive. However, having made the final sacrifice, his body silently covered the ground neither dishonourably nor miserably.

To those, who gave their lives voluntarily, death was not miserable. Everyone was keen on achieving victory forthwith, and in the beginning of battle all soldiers had the same aspiration and faced similar danger. However, all did not have equal honour or right, thus having disparate success and outcome.

However, neither arms nor youthful vigour of the soldier would ascertain mastery of the situation. This belongs but to God Almighty, in whose righteous hands lies the decision on the beginning and end of victory, and He alone bestows the laurels onto whomever He pleases.

When the day was waning, the Jacobites could accomplish little more. Retiring from their assembly areas in the hills, their cavalry abandoned the battlefield, while the infantry was left to their fate. However, deserted by the cavalry, the foot, too, gave up and threw themselves at the mercy of their conquerors, folding their colours. For a soldier to witness, this was indeed a sad prospect.

All the while, like eagles homing on their prey the English routed the fleeing Irish.

107

prædam venantium; Fugiebant Hiberni per omnes campos, errantes viatores, qvi in planitie ingenti, qvando magnô cum nubium fragore sub vesperam repentina vis nimbi & grandinis impetuosius erumpit, nescii qvid acturi sint, aut qvò se vertant, cum undiqve tempestatis violentia major, qvàm ut evitetur, occurrat, limina igitur & vestibula ædium, aut tecta montium atqve arborum qværunt, qvanta pedum velocitate possint; sic vidimus istos ferociter modò instantes subito deindè pavore perterritos jam jam per occultos tramites magis qvàm apertas vias, qvò cujusqve animus & fata ferebant, longe diversam intendere fugam, atqve effugia & subterfugia disqvirere; alii in abruptos montes, sylvas, vastas paludes & solitudines profugerunt, reliqviis susi exercitus abjectis armis discedentibus, & locum stationis nullum intrà LVI stadiorum distantiam eligentibus. Mulieres, liberi, curruumqve rectores furentibus similes itinera omnia

I luctu

The Jacobites took off across the fields like drifting rovers, who get astray when, all of a sudden, a great crash of thunder and an unexpected pour of rain breaks forth above their heads. Faced from everywhere by ferocious adversity, as quickly as they could possibly run, they sought shelter and safe haven in private houses or on the tops of mountains and trees.

So we saw them, who had so far held their ground courageously, as they were suddenly struck with fear, taking flight in all possible directions and looking for escape routes along obscure tracks rather than on the open roads. While some sought the steep mountains, forests, vast marshes and wilderness, other soldiers of the dispersed army discarded their weapons and ran off. However, within a distance of 56 furlongs from the battlefield they found little place to hide. Women, children and wagoners filled every road, and the

108

luctu ac mœrore complêrunt. Miserabilior post prælium facies erat, cum permulti & virorum & eqvorum vulneribus confixi, neq; fugam neq; qvietem paterentur, connitentes modò exsurgere subitò gravati corporis mole conciderent; aliiqve membris mutilati & saucii præ dolore ferrum in remedium poscerent, victor igitur aut gladiô aut sclopô tantum non animam agentis desiderium implevit: alii spiritum cruore ac minîs mistum evomebant, arma sua sangvine oblita arctissimo occupantes amplexu, tanqvam ad futura qvædam prælia parati, &, ut paucis dicam, è corporibus omnium sangvis, qvasi morsu Hæmorrhoidis prolectus, in terram effluxit, camposq; ita inundavit, ut vix nisi lubricò gressu pedem figere posses. Tale tamqve deforme cæsorum spectaculum in circo per aliqvot dies intacto & non mutato manebat; O horrendum obtutum! incredibile dictu, nisi spectaculo ipse affuisses, qvanto animi fervore hostem perseqve-

sorrow and lamentation of people growing mad with desperation was overwhelmingly present.

After the mêlée, the scene of battle was even grimmer. The field was strewn with injured men and horses rendered helpless by their wounds. They could neither escape nor rest; they merely struggled to get on their feet. Burdened under the weight of their bodies, with limbs maimed or wounded, they tumbled and many demanded the sword to finish their pain. Either by the sword or by musket, the victor thus fulfilled the wish of those who could hardly breathe. Others spat out both blood and menaces while trying to seize their blood smeared weapons, as if preparing themselves for future battles.

To put it candidly, the blood from the bodies of the dead and wounded sieved out onto the ground, thus inundating the plains, so that you could hardly move without slipping.

This revolting spectacle remained unchanged for days. O, what an awful sight – impossible to imagine for anyone who has not witnessed it himself.

Nonetheless, with unabated fervour the victors routed the

109

qverentur victores, caligine licet & tenebris noctis vias obscurantibus omnes; Ducum enim militumqve virtus in tenebris hostem ad perseqvendum carbunculi adinstar omnibus prælucebat & facem præferebat. Verùm enimverò ipsum noctis obscurum, qvod victorem exercitum jam detinebat, & hostem è conspectu subducebat, victis munimento & auxilio erat, nec ullo impedimento, utpote locorum scientissimis, contrà Anglis actio in tenebris difficilior fuit, ut itinerum ignaris; spe itaq; hostem ampliùs asseqvendi decollante, & signo tubâ datô, revocati in castra demum cum triumpho redeuntes phaleras eqvis, vestes & arma viris detraxerunt; hîs aucti, si non ditati, spoliis, sub dio eodem in loco, qvô hostium copias fuderant, corpora sua nocturno defatigata itinere dulci relaxârunt qviete, qvia nondum ad manum erant tentoria; ideoqve nonnullis cubile inter cadavera humus erat cruentata; alii occupati fuerunt in cadaveribus loco

I 2   sedi-

the enemy, although fog and darkness obscured the roads. The virtue of the officers and soldiers shone like a torch, allowing the Williamites to pursue their enemies into the shadows. However, as the evening progressed and the darkness grew more intense, the victors' movements were hampered and contact between the parties ceased. This helped the Jacobites protecting and aiding the victims and, since they had detailed knowledge of the terrain, darkness was of little hindrance.

Conversely, the English were unaccustomed with the ground and their activities were therefore considerably hampered by the darkness. This deprived them of any chance of pursuing the enemy further, and soon the trumpeters signalled retreat. The Williamite troops were called back to the castle, and they returned, triumphantly robbing on their way the dead enemies and horses of their decorations, clothes and weapons.

Joyful with the spoils, that day the troops rested on the battlefield. Since their tents had not yet arrived, the soldiers had had little sleep during the night while hanging about on the blood-soaked ground among the corpses.* While some soldiers were occupied with collecting the corpses, others sat

---

* Though dramatic, Claudianus' account of the final moments of the Battle of Aughrim is hardly correct. Most sources agree that the Jacobites were pursued for only about 5km, the rout being called off at nightfall, when rain was pouring and man and beast were exhausted from the day's struggle. Galster, *Danish Troops*, p. 193.

110

sedilium circum ignes in circulum disponendis, qvorum fulgore montes & campi resplenduêre. Hoc in prælio pars magna fuit rerum & potissima Dux exercitûs, qvi durante pugnâ nunqvam qvievit imperare, & ad fortitudinem animos militantium excitare, id qvod & cœteri Præfectorum, qvi vel minimâ ducendi ad prælium auctoritate pollebant, eadem animorum constantiâ executioni mandârunt, ut eximium inter eorum splendorem collaudanda sit etiam nobilitata militum virtus gregariorum, qvos licèt non excellentia generis aut familiæ amplitudo nobilitâsset, nihilò tamen minùs ut nobilitas datur præclara ob facinora vel mutis & ignobilibus locis, ubi qvis benè natus, altus & educatus est, nedum optimè meritus, ità etiam hos ad nutum Imperatoris intentos & promptos aut ad moriendum aut vincendum, mortis ipse contemptus, discrimen prælii animisqve ipsorum insita virtus, & ingenerata qvasvis ad actiones Heroibus dignas

natu-

around the camp fires, by whose light the mountains and plains shone cheerfully.

The general's untiring and ubiquitous presence with his troops played a great and decisive rôle in this battle. Throughout the battle, at no time did he cease to give directions on how his subordinate officers were to act. They, who were definitely no less experienced as to the conduct of war, executed the general's orders promptly and with sound judgment. The commanders propped up the morale of the fighting men, who should be highly celebrated for their bravery and their high calibre. The common soldiers, too, should be greatly admired even though they might not possess the dignity of noble descent and family.

Just as nobleness is shown by deeds or originating from the places where those of good birth are raised and carefully educated, so too, are those who are determined and ready to die or conquer at the will of their commander worthy of everlasting praise. Soldiers who show contempt of death, who take upon them the risk of battle, who are of high calibre and have a nature engendered in heroic actions, will be victorious and are worthy of our tribute.

※ 111 ※

natura, & deniqve victoria hæc tam egregiis redempta virtutibus in perpetuum nobilitârunt: Sed Divinæ hæc omnia benignitati accepta ferre debemus, nec unqvam committere, ut, dum caufas miramur fecundas, gloriæ primi motoris & autoris qvicqvam detrahamus. Ex omni Anglorum multitudine non ultrà qvadringentos fexaginta duos funt interfecti, qvos inter Legatus Imperatorius Holtzapelius, Tribunus Herbertus & Munchgardus Danus, qvi per gulam globo tormenti ictus fortiffime pugnando, beatiffime occubuit; Ordinum Ductores Devenishus, Pettitus, Coltus, Cornvallus, Foxius cum qvibusdam Centurionibus aliisqve fubalternis Officialibus, præterq; eos nongenti qvinqvaginta faucii, qvorum maxima pars adjutore Deô citiffime ex vulneribus curatione adhibita intentiore convaluerunt, habiles militiæ redditi & ad omnia parati. Hibernorum feptem millia in acie cæfa, & qvadringenti qvinqvaginta victoribus dediti

depo-

However, we must attribute all success to our Lord God, and though we may be greatly favoured by good fortune, we should not neglect that everything glorious comes from Him.

Of the entire Williamite army, no more than 460 officers were killed, among whom Major General Holtzappel, Colonels Herbert and Munchgaard the Dane. Having fought courageously, Munchgaard was hit in the throat by a bullet and was laid peacefully to rest. While Sergeants Major Devenish, Pettit, Colt, Cornwallis, and Fox, as well as captains and other subalterns were also among the dead, 950 soldiers were wounded, though with God's help the majority of these recovered quite quickly. The wounded were granted all possible medical care and they soon became fit enough to return to service with their units.

Of the Irish 7,000 were killed in battle, and 450 were

depositis armîs captivitatem subierunt; at Legatus Imperatorius Dorringtonus captivus plures eô præliô qvàm superiori interemptos esse, numerumq; cæsorum ad octo millia retulit. Inter captivos clarissimis Nominibus ac sangvine Nobilissimô præstantes viros seqventes numerantur:

Comites.
Dulechius.
Slanius.
Buffinus.
Kilmarius, nomine Nicolaus Brunovius.

Legati Imperatorii.
Dorringtonus.
Johannes Hammiltonus.

Prætor.
Tuiteus.

Tribuni.
Gualtherus Bourkus.

Gordenus O-Nealus.
Butlerus Kilcassilius.
O-Connellus.

Vicarii Tribuni.
Edmundus Maddenus.
Johannes Chappelius.
Johannes Butlerus.
Magennisius.
Rossiterus.
Maguirius.

Ordinum Ductores.
Patricius Lawsessus.
Kellius.

Gra-

taken prisoner, having surrendered themselves to the victors as soon as they had laid down their arms.

In captivity, Major General Dorrington told that more had been killed in this battle than in any previous encounter and that the number of dead was about 8,000.[*]

Among the prisoners of war of particularly distinct names and noble blood were the following:

Earls:
Duleek; John Bourke, Viscount Bophin; Slane; Nicholas Browne, 2nd Viscount Kenmare.

Major generals:
Dorrington, John Hamilton

Brigadier:
Tuite

Colonels (commanding officers):
Walter Bourke, Gordon O'Neill, Richard Butler of Kilcash, O'Connel

Lieutenant Colonels (deputy COs):
Edmund Madden, John Chappel, John Butler, Magennis, Rossiter, Maguire

Sergeants Major:
Patrick Lawfes, Kelly Grace, William Bourke, Edmund Butler, Edmund Broghal, John Hewson

---

[*] As to the number of Jacobite dead the estimates differ. Württemberg reported to Copenhagen that 5,000 Irish had been slain, and the French Commissary Fumeron set the count as low as 3,000. Galster, *Danish Troops*, p. 194.

Graceus.
Guilielmus Bourkus.
Edmundus Butlerus.
Edmundus Broghalus.
Johannes Hawsonius.

Centuriones.

Gualtherus Byrneus.
Gualtherus Bourkus.
Haganus.
Carolus Mac Cartius.
Cominus.
Mac Donoghius.
Clintonus.
Bellevius.
Fitz Patricius.
Blansfeldius.
Petrus Antonius.
Jacobus Garvanus.
Thomas Plunkettus.
Hubertus Dillonius.
Johannes Minnisius.
Shea.
Tearneus.
Darbeus Gradius.
Miles Bourkus.

Johannes Gouldius.
Jacobus Butlerus.
Hugo Mac Dermotus.
Gualtherus Blackius.
Gualtherus Bourkus.
Guilielmus Mac Envoius.
Brianus Murphius.

Optiones.

Henricus O-Nealus.
Thomas Gualtherus.
Edmundus Brenanus.
Mac Cartius.
Purcellus.
Murphius.
Mac Manus.
Rafterus.
Mac Mahonus.
Daffius.
Hallulius.
Qvirkeus.
Zobinus.
Devius.
Walshius.
Walcottus.

But-

Majors (company commanders):
Walter Byrne, Walter Bourke, Hagan, Charles MacCarthy, Comin, MacDonough, Clinton, Bellew, FitzPatrick, Blansfield, Peter Anthony, James Garvan, Thomas Plunkett, Hubert Dillon, Johns Minnis, O'Shea, Tierney, Darbeus, Gradius, Miles Bourke, John Gould, James Butler, Hugh McDermott, Walter Black, William MacEvoy, Brian Murphy

Lieutenants:
Henry O'Neill, Thomas Walter, Edmund Brennan, MacCarthy, Purcell, Murphy, MacManus, Rafferty, MacMahon, Davy, *Hallulius*,* Quirke, Tobin, Dewit, Walsh, Walcott, Butler, O'Cahan, Bourke, Barry, MacLoughlin, Cantlin, Brodie, Dume

---

* Probably Hall or Hull.

114

Butlerus.
Cabanus.
Bourkus.
Barrius.
Mac Loughlinus.
Cantlinus.
Dumeus.
Brodius.

Signiferi pedestris Ordinis.

Wardus.
Fitz Patricius.
Mooreus.
Mac Loughlinus.
Paineus.
Freemannus.
Stretchius.
Werdonus.
Ailmerus.
Mac Loghlinus.
Lincius.
Schaneus.
Archdiaconus.

Medgherus.
Bourkus.
Bourkus.
Kellius.
Mac Evoius.
Elemingus.
Dalius.
Loghlinus.

Signiferi eqvitatûs.

Edvardus Neilus.
Daultonus.
Terentius Neilus.
Jourdanus.
Qvinus.

Metatores.

Byrneus.
Higginus.
Biglius.
Mac Guirius.

Tesserarius.

Wholanus.

Inter

Ensigns:
Ward, FitzPatrick, Moor, MacLoughlin, Payne, Freeman, Stretch, Werdon, Aylmer, MacLoughlin, Lynch, MacShane, Archdeacon, Medgher, Bourke, Bourke, Kelly, MacEvoy, Fleming, Daly, Loughlin

Cornets:
Edward O'Neill, Dalton, Terence (Tádhg) O'Neill, Jordan, Quinn

Surveyors:
Byrne, Higgins, Boyle, Maguire

Duty Officer:
Wholan

✸ 115 ✸

Inter cæsos summæ viros exiſtimationis ſunt Comites Kilmalocus & Gallovadicus. Prætores, vulgò Brigaderi, Connellus, Guilielmus, Mansfeldius, Barkerus, Henricus, Mac Johannes, O-Nealus. Tribuni, Gualtherus Nugentius, Carolus Mooreus cum ejus Vicario Tribuni & Ordinis Ductore, David Bourkus, Ulicus Bourkus, Cohannaghtius, Mac Guirius', O-Gara, Arthurus, Felix O-Neilus, Mahawnus, Cormachus O-Neilus. Vicarius Tribuni Morganus. Ordinum Ductores, Burcellus, O-Donnellus, & Dominus Johannes Everhardus, ingentem præter numerum Centurionum & virorum minoris authoritatis. Prætor Talbottus & Dominus Mauritius Euſtacius vulneribus adeò perfoſſi, ut ſpes vitæ illis ſupereſſet nulla, ex prælio fugâ Limericum usq; ſe eripuerunt, veriti nè vel vivi vel interfecti in manus Anglorum venirent. Occupatô ca-

I 5.   ſtellô

Among those killed were the following men of the highest distinction: the Earls of Kilmallock and Galway. Brigadiers, ordinary Brigadiers, O'Connell, Williams, Mansfield, Barker, Henry, MacJohn, O'Neal. Commanding officers (colonels) Walter Nugent, Charles Moore together with his deputy (lieutenant colonel) and sergeant major, David Bourke, Ulice Bourke, Cohannaght, Mac Guirie, O'Gara, Arthur, Felix O'Neil, MacMahon, Cormach O'Neil. Lieutenant-Colonel Morgan. Sergeants-Major Barcell, O'Donnell, and Mr John Everhard, not to mention a great number of captains and men of lesser authority.

Brigadier Talbot and Mr Maurice Eustace were so severely injured that there was no hope of recovery. They had escaped from the battle and had managed to get all the way to Limerick, fearing they should end up in the hands of the English either alive or dead.

※ 116 ※

ſtellô Aghrimô multisqve intra mœnia occiſis, Tribunus Bourkus ejusq; Ordinis Ductor, nec non undecim viri autoritate præditi, & qvadraginta milites gregarii capti, qvadraginta tria ſigna militaria, qvorum in numero undecim labara fuêre, arma, tormenta, tentoria, impedimenta & cœtera inſtrumenta militiæ hoſtibus erepta. Si creduli narrationibus vulgi fides ſit habenda, Ducem copiarum etiam Regis Galliæ St. Ruth ictu tormenti cecidiſſe, credat, qvi velit. Illuſtris qvidem pugna digna, qvæ conſtanti fama & omnium ore celebretur, utpote qvæ extrema veluti alea certaminum extitit; ſed reſtant plures diei hujus caſus enarrandi, & ſeqvelæ circumſtantiæq; ſeqventes: Sanæ mentis nemo inficias iverit execrandum rerum eſſe diſcrimen, ità in regnis & rebuspublicis ſæviri in viſcera propria, ut inteſtinô cuncta bellô labaſcant, & cives à ſe invicem abalienati civium & ſociorum ſangvine & cæde lætentur. O! felix ter gemina Britannorum

When Aughrim Castle had been occupied and after many men had been slain within its walls, Colonel Bourke and his sergeant major and no less than eleven officers and 40 common soldiers were captured. The trophies comprised 43 colours, eleven beautifully embroidered standards, hand-guns and cannon. The enemy's tents, equipment and other instruments of war were also taken into Williamite possession.

If we can trust the gossip of the uncritical masses, it appears that also St. Ruth, the French captain general of the Jacobite forces, had died, allegedly by a blow of cannon.

It is beyond any doubt that the battle of Aughrim was illustrious and dignified. It is celebrated by definite reputation on the lips of everyone, inasmuch as it stood out as the final and decisive contests of the war in Ireland.

However, many of this day's events remain to be told. Moreover, we still need to learn about the consequences and circumstances which followed. No one of a sane mind can deny that such moments of bloodshed are repugnant. When such wrath erupt in kingdoms or in republics that the whole structure of society is brought to the brink of collapse by civil war, citizens turn against one another, enjoying the blood and murder of their fellow men.

O thrice as happy the three sister kingdoms of the British would be if they had not been – as, I dare say, they actually were – subject to martial scheming.

117

norum corona, nisi Romanis technis nimium qvantum fuisset, ne dicam esset, obnoxia. Præliorum hoc in Hibernia omnium erat ultimum & facilè acerrimum, eò qvòd priora tam decertandi ardore qvàm effectu longè superabat; magna qvidem & clara juxta flumen Boandum pugna pugnata est, majusqve & evidentius discrimen initum per Senum; maximum autem & notissimum apud Aghrimum jam commissum: variâ enim hîc fortunâ pugnatum, nam victis magis qvàm victoribus primordia certaminis arridebant, ut mireris eadem hosti fuisse exitio, qvæ priùs optimum ipsis successum dedêre, Sic rotæ adinstar momentô volvitur belli fortuna, incertissimo sæpé flatu horsum atqve retrorsum versabilis acta; qvod documento satis illustri hæc pugna declarat. Partium neutri studentior hæc scribo, sed qvæ & ipse miserrima vidi, & qvæ præliantium relatu hausi; qvippe qvi officiolis meis occupatus, committere nolui, ut periculosissimæ

The battle of Aughrim was the last of all the clashes in the Irish War, and by far the bloodiest.* It surpassed any previous contest in intensiveness as well as in outcome.

Although the battle on the river Boyne in 1690 and the one at Athlone on the river Shannon in 1691 were brilliant tactical achievements, the most decisive encounter happened at Aughrim in July 1691. For here at Aughrim the luck of war changed markedly during the battle. From the beginning of the battle the Jacobites were in a much more favourable position than the attackers and fought efficiently and successfully. But in the final phase of the struggle, with the Jacobite commander being killed, the Williamite assailants got the better of their opponents.

Thus, we see that the fortune of war may change at any moment, often by an unexpected incident, and it may alter over and over again. This is duly demonstrated by this battle.

By writing these things I have no intention of favouring any of the parties. My narrative is about the sad events that I have personally witnessed or have been told of by others who have been actively engaged in the struggle. Having experienced what I had, I did not wish to risk forgetting, by

---

* As far as fighting is concerned, this is not correct. There were various later clashes to be fought and the sieges of Galway and Limerick also to be taken into account. However, as to bloodiness Claudianus is correct.

118

mæ hujus peregrinationis meæ tempus qvasi per ludum perderem; testes itaq; habeo innumeros, nihil hic à me commemorari, nisi qvod perspectum & exploratum ipse habeo: At tantæ victoriæ fama omnes Hybernorum regiones brevi temporis spatio percurrit. Tertiô deinde Idus Julii motis castris mille passus processerunt Victores, eodemq; die Dux expeditam ducentorum eqvitum & dimacharum manum sub ductu Prætoris Eppingeri emisit ad castellum Portymnum, ubi hostis penarium omni genere commeatuum armorumqve copiâ refertum instruxerat, hunc locum ut interciperent, qvô occupatô Banakeria exspoliata est. Castellum Moora non multis passibus à Banakeria distans Ordinis Ductori Woodio, eò cum centum & qvinqvaginta eqvitibus emisso, ultrò se dedidit; octuaginta captivos in castra referebant præmissi, adeò ut transitus fluminis Seni omnes ad LXIV stadia usqve propè Limericum sub Regis potestate sint redacti. Triduum hoc
in

letting time slip by, the details of this, the most dangerous journey of my life, as if it were merely amusement. Thus, I have lots of witnesses, who can confirm that I have told nothing which I have not myself seen or investigated.

Word about the remarkable victory at Aughrim quickly spread through all the Irish provinces.

On 13 July the victors proceeded 1,000 paces as soon as the camps had been struck, and on the same day the commander-in-chief sent a detachment under the command of Brigadier Eppinger, comprising 200 horse and dragoons armed for battle, to the castle Portumna, in order to seize the place where the enemy had established a warehouse crammed with supplies of all kinds of food and weaponry.

As soon as we had occupied the town of Banagher it was looted. Sergeant Major Wood with 150 horsemen was detailed to take Castle Moor, not many paces from Banagher. The castle surrendered forthwith, hence leaving all the passages across the river Shannon on British hands. Moreover, eighty prisoners of war were received into the Williamite camp 64 furlongs from Limerick.

❀ 119 ❀

in loco abſumptum eſt; intereà temporis congeries cadaverum, ne fœdis avium ferarumqve laniatibus corpora eſſent objecta, more bellico ſepelire Dux juſſit. Hinc LVI ſtadia iter fecerunt ad Loughreaghiam, qvam urbem nocte prælium proximè ſeqvente depopulati ſunt Hiberni, omnibus urbis incolis natione Anglis trucidatis. Ulteriùs inſeqventi die XLVIII ſtadia Athram iter progreſſi, in lævam urbis partem haud procul à muris ſub tentoriis pernoctârunt. Athra erat urbs qvondam celebris, nunc verò bellorum civilium injuriâ nomen ejus unà cum ædificiis tantum non niſi ex ruderibus notum eſt, in muris ſaltem & turribus reſiduæ. Septimo die poſt prælium LXIV ſtadia Gallovadiam profecti urbem obſidione cinxerunt, caſtris verò locatis Angli Bobermoram magnitudine animi ſolitâ invadentes, hoſtem in fortalitium qvoddam ante urbem exſtructum repulerunt. Oriente luce duo urbis fortalitia præſidiis munitiſſima feliciter expeditâ

Three days elapsed while staying in this place. In the meantime, the general ordered that the battlefield be cleared of corpses. Thus, to prevent that they be torn to pieces by birds and wild animals, a great number of dead bodies were buried.

From here they went on 56 furlongs to Loughrea, a town that had been sacked by the Irish on the night following the previous battle, when all inhabitants of English nationality had been slain.

On the following day, we continued our march for 48 furlongs to Athenry. Close to the walls in the left part of the town, we spent the following night in tents. Athenry was once an important city. However, civil war had caused a lot of damage and, save for the remains of walls and towers, the town was no longer of any great importance, but rather a heap of rubble.

Seven days after the battle, we marched 44 furlongs to Galway, where we cordoned off the city by blockade.

At Bobermore the English troops drove the enemy soldiers into a redoubt thrown up before the city. At sunrise, having dispatched an advance detachment, Major General

※ 120 ※

ditâ delectorum manu expugnavit Legatus Imperatorius Maccajus, qvibus occupatîs obsidionem tolerare cœteri non poterant. Secuta igitur est brevis ad refocillationem reqvies: namq; novas ferentem pacis conditiones tympanistam Prætor urbis emisit, Dux Anglorum postulatis ejus libentissimé hac ratione annuit, ex urbe confestim ut exiret præsidium cum omnibus sed propriis sarcinis, sex tormentis, tibiis sonantibus signisqve agitatis: Post Anglis traditum est suburbium. Die inseqventi Dominicâ hostes trium legionum globis instructi ex urbe egrediebantur; Dominus d'Ussone Præfectus Gallorum maturius horâ qvintâ, ut antè postulaverat, solus profectus est, qvem horam post septimam cœteri sunt secuti; Hos enim Gallus suâ præsentiâ suoq; ductu in conspectu nostro dedignatus est; nam ad comiserationem magis qvàm indignationem etiam hostes flectere suos poterat turba colonorum & militum miscella. Erant qvidem omnes juvenes
robu-

Mackay successfully captured two well-defended bastions. When these had been occupied the rest could not withstand a siege. Then, as soon as they had pitched camp, they marched into town with their usual style.

It had happened so that, after a brief operational pause allowing the troops some rest, the city's commandant had sent a drummer offering new terms of surrender. The English general had agreed to the terms, which were quite reasonable. The garrison would leave the city without delay, bringing everything with them apart from their baggage and six guns, but neither with sounding pipes nor with flying colours. Then, the suburb was handed over to the English.

On the following day, a Sunday, the three regiments of enemy troops had left the city. According to previous agreement Monsieur d'Usson,* the French Lieutenant General, set out alone earlier than five o'clock, while the remainder followed at seven. For before our very eyes, the Frenchman had shown disdain of the Irish. For the crowd mixed of farmers and soldiers had roused compassion rather than fury in their enemy.

The Jacobites were definitely youthful and strong, being

---

* D'Usson had taken over as commander-in-chief upon the death of St. Ruth.

121

robusti, sed agrorum ac pecoris magis qvàm belli cultores. Pompam ex congruo licitam qvis contemnit? Nonnulli solô gladiô ac præacutis cuspidis hastis tantùm erant armati, alii sclopos ferrugine exesos & vix bello aptos, præтereaqve nihil gestabant, plerosq; vestes discolores sed laceræ tegebant, paucis justa aderant ad manus arma, qvibus hosti resistere possent. Viris oppidô excedentibus comites hærebant mulieres liberorum & infantium bajulæ. Tormentorum unum, qvod ferreum erat, rotis in itinere fractis ad mille passus ab urbe relictum est. Urbem posteà cum præsidio trium legionum peditum Domino Henrico Bellasio Dux tradidit, & in castris bidui spatio exercitus commorabatur. Gallovadia est urbs maritima ad fluminis Ausobæ ostia sita, muris, vallô & propugnaculis innovatîs munita, qvò piscium saliendorum & commercii gratiâ multi se conferunt navigantes; olim exile fuit piscatorum receptaculum, nunc antiqvitate, qvam ædificia
urbis

used to cultivating fields and tending cattle, however, rather than waging of war.

Who would not feel sorry for such a column marching out having surrendered? Some were armed with swords and pikes, but others brought nothing but rusty muskets that were hardly fit for war. Many wore discoloured and tattered clothes. Indeed only few carried reasonable implements, with which they might resist the enemy.

Womenfolk carrying small children and babies hung on to the soldiers as they filed out of the town. One cannon, which was made of iron, was left at 1,000 paces from the city since the wheels of the carriage had broken down during the march.

Then, in the presence of his three infantry regiments the commandant handed over the city to Mr Henry Bellasis, and the Williamite army stayed in camp for two days.

Galway is a coastal city where many ships have hove to because of the salty fish and the trade. It is sited at the mouth of the river Corrib, it has secure walls, a moat and new fortifications. Once the fishing opportunities were meagre, but now there is an ample sufficiency of fish. Moreover, the city is fashionable due to its antiquity, to which the buildings of

※ 122 ※

urbis teſtantur, amplitudine & portus aptitudine piſciumq; capturâ clarum & nobile emporium. Qvinto deindè Calendarum Auguſti, præſidiô in urbem introductô, LXIV ſtadia Athram usqve ſunt remenſi. Intereà claſſem Anglorum viginti duabus conſtantem navibus Gallovadiam adveniſſe, lætus afferebatur nuncius, qva de cauſa Dux Ginkelius unà cum Duce Würtenbergico in urbem eqvô vectus rediit. Poſterà die XLVIII ſtadia Loughreagam, indeqve longiùs ſeqventis ab ortu lucis LXXX ſtadia profecti, tandem ipſis Calendis Auguſti XLVIII ſtadia Bannakerbrigam pervenerunt. Subjectâ jam Regis poteſtati Regione Connaciâ ulteriùs bellum ſerpſit in Regionem Momoniam. Connacia eſt vaſta Regio, qvam ad Orientem pars Lageniæ, ad Septentrionem verô pars Ultoniæ diſtincta flumine Raviô attingit, ad Occidentem Oceano Occidentali clauditur, ad Meridiem Momoniæ proxima eſt, & Senô fluviô clauſa. Hæc Regio ut Septentrionem verſus &

Meri-

the city bear witness, for its excellent harbour facilities and for its prolific trade.

Then on 28 July 1691, as a new Williamite garrison had occupied the city, we retraced our steps 64 furlongs to Athenry.

Marching, we heard the joyful announcement that an English flotilla consisting of 22 ships had arrived in the Galway roads. For this reason Lieutenant Generals Ginkel and Württemberg rode back to that city.

At sunrise on the following day, 1 August, having marched 48 furlongs to Loughrea and then 80 furlongs further, we finally came as close as 48 furlongs from Banagher bridge.

The province of Connacht had already been subjected to the King's authority, and now the war had spread into the province of Munster.

Connacht is a vast province. It borders on parts of Leinster in the East and to the north, on a part of Ulster, the dividing line being the river Erne. To the West, Connacht's coastline borders on the Western sea. To the South it neighbours Munster and is delineated by the river Shannon. Although to the North and South, this province has only narrow borders,

※ 123 ※

Meridiem arctiores terminos obtinet, ita Orientem versus & Occidentem se latius extendit, & si ambitum ejus permetiaris, milliaria habebis circiter qvadringenta Anglicana. De natura hujus insulæ incolarumqve ingenio aptè hoc afferri potest veriverbium, qvod nec cœlo nec solo læta sit Regio. Cœlo enim non undiqvaq; clementi & temperato fruitur, ut cœteræ ipsi conterminæ regiones, propter pluralitatem locorum uliginosorum atqve palustrium, qvæ gramine qvidem sunt obducta, sed omni stagnantium profluvio aqvarum carent; ex continuis ergò vaporibus perpetuò in altum sublatis densissimæ caligines nebulæqve sæpe periculosæ decidunt: Sterile & nudum plerisqve in locis solum est ab asperitate cœli & montium collusiva, gregibus qvàm hominibus alendis benignius. Incolæ etiam hujus Regionis pabulationi pecorum & piscationi magis, qvàm agriculturæ student; agrorum igitur plures sunt effœti frugumqve vacui atq; inanes. Non
K tamen

it appears wider if observed east-west. Its circumference is about 400 English miles around. The nature of this province and the disposition of its inhabitants are not very pleasant. Neither the sky nor the earth pleases the eye. In no way and nowhere does it enjoy a mild and moderate sky like that of the neighbouring provinces. Because of the many swampy locations which are covered by grass but lack the steady inundating flow of water, the province appears bleak.

Because of the permanent heat, which rises continuously up into the skies, a very intense fog, which is often dangerous, descends. In many places the earth and the mountains are infertile, exposed as they lay to the coarseness of the skies. These places are more apt for nourishing herds of animals than for human subsistence.

For the same reason, the Irish living in this province are more thorough in foraging for their beasts and in fishing than they are with their agricultural pursuits. Thus many fields are worn out thus giving no produce. However, nowhere is

124

tamen horum nullibi locorum aptiores dantur frugibus agrorum conserendis, sed qvi semina ad seram producunt maturitatem, eò qvòd maturandæ tempore frugis æstu Solis destituuntur; multaqve item montium juga aspera sunt atq; deserta, qvorum tamen radicibus planities adhærent ingentes adeoque luxuriosæ herbis, non adspectu modò jucundis, sed gratissimo etiam mellis sapore adeò edulceratis, ut, nisi exigua tantùm parte diei pecora his impleantur, pabuloqve diutiùs prohibeantur, suprà modum pasta diffiliant; Itaqve terra hæc mellis præstantissimi, pecoris, piscium ferarumqve dives est. Post biduanam hoc in loco reqviem exercitus ulteriùs trans pontem Banakeriæ flumini Seno impositum XL stadia Biram tendebat. Proxima verò dies ad qvietem militibus data est. Jamqve nonbidui longiùs itinere à Nenagha aberat exercitus, cujus in præsidio Longus Antonius Carollus Jacobi Prætor relictus erat; Dux Anglorum cum expeditis

offered better opportunities for sowing than in these fields. But since they are allowed to mature so late, they are scorched by the sun before having had time to develop.

Moreover, many mountainous plains are barren and forsaken. On the foothills, however, large plains present abundant pastures for animal grazing. The grass provides delightful vistas and is also sweetened with a pleasing taste. The supply is so ample that, if the cattle were left alone there the whole day they would graze until bursting. The land is rich with fine honey, cattle, fish, and wild animals.

After a two-day rest and recuperation in this place, the army marched on to Banagher bridge. This is on the river Shannon, 40 furlongs from Birr. Next day, again the soldiers were granted a break. And soon the army was no more than two days travel away from Nenagh, a town which the Jacobite Brigadier Anthony Charles Longus had been tasked with defending. In order to reach an agreement with him, the

※ 125 ※

ditis cohortibus eqvitum, dimacharum peditumqve Prætorem Levefonium eò præmifit; Sed Prætor caftelli, cognitò emiſſorum adventu, Panicò qvaſi qvodam metu perculſus ad pontem qvadringentos paſſus à caſtello ſtructum, ut trajectum ibi defenderet, aufugit, ſed partem Anglorum à dextra & ſiniſtra ſimul advolantem & tranſitum inhibituram pontemqve deſtructuram animadvertens, maximâ ad Nenagham recedens celeritate, facibus arci ſubditis, indé mox demiſſis manibus fugit; ignis tandem à captivis qvibusdam in caſtello Anglis ob feſtinationem relictis exſtinctus eſt; Leveſonius autem ad triginta duo ſtadia & viciniam Limerici hoſtem perſecutus, opes & impedimenta omnia victorum victor obtinuit. Ab ortu lucis LXIV ſtadia Burraſhiam, & ſeqventi die ultrà XLVIII ſtadia ad tranſitum Nenaghæ progreſſi, ſex ibi dierum ſtativa habuêre. Hinc Tertiô Idus Auguſti ſtadia XLVIII Skilleam, inde totidem ſtadia Tullam usqve pro-

K 2   ceſſe-

English general detailed Brigadier Leveson in advance together with some well-equipped regiments of horse, dragoons, and foot. However, being the commandant of the castle, Brigadier Longus, as soon as he had realised that the emissaries were on their way, he hurried to the bridge 400 paces from the fortress in order to defend the crossing. Nonetheless, as he observed some of the English troops closing in from right and left he decided to prevent the passage of the river by destroying the bridge. He withdrew, then, promptly to Nenagh where he set fire to the castle and fled as fast as he could.

Eventually the fire was extinguished by prisoners of war, whom the English had left behind in the small fortress, having been in a hurry. Leveson now followed the enemy for 32 furlongs, thus closing in on Limerick. Being the victor, he impounded the possessions and horses of those vanquished.

At daybreak we marched on for 64 furlongs to Borrissokane,* and on the following day another 48 furlongs to the pass at Nenagh. Here we pitched camp and stayed for six days. On 11 August, we proceeded from here 48 furlongs

---

* Claudianus only refers to this location as "Burrashia," and it is noteworthy that there are in fact several place names with the root "Burrish-" in the vicinity.

※ 126 ※

cesserunt; post unius tantum diei otium ad Abbiownibrigam tria millia passuum, & totidem passus Cahironlisham iter facientes pristinam sedem receperunt. Undecimum jam diem eodem in loco ad qvietem militibus Dux dederat ad exspectanda tormenta & mortaria Athloniæ relicta. Viginti novem pontones intereà per flumen Senum ad castra transvehebantur. Deindè octavô Calendarum Septembris, XL stadia Limericum emensi, eodem die tria ante urbem structa fortalitia occupârunt. Proxima nocte ictu sclopi per gulam percussus Tribunus eqvitum Donepius animam exhalavit. Seqventi die uxor qvædam eqvitis Donepiani puerulum sinu gestans ictu tormenti in tentorio suo ità à tergo vulnerata est, ut spina dorsi in viscera ejus contorta intrà duarum spatium horarum exspiraret; puer contrito capite & cerebro latè disperso subitanea morte exstinctus est. Viginti qvatuor abhinc stadia erat mons saxeus flumini

to Killoscully,* and a similar distance further to Tulla.†
Having rested for a day, we marched 3,000 paces to
Abbeyowney, and the same distance to Caherconlish where
we pitched camp in the unspoiled surroundings.

Here the general granted the soldiers eleven days of rest
while awaiting the guns and mortars coming up from Athlone.
In the meantime, 20 new pontoons were carried across the
river Shannon to the campsite. Then on 25 August, we went
40 furlongs to Limerick, and on the same day we manned
three redoubts, which had been built in front of the city.

The next day the commanding officer of 2nd Cavalry
Regiment, Colonel Donep, expired, having been hit in the
throat by a cannon ball. The day after, the wife of one of
Donep's cavalrymen, who was bearing a little child in her
womb, was so badly injured by a cannon ball coming in from
behind that she died within two hours, her vertebrae having
been crushed inside her. The child was killed instantly, his
head smashed and his brains strewn around.

There was a rocky mountain 24 furlongs away near the

---

* By then Schoulea.

† Tullow seems most logical, although it could be Tulla near the town of Tipperay.

※ 127 ※

mini Seno vicinus, mediocri inftructus caftellô, qvod centum & viginti latronum præfidiis, muris, afperô & perangufto aditu & eximia erat magnitudine munitum, qvem ad occupandum locum Vicarius Tribuni Fromholtus Wittinghoffius cum trecentorum peditum & centum eqvitum delecta manu emiffus eft; Præfes verò difficultate loci & inacceffibili hujus fummitate Petræ fretus obfidionem decrevit tolerare, eandemqve pacis conditionem fe initurum & præftolaturum, qvam præfidiarii urbis Limerici inirent, refpondit: datô tamen oppugnandi figno fine ulla pacis conditione rupem & caftellum unà fecum victoris gratiæ dedidit: Itaqve fubjecto muris pulvere nitrato, latronum hoc receptaculum refugiumq; in aëra difperfum eft; tria alia mediocri munita præfidiô caftella, qvorum primarium Carrig-Ganellum, per idem tempus in Anglorum poteftatem funt redacta; omnesqve in caftra captivos fecum inermes victor abduxit. Inter

K 3   hæc

river Shannon. On it there was a second-rate castle that was protected by its walls, extraordinary bulk, a rough and constricted pass, and 120 mercenaries. In order to seize it, Lieutenant Colonel Fromholt Wittinghof* was detailed with a task force of 300 foot and 100 horsemen.

The garrison, however, confident because of the difficulty of the surroundings and the inaccessible summit of the mountain decided to sit out the siege. On being challenged to surrender, the commandant responded that he expected and would accept similar terms like those offered to the governors of the city of Limerick. However, when the sign for the assault was given, he surrendered without having agreed to any terms. The cliff and the castle together with himself were handed over to the victors. Subsequently, when gun powder had been applied to set the walls ablaze, this insignificant refuge of mercenaries was blown to smithereens.

At the same time, three other castles – the largest of which was Carrig-Ganellus, and all of them occupied by unassuming garrisons – fell into English hands. The victors carried off with them the defenceless captives.

---

* Claudianus writes: Vicarius Tribuni Fromholtus Wittinghoffius. However, there was no such officer with the Danish troop contingent. Claudianus has mentioned earlier a Major Vittinghof (who was killed) and a Sergeant-Major Formholt Witinghoff (who was wounded) and might have confused his notes.

128

hæc Limericum advenerunt tormenta majora bellica & mortaria; Octodecim navium classis Anglicarum aplustris usa Gallicis in speciem Hibernos juvandi urbis usqve portum penetravit. Hiberni qvi ultra flumen ab urbe mille passuum ad Cattalogiam relicto suorum exercitu consederant, repente hoc navium aditu exciti, tripudiis & corporis agitatione plausuqve militum immodicam & inopportunam animi lætitiam ostentare cœperunt, utpote advenientem ex insperato salutem sibi gratulantes; Angli effusæ causam lætitiæ comperti pro demissis signis Gallicis aplustria Anglorum in malorum fastigiis rursus defixerunt, & statim vehementissimo tormentorum fragore é navigiis in castra hostium tam atrociter detonuerunt, tutiora in loca se agminatim ut retraxerint, nautarum dolo se esse deceptos videntes, & non auxilium à Gallis, ut speraverant, sed terrorem ab Anglis adesse, præcipuum autem id ab Anglia erat Auxiliorum.

Ali-

Siege guns and mortars now arrived before Limerick. A flotilla of eighteen English ships reached Ireland, heaving to at the city's harbour. They flew a false flag belonging to the French in order to give the appearance of long awaited French support for the Irish.

While their army being nowhere near, the Irish, who stayed at Cattalogia,* 1,000 paces from the city on the other side of the river, were happy with the arrival of these ships and started to show their unreserved joy. Jumping and dancing, and clapping their hands, they thanked for the perceived support arriving so unexpectedly. The English, having acknowledged the cause of their joyfulness, now hauled down the French flags, again hoisting the English ensign to the summits of their masts. Soon, a vigorous salvo from their cannon thundered from the ships. Cannon balls hit the enemy so hideously that the Irish hurriedly withdrew to more secure places, realising that they had been deceived by the naval men's trick. It dawned upon them that what was present was not assistance from the French as they had hoped, but terror from the English. Nonetheless, this was primarily auxiliaries from England.

---

* This does not correspond to any known place in Limerick, unless being a Latinisation of the old Cattle Market Lane.

※ 129 ※

Aliud etiam erat castellum Connellum, qvadraginta circiter stadia Limerico distans, eò Princeps Darmstadicus cum expedita missus est trium legionum peditum & septingentorum eqvitum manu, ut ad deditionem id compelleret, qvô occupatô duo alia castella simili modô deditâ in fidem magna cum gloria acceperat, multa qvoqve ignobilia oppida, qvorum incolæ latrones erant, in Regis potestatem venerunt. Jam tota Hibernia, jam urbes omnes exceptâ Limericô urbe Regis Guilielmi erant, illud qvanqvàm unica omnium urbs superesset, tamen resistere & viribus Anglorum se opponere non erubuit, more angvium, qvi capite & corpore obtritô postremùm caudâ minantur. In molem igitur tormenta & mortaria attrahi Angli curabant, humo ut æqvarent fundamenta muri atqve valli, ne qvidqvam urbis exstaret vestigium, qvibus dispositis urbem sub noctem obscuram decem tormentis bellicis acriùs infestare & in muros sævire, ignesqve è

K 4   pyro-

Castle Connel would prove to be a different, challenge. It lay about 40 furlongs from Limerick, and the Prince of Darmstadt was now detailed with a strong detachment of three regiments of foot and 700 horse in order to coerce it into submission.

When this had been gloriously accomplished, he chose to take two more minor castles in a similar manner. Many unknown towns, too, the inhabitants of which were rapparees, came under King William's rule.

Now, in all of Ireland every city but Limerick was in King William's hands. Although Limerick was the only city remaining in Jacobite power, it was not, however, ashamed of resisting and opposing the English. Their last struggle was like a snake that makes a final menace with its tail, though head and body has already been destroyed.

Thus, the English carefully positioned their siege guns and mortars onto the heaps of earth they had levelled with the wall. As soon as the guns were in position, obscured by night, they started to demolish the city. While with ten siege guns they began their devastation of the walls, fire-spitting mortars

130

pyrobolorum machinis ad qvatriduum tectis injicere cœperunt. Pridiè Nonarum Septembris sub vesperam, urbi viciniores esse ut possent, moles tormentorum & accessus variârunt, qvam ob causam novi operis aggerem viginti qvatuor tormentorum capacem à latere urbis Orientali exaggerabant, ingentem vim materiæ milites, eqvites autem fasces ramorum stipitesqve arborum attulerunt; paucas intrà horas opera ista tanto militum ardore sunt absoluta, ut agger summum muri æqvaverit fastigium, nec oppidani, qvicqvid molem ad impediendam excogitari poterat, segniter exseqvebantur, majore tamen nisu qvàm effectu. Nec ergò posterus lætior erat dies, qvippe muros tam sævum in modum concusserant, ut sub vesperam per ruinam mœnium perforatam decem viri ordine urbem intrare potuissent; ictibus crebris sine intermissione biduô adhuc globos evomuerunt igniferos, qvi per ætheris auram volantes subitò delapsi in
tecta

threw incendiary bombs onto the houses for four days, so that no urban feature remained undisturbed.

In the evening of 4 September, we shifted the cannon and moved closer to the city. For this purpose we threw up a twenty four gun battery. Foot soldiers brought huge quantities of materiel from the east of the city, and the cavalry collected branches and logs. The soldiers toiled effectively and, within a few hours, this work was completed, so that the battery was at the same level as the top of the wall. The citizens of Limerick, of course, did their best to obstruct the construction work, though to little avail.

Thus, for the defenders the day was no happier than the one before, since during the evening the wall was breached to such an extent that ten men could have entered the city, line abreast.

For two days in a row and without interruption, we threw red-hot balls, which were scattered randomly onto houses and

※ 131 ※

tecta terramqve validiſſimô fragore eructabant flammas & mille mortes ſpirabant, ut ignes tribus in locis accenſi, ter infelicibus ad extremum noctis arderent incendiis. Angli intereà temporis tormenta coeterasqve machinas capiti molis Cromvellianæ imponentes non qvieverunt. Moles illa vallum erat à Cromvello ante 65 annos eductum, qvô Hibernos ad deditionem adegerat, idq; jam ab hoſte obſeſſum primùm in Anglorum ceſſit poteſtatem, urbi rurſus interitum minaturum. Decimô Octavô Calendarum Octobris cum jam adveſperaſceret, pro victoria illa ſpecioſa Hungarica à Cæſare contra Turcas obtenta, tota per Anglorum caſtra, omnia tormenta tam majora qvàm minora triplici lætitiæ ſignô ſunt exploſa, & magnificè feſtivo fiſtularum, tubicinum ac tympanorum ſtrepitu, igniumqve ſplendore aliisq; modis triumphatum eſt, qvo in prælio tredecim millia Turcarum, à parte verò Cæſaris octo millia, qvorum numerum ad qvatuor

K 5   tan-

streets. The balls fell with deafening noise and caused thousands of deaths. During that night three locations were razed to the ground.

The same night, the English carried on their siege activities, positioning guns on the top of the walls of Cromwell's Fort. This fort had been built by Cromwell 65 years earlier in order to persuade the Irish to surrender. As, now, it was again taken by the English, it threatened anew the city with ruin.

On 14 September, as the day waned, throughout the English positions gun salutes were fired as a sign of great joy. The occasion for this celebration was the splendid victory won by the Hungarians and the Emperor against the Turks.* Moreover, we witnessed the most magnificent concerts of pipes, trumpets and drums, and a splendid firework. In the aforementioned battle 13,000 Turks were killed, while 8,000 souls were claimed on the part of the Emperor. Later, a report from the Emperor's forces brought this number down to

---

* A victory in one of the numerous battles fought by the Germano-Roman Emperor Leopold I against the Turks in the Great Turkish War.

❈ 132 ❈

tantùm millia virorum cæfa redigunt relationes Cæfareanorum, tormenta centum & qvinqvaginta octo cum impedimentis omnibus coeterisqve belli præparatoriis capta funt atqve direpta. Nihil intereà agebatur dignum relatu, nifi qvòd diros globos facesq; & qvicqvid alendo igni aptum erat ingererent obfeffis. Multi Anglorum ad pabulatum egreffi à latronibus opprimebantur, alii capti, pluresqve occifi, nam hoftis in fylvis campo adhærentibus armatos abfcondidit latrones, qvi prætereuntes ex improvifo adoriebantur. Decimô Calendas Octobr. ad hoftem è Comitatu Clariæ depellendum legiones Danicæ Regis nempè ac Reginæ cum alia ex univerfo exercitu felecta undecim legionum manu flumen Senum, ficuti pridiè præceptum erat, tranfibant, ponte navali flumine impofitô: horâ tertiâ pomeridianâ incepta eft pugna, qvæ ad qvintam usqve horam tam acriter duravit, ut hoftes fuis è foveis, fedibus & munimentis ejecti,
cater-

merely 4,000 men. Moreover, 158 guns were captured together with wagons and other supplies.

Little more worth mentioning happened that night, but we continued the bombardment and keeping the fires of the burning city alive. Many English soldiers going foraging were assaulted by rapparees, some were captured, and several killed. Apparently, the enemy hid the armed mercenaries in the woods close to the battlefield, from where they ambushed without warning.

On 22 September, the Royal Life Guards and the Queen's Regiment crossed the river Shannon in order to rout the enemy in County Clare. Together with eleven other regiments selected from the whole army, the Danes went across as soon as the boat-bridge had been laid on the river. At three o'clock in afternoon, the battle commenced. It went on until five o'clock and was fought with such fury that the enemy was driven out of all his positions, huts and shelters, and pushed

133

catervatim in urbem, tanqvam greges ovium in ſtabulum, convolarent, & qvi nondum ad pontem usqve ductarium pervenerant, cum ponte ab ipſis oppidanis ſubducto caperentur, relictis in prædam victori duodecim ſignis militaribus, magna vi pecorum dimacharumqve eqvis, præter opima ſpolia qvæ obtinuerunt Angli, qvi in molem ab hoſte deſertam plura intulêre tormenta, portam urbis & pontem ut decuterent. Sic hoſtes terreſtri ſimul navaliq; premebantur obſidione; ſed nec alia unqvàm urbs fortiùs obſidionem tulit. Hiberni verò cum omnia ſibi indies exaſperari, & ſe ad ultimam usq; penuriam eſſe redactos, nec qvicqvam ſupereſſe ad reparandas vires, jam jam penè exhauſtas, bellumqve magis ingraveſcere & innovari viderent, mitigata mentis feritate ſeditioſa iſta deferbuit vehementia, ut tandem obſidionis ærumnas pertæſi deditionem meditarentur, & poſt colloqvium cum hoſte, mutuum inirent conſilium de induciis
&

back into the city in small disorganised crowds, just as herds of sheep are hustled into their stable.

Many Jacobites, who had not yet managed to get across the draw bridge, were caught in the open since the citizens had now raised the bridge. The victors took twelve colours, a great number of cattle and horses belonging to dragoons, besides other spoils. The English also took possession of many guns, which had been deserted by the enemy when making for the bridge.

By now, the enemy was completely contained by the besiegers on land as well as by the naval blockade. Never has a city ever borne a siege more courageously.

Nonetheless, the Irish realised that their situation worsened by the day and that their stock of supplies was running low. There was nothing left by which they might regain their strength – which was now almost exhausted – and that the burdens of the war grew even heavier. The defenders' mood fermented as the fierceness of their minds had softened. Wearied by the hardships of the siege they finally considered surrendering.

At a conference with the enemy they agreed on cessation

134

& pacis recuperandæ conditionibus. Intereà fidei causâ in urbem mittebatur Dux Schraumoreus, cujus obses Sarsfeldius urbe egressus in castra venit. Tutæ jam tranqvillæq; res erant omnes; induciæ autem & pacis consultationes in terminis suis octiduô sunt procrastinatæ, qvia nondum præstò aderat concilii bellici Præses & Judicum Princeps, sed ipsis Calendis Octobris Dubliniô in castra gratus omnibus exspectatusqve venit, statuitq, cum eis de omnibus pactionibus præsens agere. Posterô igitur die in Prætorium castrense ambarum Legati partium convenerunt, ubi fœdera pacis manu omnium sunt subscripta atqve sigillis obsignata. Summam legum & conditionum paucîs ut in compendium redigam; actum & transactum est; ut priscæ in statum libertatis redirent omnes, & suæ libertate conscientiæ perfruerentur, prout erant annô, qvô Rex Jacobus ad Regium dignitatis fastigium fuerat evectus. Deindè qvorum animis Galliam cum copiis

of hostilities and articles of the peace agreement.

Having proven his reliability Lieutenant General s'Gravenmoer was now sent into the city, and Sarsfield was exchanged for him as a hostage and left the city to go into the English camp. Now, all was safe and calm. However, though hostilities had ceased, the consultations regarding the peace articles were procrastinated for eight days, since the chairman of the war council and the lord justice were not yet present.

Then, on 1 October he arrived in the camp. Esteemed in Dublin and impatiently expected by everyone he decided to negotiate all the articles with the Jacobites. Thus, the next day representatives from both parties met in the general's tent, where all the articles of peace were signed and sealed by the hands of everybody.

The main elements of the laws and conditions for war termination may be summarised as follows: they should facilitate that the Irish were granted a state of new freedom and that they might enjoy full freedom of confession, just as in the year in which King James had been elevated to the summit of dignity of Monarchs.* Moreover, since many Irish fighting men desired to go to France to fight with the French

---

* Actually the wording allows for freedom of confession as in the time of King Charles.

※ 135 ※

piis Gallicis transvehendi cupido incef-
ferat, non impediti ad tria usqve millia
virorum abirent. Hiberni intereà dum
transportatio fieret, in vetère urbe, qvæ
Anglicana dicitur, & Infula, Angli verò
in nova urbe, qvæ Hibernica feu fubur-
bana nominari folet, commorarentur,
qvibus omnia urbis munimenta & propugnacula extemplò tradita funt. Urbs
ipfa & tecta ædificiorum globis ignife-
ris erant male multata: In templo erat
Epifcopi cujusdam fepultura hôc orntaa
Epitaphio:

Nemo mihi tumbam ftatuat de
marmore faxit,
Urnula Epifcopolo fatis hæcce
pufilla pufillo
Angli qvis vivus fuerim & te-
ftentur Hiberni,
Cœlicolæ qvis fim defunctus
teftificentur.

Variæ

colours, this was allowed, and hence about 3,000 men left.

Until there was shipping, the Irish remained in the old city of Limerick, which is an island called English Town. The English, then, stayed in the new town, which is a suburb called Irish Town, where to all the defence materiel was moved directly.

The city itself and roofs of the buildings had been badly damaged by red-hot balls; and in a church a grave of a bishop was adorned with this epitaph:

> To me, since I have met my doom,
> Let none erect a marble tomb
> Or monument; this humble urn
> will serve a little Bishop's turn.
> Let Albion and Hibernia fair
> What I have been in life declare:
> What I am truly since I fell,
> Just Heaven above can only tell.

❊ 136 ❊

Variæ legiones in gratiam & tutelam Regis recepti ad fidem fe Sacramento jurisjurandi obftrinxêre, reliqviis ad Parentes, domos & amicos redeuntibus. Sic profpero fortunæ flatu ad optatum perducta funt finem magna belli molimina, & novum pacis velut ex triftiffima crudelitatis caligine exortum rurfus illuxit fidus, qvod face belli exftinctâ difcordiarumqve fluctibus repreffis magnam tempeftatem fubita ferenitate discuffit, lucemqve regno reddidit obtenebrato; Hoc ergo modò revirefcit & utinam revirefcat longa pace refocillatum, & velut ex morte refurgens reflorefcat renata Hibernorum Respublica; ut uno fub capite membra coalefcant & convalefcant omnia, qvæ fub pluribus in monftrofum & multiceps corpus abirent, femper in fua ipfius carcinomata defæviturum: Qvis non mirabitur tot triumphos & trophæa invicti Anglorum exercitus, finemqve belli inteftini exoptatum tot præliis, multis fudoribus & incredibili celeritate redem-

While the regiments, which had been received into the grace and protection of King William, now swore loyalty to him by a military oath of allegiance, the rest returned to their parents, homes and friends.

Thus, by a stroke of good fortune, the great efforts of war were led to the desired end and a new star of peace shone again. As soon as the embers of martial conflagration had been stamped out and the waves of discord calmed, light returned to the darkened kingdom. With sudden serenity, the kingdom of Ireland came out of the sad darkness and great calamity which had shattered her.

Therefore the state of the Irish, which was thus reborn, came back to life. May it fully revive, warmed into life anew with long lasting peace and, having risen from death, blossom again. May it re-unite its citizens under one ruler and regain all the strength, which had been absorbed by an atrocious and many-headed monster.

Who will not marvel that so many triumphs were achieved and so many trophies taken by the invincible English army; and that the end of civil war, longed for through so many battles, was paid for by the soldiers' toil and remarkable swiftness.

※ 137 ※

demptum, tot ardua montium, tot lubrica vallium, tot propugnacula moenium intrà biennium superata, tam pertinax ad resistendum Regnum Hibernicum etiam antè Hybernia, in jus ac potestatem Regis Guilielmi devenisse: Habes, benevole Lector, qvisqvis sis, sive peregrinus, sive Civis, Historiam de Bello Hibernico literis à me consignatam, qvi plurima horum ab ipso rerum exordio ad ultimam usqve periodum & vidi, & militantium relatu comperta, non interpositâ morâ, nè qvid oblivione intercideret, in literas retuli, & pyctatio, qvod semper erat ad manus, commisi. Fateor, me parciorem justô fuisse in exaggeranda Danicorum virtute militum æq; ac Ducum, qvorum fortitudini præclarorum magna pars facinorum & progressuum debetur; Sed malui hoc ab exteris, qvàm à me tanqvam commilitonum minimo & Sympatriota digna virtutibus eorum prædicatione, literis ac monumentis efferri & decantari; aliàs forte nobis aliundè

Many difficult mountain paths had been negotiated; many uncertainties of valleys, many palisades and walls were overcome within two years. Moreover, in spite of the winter's tenacious resistance, the Irish had now eventually submitted to the justice and power of King William.

Sincere reader, whomever you are, whether foreigner or citizen, you have now perused the history of The Irish War as I have seen it. I was present from the very beginning and many of these events I have seen with my own eyes all the way to the end. However, other occurrences I have gathered without delay from the accounts of my fellow soldiers in order to ascertain that nothing is lost to oblivion.

I have written it all down on a little pad which was always at hand. I admit that I have been sparing in praising the virtues of the Danish soldiers and commanders, though a considerable part of the conquests and other advances of this war was owed to their fortitude.

Rather than from me as a fellow partisan, I have wanted that their praise be sung by others or brought about by monuments. Others have lavishly eulogised their own deeds and glorified their own soldiers. That practise is amply familiar: Self-praise is no recommendation.

undè objiceretur gloriosi characterismus militis satis notus & tritus : Propria laus sordet.

COROLLARIUM SUPPLEX.

Milite sic Vestrô gestum, Rex Maxime, bellum
Descripsi, cujus testis & ipse fui,
Munera Bellonæ canto & certamina Martis,
Monstráq; qvæ secum Martia castra dabant,
Donec Ivernorum pressi pede lassus arenas,
Hinc procul à Patrio promtus abire solo,
Sæpiùs ergò animam per mille pericula duxi,
Illæsam toties sæva per arma tuli.

Post

A Humble Gift

Greatest King, I have described the war that I witnessed myself while it was fought by your army. I have told about Bellona's duties and the battles of Mars. I have described the monstrosities of the army's camps en route to Ireland. Having travelled such long distance from my parental land, wearied I set foot on the sands of Ireland. Therefore, I have suffered a thousand perils, but I emerged unscathed from countless clashes.

139

Poſt motus animi & certamina tanta,
qvietem
Otiaq; Iverni dulcia pacis habent;
Aſt ego Bellonæ pertæſus munera a-
varæ,
Tentavi patrios pauper adire focos.
Martis me pullum tenuit tres Marspiter
annos,
Principioq; ſagum, fine reſumo to-
gam;
Muſarum in caſtris merui hanc per A-
pollinis arma,
Ne poſthàc pugnas Marte, ſed Arte
feram.
Hoc tibi confectum parvum, Rex
Maxime, munus
His chartîs veſtros volvitur ante pe-
des;
Ad tua confugiens, ſupplex ſubſellia
adoro,
Ut mihi parva Deûm gratia parta
fiet.

L   In-

A Humble Gift

After all the commotion of mind and of great battles, Ireland is calm and at peace. However, feeble and wearied by Bellona's tasks, I returned to my parents' hearth. For three years, Mars was my father and I took up the cloak, though in the end I chose the toga.* Not again shall I be persuaded by Mars; rather arts will guide me, and much do I owe to the Muses and to the arms of Apollo. This little gift, written in these leafs for you, noble King, is hereby submitted before your feet. I humbly implore that a little of the grace of God, which takes refuge at your court, might befall me.

---

* It is likely to mean, "while first I donned the uniform, later I became a civil servant."

Emendanda.

In præfatione pag. 2. lin. 9. lege eruditionis. P. 9. l. 21. l. sapientissimus. P. 10. l. 23. l. constantissimè. P. 12. l. 23. l. sacris pro succis. In libro ipso p. 4. l. 18. l. pergentes. Pag. 8. l. 5. l. Nobilis, ibidem l. 19. l. Carrigfergum. P. 10. l. 9. l. Lageniam. P. 13. l. 8. l. altitudinem. P. 19. l. 4. l. contemplatio. P. 20. l. 2. l. atqve. P. 23. l. 10. l. bombardarum. P. 41. l. 3. dele (magni). Pag. 54. l. 8. l. vehementem eruptionem. P. 69. l. 23. dele (.) P. 79. l. ult. l. contulit. P. 82. l. 11. undæ pr. unde. P. 104. l. 5. l. aridæ pr. arridæ. Reliqva Lector benevolus facilè corriget.

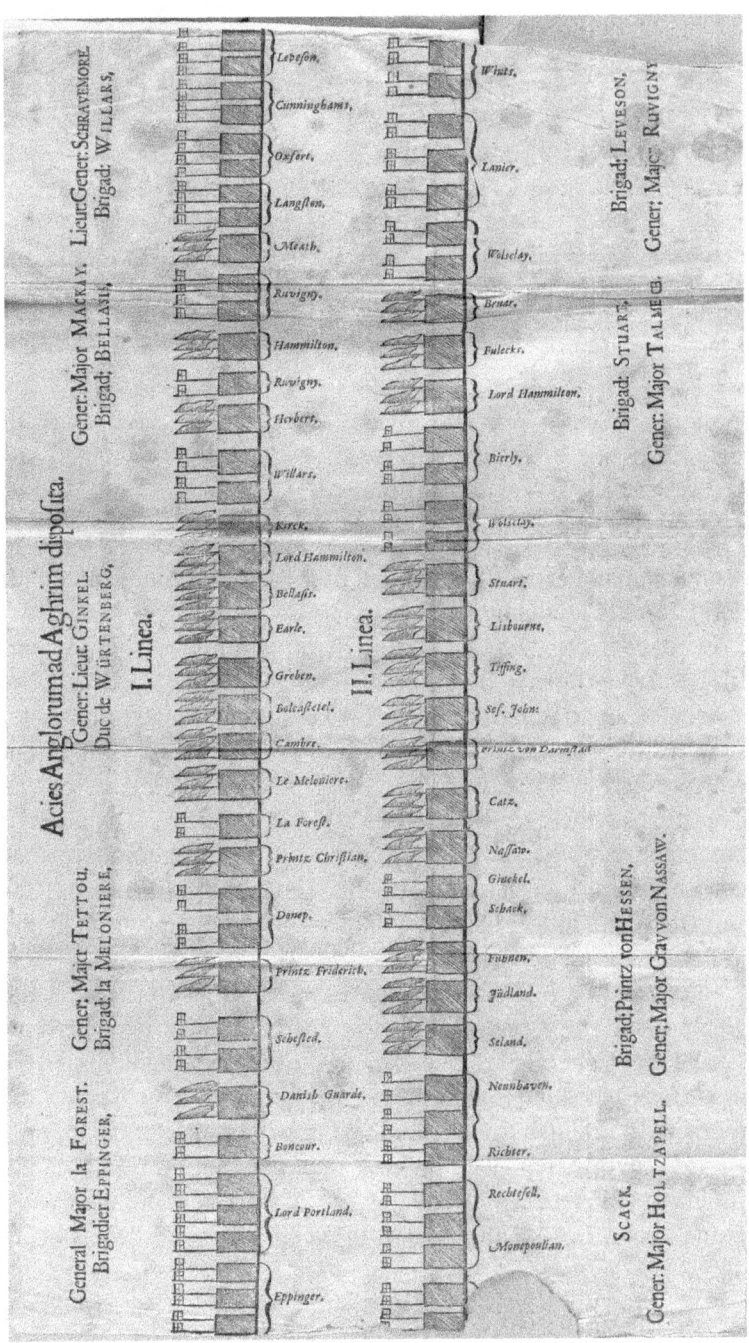

Epilogue

In the autumn of 1691, by the fall of the last Jacobite stronghold, Limerick, Claudianus' martial exertions in Ireland were over. On 3 October 1691, the articles of capitulation were signed and Limerick was opened up to the Williamite forces.

Thus, a garrison of more than 10,000 well-armed troops with supplies for 2–3 months had now surrendered. Those of the Irish who wanted to do so were now free to leave for service on the Continent with King Louis XIV's armies, and the Royal Navy would provide the necessary transport to bring them there – or perhaps merely to get rid of them. Those who did not opt for service with Louis' colours could either go home or join the Williamite forces.

As the war in Ireland had now come to its conclusion, the General Officer Commanding the Danish expeditionary corps, Lieutenant General the Duke of Württemberg-Neustadt, turned his attention to the future: the campaign in Flanders. However, for the moment the Danish troops remained in winter quarters in Ireland. The cavalry was in Clonmel, Cashel, Carrick and Fetard; the infantry at Waterford, Youghal, Cork and Kinsale, but orders had come from Lord Nottingham to keep ready for transfer to

Flanders.[1] In early 1692, the Danish contingent eventually moved across to the continent of Europe. While Claudianus initially went along with his regiment to fight for another four years, he returned to Denmark in 1696 to commence his studies of theology.

The fight in Ireland – and in Flanders for that matter – in the last decade of the seventeenth century had not only been a consequence of national interests. It was just as much an activity agreed to and performed in the context of membership of a wider multi-national community, whose member states shared some common values.

In the closing decades of the seventeenth century and the opening ones of the eighteenth, the peace and well-being of many European countries were menaced by France, personified by King Louis XIV. The Grand Alliance fighting in the War of League of Augsburg, or the Nine Years War, 1688-97, and the War of Spanish Succession, 1701–13, as well as the coalition-of-the-willing struggling in Ireland 1689–91, were the European states' responses to that threat.

Denmark's long-term strategic interests were closely linked with those of other non-French European states. However, the double monarchy of Denmark-Norway had additional security worries of its own. The war with Sweden 1675–9 had drained the treasury and the huge army, which was then believed to be necessary for defensive purposes as well as for recovery of territories lost, had to be paid, trained, equipped and held ready for action. For these reasons, funds and war experience were essentials to fulfilling immediate as well as long-term security needs.

The coalition treaty of 1689 between Britain and Denmark had specifically aimed at providing a Danish contribution to the multi-national coalition-of-the-willing assembled in order to rid the British crown of the Hiberno-French menace in Ireland, and it was in this greater political context – though probably unknown to him at the time – that Andreas Claudianus went abroad with Prince Frederick's Regiment.

---

[1] Daniel Finch, 2nd Earl of Nottingham, until 1693 Secretary of State under King William and Queen Mary.

At the operational level the whole coalition shared common purposes. As far as Württemberg was concerned, his specific war aims as a subordinate commander were to engage his troops in the best possible way with a view to winning battles and securing smooth co-operation with other arms, as well as with the non-Danish contingents. Moreover, as His Danish Majesty's general officer commanding the Danish contingent, his obligations were to make sure that Danish interests were adequately served. These included not only maintaining good relations with the lead-nation, Britain, but just as much preserving the fighting power of his own contingent by keeping up discipline, health, unit strength, equipment and troop morale.

Geographically, and with the benefit of hindsight, we may suggest that there were at least three intermediate aims in the war on land: securing a beachhead and a foothold in Ulster; conquest of the capital Dublin and the associated terrain – that is, northern and eastern Ireland; and finally taking the harbours through which French support of the Jacobite army might otherwise be received – in other words taking all the rest of southern and western Ireland. Prince Frederick's Regiment did their bit throughout the conflict to achieving these aims.

Tactically, the objectives which had to be taken in order to achieve the operational aims were all connected with the conquest of positions – castles, fortified towns, harbours etc. – and with the defeat of enemy commanders, army units and irregular forces. Seen in Claudianus' perspective and in chronological order, the primary objectives would have included the establishment and expansion of a reasonable foothold in Ireland through breaking out of the strictures of the beachhead in Ulster in order to proceed towards Dublin; the successful march to and passage of the Boyne, which opened the way to Dublin, and the eventual conquest of Limerick. Probably, the crossing of the Boyne must have been Claudianus' first and a very daunting challenge, although definitely not the only one. The successful defeat of the Jacobite army, including the French brigade, on the Boyne was indeed a deadly blow to King James' designs.

After the conquest of Dublin, which fell without resistance, the failure to take Limerick during the campaigning season of 1690 was a severe setback forcing the soldiery to suffer the hunger, cold and privations of the Irish winter.

The most remarkable feat at the tactical level in the final stages of the war, the campaigning season of 1691, were without any doubt the bloody battle of Aughrim, where Prince Frederick's Regiment fought courageously and efficiently.

While Aughrim was hard fought, and Williamite success far from certain until the death of French Lieutenant General St Ruth, the 1691 siege of Limerick was rather, to a certain extent, a matter of waiting, and when Limerick had eventually fallen the war in Ireland was practically over.

In Flanders new tasks were waiting for the Danish Contingent and, though Claudianus set foot on his native soil in 1696, it was not until 1697 that the – now somewhat depleted – Danish contingent as a whole could finally return to Denmark.

Upon return, the three Danish cavalry regiments were broken up, as they had been formed solely for the expedition. Over the following years, the infantry regiments were to change names or amalgamate so that today the only one still remaining largely unchanged is the Royal Life Guards. Prince Frederick's Regiment was amalgamated in 1729 with the Funen Regiment, whose successor regiment ceased to exist in 1991.

Conclusively, it merits attention that so few reliable eye witness accounts are available. This, we believe, encourages further research of this most crucial contest, and the emerging technique of battlefield archaeology might well be applied to the bloody fields at the Boyne, Cork, Athlone and Aughrim, the latter still being largely unmolested by developers and therefore open to this kind of research.

Annex A – Order of Battle of Prince Frederick's Regiment

Commanding Officer: Colonel Heinrich Wulf Kalneyn

A Company:
Major von Vittinghof
Lieutenant Fischer
Second-Lieutenant Schacht
Ensign Jasmund

B Company:
Captain Brünau
Lieutenant Elschner
Second-Lieutenant Fabricius
Ensign Koss

C Company:
Captain Brockdorf
Lieutenant von Osten
Second-Lieutenant Diekman
Ensign Johan Grün

D Company:
Captain Baron Johan Mauritz von Ueffeln
Lieutenant Benninger

Second-Lieutenant Dalboe
Ensign Chaillou

E Company:
Captain J.W. Münschefall
Lieutenant Leegaard
Second-Lieutenant Schneman
Ensign Stockfleth

F Company:
Captain von Schiller
Lieutenant Gyllerup
Second-Lieutenant Wohnsfleth
Ensign Bauman

Annex B – Glossary

Place Names

Abbiownibriga	Abbeyowney
Armacha	Armagh
Ballicomera	Ballicumber
Ballifarcellum	Unknown
Ballimona	Unknown
Blacburna	Blackburn
Boanda,	Boyne
Boreum promontorium	Malin Head
Brigus	Barrow
Burrashia	Borissokane
Buvinda	Bandon
Cahironlisha	Caherconlish
Calatum	Appleby
Capoga	Cappoge
Capogum	Cappoge
Clitoro	Clitheroe
Connacia	Connacht
Corballiensis	Garbally
Corcagia	Cork (Ir. "Corcaigh")
Dabrona	Avonmore

Annex B – Glossary

Dunkerana	Dundalk
Dunohil	Donohil
Eboracum	York
Eoyrus	River Nore
Ermonia	Ormond
Ernus	River Erne
Glandologia	Glendalough
Gurtnaporia	Gortnahorna
Highlac	Hoylake
Hykinselagh	Kinsale
Ifamnium	Unknown
Igrina	Unknown
Jagolia	Yougal
Kevineus	Lugduff (Wicklow Mountains)
Kilcassilia	Kilcashel
Kilcoole	Kilcullen
Knochdon	Unknown
Lagenia	Leinster
Legocorriacum	Rich Hill (Legacorry)
Liferpalum	Liverpool
Liffius	Liffey
Liscappal-Iskerum	Liscappul-Eskerkeel
Lisnagarva	Lisburn
Listrensia	Lister Dyb (North Sea off Southern Jutland)
Logia Flu	River Bann and/or Lough Foyle
Lorgina	Lurgan
Loudia	Louth
Luuius	River Lee
Maira	Moyra
Merseum	Mersey
Momonia	Munster
Naegho	Lough Neagh
Neorus	Lagan Water
Otlega	Otley
Portadunum	Portadown
Prestonia	Preston
Ravius	River Erne (Connacht)

Svirius	Suir
Robogdium	Fair Head
Roboretus	Derry
Sauranus	Suck
Senus	Shannon
Shipdonia	Skipsea
Skillea	Killoscully
Skiptonia	Skipton
Therneus	Cuilcagh
Tulla	Tullow
Ultonia	Ulster
Uraschree	Urraghry
Vinderius	Bay of Carrickfergus
Wellas	Wells

Titles and Military Ranks and Units, Military Weapons, Equipment & Tactical Expressions

Acies	Line-of-battle, battle formation
Agmen	Marching column or a particular line-of-battle
Ballista	Gun
Castrum	Camp, fort
Centuria	Company i.e. subunit of a legio (regiment)
Centurio	Captain/major/company commander
Chiton	Tunic
Cohors	Company, subunit of a legio comprising more centuriae, though with Claudianus apparently synonymous with centuria.
Contubernium	Tent
Cornicen	Bugler, cornet
Danorum	Danes
Decurio	Cavalry officer
Dimachae	Dragoons

Annex B – Glossary

Dux	Duke, Commander
Eques, equites	Cavalrymen
Exercitus	Army
Fortuna bellica	Fortune of war
Gladius	Sword, sabre
Glandium	Ammunition, gun or musket balls
Globus	Ball
Globus plumbeo	Hand grenade
Hasta	Spear
Hastati	Frontline footsoldiers
Impedimenta	Heavy baggage
Imperatoris consilium	War council
Imperatorius	infantry
Legatus Imperatorii	Major-General/Lieutenant-General
Legatus militiae	Major-General commanding the
Legio	Regiment
Legione Regia Danica	The Royal Life Guards
Legioni praefectus	Commanding officer
Lorica	Body armour
Machina	Siege engine/equipment
Machinarorum armorum	War machinery, weapons and equipment
Magister Equitum	Deputy commander and general of horse
Manus	Task force, detachment
Metator	Surveyor
Oppidum	Irish fortress, usually on a hill top
Optio	Lieutenant
Ordinis Ductor	Sergeant-major
Pilum	Javelin, pike
Praetor	Brigadier
Prefectus	Commander of allied army
Prefectus Castrorum	Commandant (camp/garrison)
Pulveris nitrate	Gunpowder
Questor	Quartermaster
Regia cohorte Danorum	Company, Royal Life Guards
Regia peditum Legio	Royal Life Guards (foot)
Reginacohortis/legionis	The Queen's (company/ regiment)

Selecta modo manus	Task force
Signifer	Standard bearer (infantry)
Signifer equitum	Cornet
Sphaere	Ball
Tabernaculum	Tent, HQ
Tentorium	Tent
Tessarius	Duty officer, sometimes commander of the guard of a castra, the one responsible for passwords (challenge/countersign)
Tormentum (bellicum)	Gun
Triarii	Seasoned soldiers
Tribunus	Commander, commanding officer
Tunica	Tunic, coat
Turma	Cavalry unit, troop
Vexillarius	Ensign/Commander of a detachment
Vexilliferus	Ensign
Vicarius Tribuni	Deputy (brigadier/captain-lieutenant)

Index

Abbeyowney................ 295, 330
Aristotle........................ 25
Armagh............ 75, 87, 89, 91, 330
Athenry.................... 281, 287
Athlone... 141, 143, 181, 187, 189, 191,
 197, 205, 227, 229, 277, 295,
 327
Aughrim.. 107, 235, 247, 249, 261, 275,
 277, 279, 327
Avonmore................... 65, 330
Ballicumber................. 187, 330
Ballinasloe.............. 233, 235, 239
Ballyboy................... 185, 187
Ballymona..................... 187
Ballymore............. 185, 187, 197
Banagher.............. 279, 287, 291
Bandon... 111, 155, 157, 165, 213, 223,
 330
Barrow............. 65, 129, 135, 330
Belfast...................... 59, 85
Bennetsbridge................... 129
Bircherod, Jacob Thomassøn...... vi, 3
Blackburn................ xii, 57, 330
Blackwater..................... 171
Boyne... 65, 95, 97, 107, 115, 117, 121,
 179, 277, 326, 327, 330
Brandenburg...................... x
Brockdorf.................. 155, 328
Caher......... 137, 159, 161, 295, 330
Caherconlish........ 137, 159, 295, 330
Cambrensis..................... 67
Cappoge.................... 93, 330
Cappoquin..................... 171
Carrick [on Suir]. ... 133, 135, 181, 324
Carrickfergus.......... 59, 69, 85, 332
Cashel.......... 135, 183, 233, 324, 331
Castledermot................... 129

Cattalogia..................... 299
Charles Fort............... 163, 169
Christian V, King...... iii, viii, ix, 3, 85
Cicero.................... 17, 25, 27
Clare, Co. 35, 307, 313
Claudianus, Andreas (Stenstrup)..... 1,
 iii-vii, x-xii, 3, 15, 17, 25, 31,
 51, 55, 67, 69, 81, 89, 107,
 121, 127, 159, 163, 169, 179,
 195, 207, 211, 213, 227, 233,
 237, 239, 241, 243, 247, 251,
 277, 293, 297, 325, 327, 332
Clinton..................... 93, 269
Clitheroe............. xii, 55, 57, 330
Clogheen...................... 161
Clonmel. .. 135, 137, 155, 181, 183, 324
Connacht (Connaught)....... 63, 67, 93,
 129, 143, 159, 173, 191, 197,
 233, 287, 330, 331
Cork.. 69, 133, 139, 161, 163, 171, 324,
 327, 330
Corrib..................... 65, 285
Cromwell.................. 79, 305
Cuilcagh Mountain............... 195
Cullen................ 127, 159, 331
Cunningham, Albert............. 241
Curachmore................ 177, 181
Danish Contingent. .. iii, vii, x, 91, 107,
 241, 325-327
Danish expeditionary force.... iii, x, 53,
 207
Darmstadt, Brigadier the Prince of.. 221,
 301
Donep, colonel.............. 87, 295
Donohil................... 137, 331
Dorrington, major general......... 267
Douglas, lt. general....... 141, 151, 191

Index

Drogheda. 69, 95, 99, 117
Drumnochum, Castle. 121
Dublin.. . . ii, 69, 89, 119, 121, 123, 125,
127, 187, 191, 311, 326, 338
Duleek. 117, 267
Dunbrigam. 85
Duncan, Castle. 121, 175
Dundalk. 91, 93, 331
Dungarvan. 171
Dunmore. 119
d'Usson, major general. 283
Edinburgh. 51, 53
Ehrencron-Müller, H. . . . . vi, vii
English Town. . 159, 197, 199, 203, 207,
211, 217, 313
Epicurus. 21
Eppinger, Brigadier. 243, 279
Erle. 249
Erne. 65, 67, 287, 331
field Artillery. xi
Flamborough Head. 51, 53
Flanders. . . . . iii, 324, 325, 327
Formholt Witinghoff.. . . . . 155, 297
Foulkes. 249
Foyle.. . . . . 83, 331
Frederick III, Dano-Norwegian King. viii
Frederick IV, Dano-Norwegian King. . iv
Galgorm Castle. 85
Galway. . ii, 69, 143, 181, 233, 273, 277,
281, 285, 287
Garbally. 233, 235, 239, 330
Ginkel, lieutenant general, Baron. . . 175,
181, 185, 187, 209, 233, 245, 287
Gisburn. 57
Glendalough. 67, 331
Gowran. 129
Gregorian calendar. xi
Harmann, sergeant. 155
Herbert. 249, 265
Hjerpsted. 47, 49
Hobbies. 131
Højer.. 49
Holtzappel, major general.. . . . . 245, 265
Holycross. 183
Homer. 33
Hoylake. 55, 59, 331
Huguenots. . . . . viii, 141
Hull.. . . . . 53, 55, 269
Igrina. 331
Irish Town. . . . 155, 159, 197, 211, 217,
223, 313
Jacobites.. 103, 139, 141, 153, 175, 189,
197, 207, 225, 227, 233, 237,
255, 257, 261, 277, 283, 309,
311
James II, King of England (alias James VII
of Scotland). . . . . . . vii, 45, 81
James' Fort. 165, 167, 169
Jomini, Antoine Henri Baron de. 17
Juel, Baron. 87
Kaas, lieutenant. 227
Kalneyn, Colonel Heinrich Wulf . . xi, 55,
155, 177, 328
Kilcashel. 233, 331
Kilcommadan. 235, 237, 241
Kilcullen. 127, 331
Killaloe. 147, 195
Killoscully. 295, 332
Killoskehane, Castle. 183
Kilmacthomas.. 171
Kilrush. 127
Kilworth. 161
Kinsale. 69, 163, 169, 324, 331
Knochdon, hill. 233, 331
Lagan Water. 65, 331
Lancaster. 57
Lange, second lieutenant. 227
Larne. 59
Leighlinbridge. 129
Leinster. 63, 93, 117, 129, 131, 173,
287, 331
Liberal arts. 23, 29, 33
Liffey. 65, 123, 125, 331
Limerick. . . 69, 141, 143, 147, 159, 175,
177, 181, 191, 195, 197, 211,
273, 277, 279, 293, 295, 297,
299, 301, 303, 313, 324, 326,
327
Lisburn. 87, 331
Liscappul-Eskerkeel. 233, 331
Lismore. 171
Lister Dyb. 47, 331
Liverpool. 55, 57, 331
Loges, Captain des. 227
Longus, Brigadier Anthony Charles. 291,
293
Lough Foil. 65
Lough Neagh. 65, 87, 331
Loughrea. 281, 287
Louis XIV, King of France. . . . . viii, 325
Louth, Co. 93, 129, 331
Lurgan. 87, 331
Lüttich. 107
Mackay, major general. . . 201, 221, 245,

Index

Martis Comes. vii
Mary II, Queen of England & Scotland
. . . . iii, ix
Mavors Irlandicus. . . . . iv, vi, 3
Meath, Co. 63, 117, 125
Melonier, brigadier. 219
Mersey. 57, 59, 331
Moor, castle. 159, 271, 279
Morton, Castle. 127
Mount Etna. 11, 253
Mount Kevin. 67
Mullingar. 181, 187
Munchgaard, lieutenant colonel. . . . 177, 219, 265
Münschefall, Captain J.W. 155, 329
Munster. . . 63, 129, 131, 159, 171, 173, 287, 331
Nestor. 33
Newtown. 187
Nore. 135, 331
Normann, Olav. 207, 209
Ormskirk. 55, 57
Otley. 55, 57, 331
Passus. xii
Portadown. 87, 331
Portumna, castle. 279
Preston. 55, 57, 331
Prince Frederick's Regiment. . . ii, iii, vi, vii, x, xi, 49, 55, 85, 87, 89, 155, 171, 175, 177, 189, 197, 201, 227, 241, 325-328
Privateers. 53
Prudence. 17
Queen's (Regiment). . 107, 181, 307, 333
Rapparees. 139, 147, 149, 175, 185, 301, 307
Rathcormack. 161, 181
Ribe. 11, 47, 61
Rich Hill. 87, 331
Roscrea. 183
Roughty. 65, 67
Salterbridge. 171
Sarsfield, general. . . . 147, 179, 205, 311
Scanian War. viii
Schiller, captain von. 189, 329
Schomberg, Marshal Frederick Duke of
. . . . 59, 115
Sciticus. 71
Shannon. . . 65, 129, 135, 143, 147, 159, 175, 191, 193, 197, 205, 213, 221, 227, 233, 277, 279, 287, 291, 295, 297, 307, 332
siege Artillery. . . . . xi, 147, 151, 205
Skipsea. . . . . xii, 55, 57, 332
Skipton. 55, 57, 332
St. Ruth, Jacobite captain general, Marquess de. . . 205, 275, 283
Stadium. xii
Stenstrup. . . . . iv, vii
Streamstown. 187
Stuffard, judge advocate. 201
Suck. 65, 163, 233, 332
Suir. 65, 133, 135, 175, 332
s'Gravenmoer, Lieutenant-General Heer van. 311
Tallum. 171
Tettau, Major-General Ernst von. . . 165, 175, 207, 219, 245
Thomastown. 129
Three Sisters. 135
Thurles. 135, 183
Tipperary. 139, 161
Tulla. 295, 332
Ueffeln, Captain Baron Johan Mauritz von
. . . . 201, 328
Ulster. . 63, 67, 83, 85, 93, 97, 117, 187, 287, 326, 332
Ulysses. 33
Urraghry. 237, 332
Viceroy. 123
virtue. . . 3, 21, 29, 41, 75, 79, 103, 251, 261
Vittinghof, Major von. 155, 297, 328
Walsingham. 71, 73
Walther, colonel. 145
War in Ireland 1689-91. . . . . ii, vi
War of two Kings. iii
Waterford. . 69, 133, 135, 151, 171, 177, 181, 183, 324
Wedell, captain. 227
Westphalia, Peace of. vii
White Falcon. 49
William III, King of England & Scotland
. . . . iii, ix, 45, 55, 107
Williamite coalition. x
Wood, sergeant major. 207, 279
Wulfen, lieutenant. 227
Württemberg, Lieutenant General Ferdinand Wilhelm Duke of
. . . . 45, 51, 53, 55, 107, 155, 175, 177, 181, 201, 203, 245, 267, 287, 324, 326
Yougal. 69, 331

About the Translators

Kjeld Hald Galster, born 1952, is a military historian and a retired military officer. He has held positions as senior researcher, Royal Danish Defence College and (external) associate professor of the Saxo Institute, University of Copenhagen. He has lectured at Trinity College, Dublin and The Royal Military College of Canada; and he has published widely in Canada, Ireland and Denmark.

Rasmus Wichmann, M.A., born 1985, has held positions as a curator at various museums and as a fellow at the Royal Danish Defence college. His degree was in History, Philosophy and South-East Asia Studies.

www.ingramcontent.com/pod-product-compliance
Lightning Source LLC
Chambersburg PA
CBHW062012180426
43199CB00035B/2569